TEACHING
SECONDARY MATHEMATICS
WITH ICT

Learning and Teaching with Information and Communications Technology

Series Editors: Tony Adams and Sue Brindley

The role of ICT in the curriculum is much more than simply a passing trend. It provides a real opportunity for teachers of all phases and subjects to rethink fundamental pedagogical issues alongside the approaches to learning that students need to apply in classrooms. In this way, it foregrounds the ways in which teachers can match in school the opportunities for learning provided in home and community. The series is firmly rooted in practice and also explores the theoretical underpinning of the ways in which curriculum content and skills can be developed by the effective integration of ICT in schooling. It addresses the educational needs of the early years, the primary phase and secondary subject areas. The books are appropriate for pre-service teacher training and continuing professional development, as well as for those pursuing higher degrees in education.

Published and forthcoming titles:

Adams & Brindley (eds): *Teaching Secondary English with ICT*
Barton (ed.): *Teaching Secondary Science with ICT*
Florian & Hegarty (eds): *ICT and Special Educational Needs*
Johnston-Wilder & Pimm (eds): *Teaching Secondary Mathematics with ICT*
Loveless & Dore (eds): *ICT in the Primary School*
Monteith (ed.): *Teaching Primary Literacy with ICT*
Monteith (ed.): *Teaching Secondary School Literacies with ICT*
Hayes & Whitebread (eds): *Supporting ICT in the Early Years*
Stern: *Teaching RE with ICT*
Way & Beardon (eds): *ICT and Primary Mathematics*

TEACHING SECONDARY MATHEMATICS WITH ICT

Edited by

Sue Johnston-Wilder and David Pimm

Open University Press

Open University Press
McGraw-Hill Education
McGraw-Hill House
Shoppenhangers Road
Maidenhead
Berkshire
England
SL6 2QL

email: enquiries@openup.co.uk
world-wide web: www.openup.co.uk

and Two Penn Plaza, New York, NY 10121–2289, USA

First published 2005

A catalogue record of this book is available from the British Library.

ISBN 0 335 21381 2 (pb)   0 335 21382 0 (hb)

Library of Congress Cataloging-in-Publication Data
CIP data applied for

Typeset by RefineCatch Limited, Bungay, Suffolk
Printed in Great Britain by MPG Books Ltd., Bodmin, Cornwall

To Peter and Eileen,

who were inadvertently party to the rigours of
twenty-four hour transatlantic working, and kept smiling,

with love.

CONTENTS

This book is supplemented by a linked website:
www.openup.co.uk/ict/johnston-wilder

LIST OF CONTRIBUTORS

Douglas Butler, Oundle School, has taught secondary mathematics for many years. He served as Head of Mathematics and then Head of Careers Education. He also chaired the MEI project in the 1980s. He founded the iCT Training Centre in 2000. This is based at Oundle School, and runs courses all over the UK and abroad, with the aim of helping teachers get to grips with the many possibilities of using computers in the classroom. This Centre also researches and creates resources for the educational use of ICT. He is author of *Using the Internet – Mathematics* (2000) and co-author of the software *Autograph 3* (2004).

Alison Clark-Jeavons, University College Chichester, was formerly an 'advanced skills' teacher of mathematics and is now a senior lecturer at University College Chichester. Alison is researching the effective use of the interactive whiteboard in the mathematics classroom in collaboration with colleagues and teachers and has a particular interest in teachers' professional development with respect to ICT.

Jenny Gage, University of Cambridge, is the co-ordinator of the Motivate video-conferencing project for schools, which is part of the Millennium Mathematics Project. Before this, she was a secondary maths teacher for 15 years. She is also doing research into the use of graphics calculators in the teaching and learning of algebra at ages 11–14.

Dave Hewitt, University of Birmingham, is a Senior Lecturer in Mathematics Education. Previously, he had taught in secondary schools for 11 years, including being Head of Mathematics for five of those years. Dave's research interests relate to ways in which the powers all of us possess and used as young children in our early pre-school learning can be accessed and utilized more frequently and effectively within the mathematics classroom. Recently, this has led to a particular interest in the teaching and learning of algebra and the use of computer software.

Nicholas Jackiw is the inventor of *The Geometer's Sketchpad*. He also works as the Chief Technology Officer at KCP Technologies, where *Sketchpad* and *Fathom* are under continual development.

Peter Johnston-Wilder, Warwick University, has been a secondary maths teacher and a lecturer on courses for intending and in-service teachers. He was joint editor of *Micromath* for six years and has been an examiner for A-level Statistics. He is currently conducting research in statistical education.

Sue Johnston-Wilder, The Open University, has been involved with ICT for many years. She was Director of one of the NOF-funded ICT providers. Sue now works on new courses for teachers of mathematics, and her current research is related to using ICT to meet diverse needs in mathematics education.

Kate Mackrell, Queen's University, Canada, has specialized in the use of interactive geometry software. She worked in computing before going into secondary mathematics teaching. She taught in a variety of contexts before starting to work in teacher education at the University of Brighton. A particular interest has been in the development of mathematical thinking through the use of ICT. She contributed to the development of the ATM *Active Geometry* files. Kate is currently studying for a PhD at Queen's University in Ontario, Canada, exploring the use that teachers make of interactive geometry in their teaching.

John Mason, The Open University, is well known for many books including *Thinking Mathematically* (with Leone Burton and Kaye Stacey) and *Learning and Doing Mathematics*. More recently he has published *Researching Your Own Practice: The Discipline of Noticing*. He has a wealth of experience of helping practitioners to develop their own practice, and to turn that into research.

John Monaghan is a lecturer in mathematics education at Leeds University. He has a special interest in students' understanding of algebra and calculus and the use of new technology. He has edited and contributed to several books and journals on the subject of computer algebra.

Adrian Oldknow, Professor Emeritus, University College Chichester and Visiting Fellow, Mathematical Sciences Group, Institute of Education, University of London, has taught mathematics and computing at all levels in secondary schools, further education and universities, including pre-service and in-service teacher education. He chaired the Mathematics Curriculum ICT support group for the DfES 1993–99 and maintains an active involvement with many mathematics and computing subject professional associations. He currently chairs the Professional Development Committee of the Mathematical Association and is Treasurer of the Joint Mathematical Council. He chaired the Royal Society and JMC Working Group which produced the report 'Teaching and Learning Geometry 11–19' in July 2001. He is co-author of *Teaching Mathematics using ICT* with Ron Taylor.

David Pimm, University of Alberta, Canada, has worked in the UK, the USA and Canada in mathematics education and has published and edited many books and other resources. His main area of interest is mathematics and language, including forms of mathematical communication enabled by current developments in technology.

Nathalie Sinclair, Michigan State University, United States, has recently completed a post-doctorate programme at Simon Fraser University in Canada, and is now an assistant professor, cross-appointed between the Department of Mathematics and the College of Education at MSU. She has taught secondary- and middle-school mathematics, and has worked extensively with teachers and students in designing and using various technology-based environments.

David Wright is Teaching Fellow in Mathematics Education at the School of Education, Communication and Language Sciences, University of Newcastle upon Tyne. He is also an editor of the professional journal *Micromath*.

SERIES EDITORS' PREFACE

Seymour Papert, in his seminal volume *Mindstorms: Children, Computers and Powerful Ideas*, perspicaciously saw the role of ICT in mathematics long before the 'C' appeared in ICT courtesy of the Stephenson Committee (Stevenson, 1997):

> learning to communicate with a computer may change the way other learning takes place. *The computer can be a mathematics-speaking. . . . entity.* We are learning how to make computers with which children love to communicate. When this communication occurs, children learn mathematics as a living language. Moreover, mathematical communication [. . . is] transformed from the alien and therefore difficult thing [it is] for most children into [something] natural and easy. The idea of 'talking mathematics' to a computer can be generalized to a view of learning mathematics in 'Mathland'; that is to say, in a context which is to learning mathematics what living in France is to learning French.
>
> (p. 6)

Communication is, of course, essential to any learning – and we refer here not to transmission but to the social constructivist view of building knowledge. Students 'talking mathematics' through ICT is indeed a powerful idea and this volume approaches an exploration of communication in mathematics through a variety of perspectives and strategies.

The recently published OFSTED (2004) ICT in Schools report describes children at Key Stage One generally making good use of ICT in mathematics (p. 29). At KS2, we read, they make 'effective' or 'very good' use of ICT.

In secondary schools, however, the picture appears more varied, with pupil achievements good or better in just over half of lessons observed. The inspectors report that:

the impact of ICT on pupils' achievement tends to be most pronounced where departments use it in an extensive and sustained manner with pupils having regular access to ICT resources.

(p. 39)

The Smith report (DfES, 2004), *Making Mathematics Count*, reinforces the importance of ICT in teaching and learning mathematics, and the UK government has responded very positively to the recommendation that teachers be 'fully informed about the role and potential of ICT to enhance the teaching and learning of mathematics and have access to state-of-the-art hardware and software' (p. 122). They also recommend more systematic integration of ICT in teaching and learning, as part of new approaches to pedagogy and, in particular, suggest the use of ICT should be adopted to ensure that all students acquire an appreciation of the power and applicability of mathematics. Evaluation of the experiences of older learners shows that 92% find the use of ICT motivating and that most feel ICT enables them to produce a higher standard of work more quickly. Sixty-four per cent of learners said that ICT helped them to learn and in particular to concentrate.

There is serious concern that students have little exposure to how ICT can be used to enhance each of these aspects of mathematics, even though employers today increasingly want a combination of mathematical skills harnessed to ICT skills.

(p. 86)

Our assumption as editors is that, as a reader of this book, you are a mathematics teacher or mathematics educator with an interest in ICT. As a teacher of mathematics, you are part of a community that includes teachers like James and Ruth.

Ruth started teaching in 1966 and is currently a Learning Support Assistant. In the following passage, she recalls her early experiences teaching mathematics using technology.

My first memory was of a VIth form visit to Bradford Technical College to see two computers. One was like a table top-analogue – I didn't understand it at the time and can't remember much about it. The second filled a large room. It used reels of paper tape. We put a numerical question into the code of holes on the paper tape. The answer came back to us as another piece of paper tape. We translated the pattern of holes in order to see the answer.

In my first maths teaching post, I taught in a girls' secondary school with smallish classes. I felt I was being 'progressive' when I ordered a set of slide rules and taught their use, relating them to log table methods. They were quite an expensive item and I took care of them, putting each one back into its plastic sleeve and checking them back into the box. On the whole, the girls did not like them, preferring to use log tables. I think that in mixed/boys schools they were more accepted because of their association with engineering metalwork and technical drawing and were sometimes seen as a status symbol associated with male-dominated occupations.

James is a young maths teacher with a six-year-old child of his own, Samuel. One day, Samuel was waiting for dad to change the baby's nappy. He wanted to know about the dynamic geometry software on dad's computer. Dad said it was quite hard, showed him briefly and said they would do more on his return. When he got back, Samuel had already created an interactive geometry page. For James, this incident made him reflect on his own teaching – particularly about what he can expect from his secondary pupils if his 6-year-old can do this

Meanwhile, many young people are growing up impatient for their teachers to wake up to the possibilities that teaching with ICT will awake for them. Ofsted inspectors write 'one of the main barriers to improving achievements in subjects is teachers' lack of awareness of what pupils can do.' (Ofsted, 2004:51)

This book will enable development of reflective practice and will support the implementation of ICT by means of effective learning tasks. It is then up to the reader to try these things out with learners, listening to and watching responses.

The first two chapters of the book provide an introduction, specifically for the benefit of teachers new to teaching mathematics or to ICT. The central chapters are about current curriculum and developments and the final chapters look to the future. Several chapters include case studies and practical examples, as well as discussing more general themes and issues.

The book contains references to research, and is supported by a website, giving access to demonstration copies of software and sample files. The book will inform your visits to the classrooms of colleagues teaching other subjects or teaching mathematics in other schools. It will also serve to inform your future reading of case studies by colleagues. We hope you too will be prepared to share with colleagues some of your experiences of teaching using ICT, and we recommend you start by keeping a reflective diary. Later, you may wish to report on your developing use of ICT in your own practice, to *Micromath*, which is a professional journal aimed at sharing experiences such as your own to support those colleagues who are on paths similar to your own.

Perhaps, as general series editors, we can leave the last word to Papert too:

> We are at a point in the history of education where radical change is possible, and the possibility for that change is directly tied to the impact of the computer [. . .] there will be new opportunities for imagination and originality. There might be a renaissance of thinking [. . .]
>
> (pp. 36–37)

We commend this book to you as an opportunity to be part of that renaissance in mathematics education.

Anthony Adams & Sue Brindley

References

DfES (2004) *Making Mathematics Count*. London: HMSO.

Ofsted (2004) *ICT in Schools: the Impact of Government Initiatives Five Years On* (HMI 2050). London, HMSO.

Papert, S. (1980) *Mindstorms: Children, Computers, and Powerful Ideas*. New York: Basic Books.

Stevenson, D. (1997) *Information and Communications Technology in UK schools: an independent enquiry*. London: The Independent ICT in Schools Commission.

Introduction

1

TECHNOLOGY, MATHEMATICS AND SECONDARY SCHOOLS: A BRIEF UK HISTORICAL PERSPECTIVE

David Pimm and Sue Johnston-Wilder

Throughout recorded history, devices have been created in order to assist with the *doing* of mathematics, especially for the carrying out of algorithmic computations and the coming up with (and holding by means of tables) the values of particular functions. Such devices have ranged from ancient Babylonian table texts (e.g. of multiples, squares or square roots), Napier's rods and slide rules to mechanical (hand-powered) and electronic (desk to hand-held) calculators, as well as, most recently, computers.

Some of these devices are purely about enhanced or substitute performance, while others have greater or lesser pedagogic intent present in their design. Some, such as pocket calculators, are to be found all over the adult world, while others, such as geoboards or Dienes multibase blocks, are only to be found in school classrooms. Some computer software, such as the spreadsheet, was primarily designed for business applications, while others, such as recent interactive geometry environments, were designed with mathematics classrooms specifically in mind.

In this opening chapter, we take a brief look at aspects of electronic technology's increasing incursion into the UK school mathematics scene over the past 30 years. We discuss the changing relationship between school mathematics teachers and calculators, computers and computing (programming), as well as the marked rise of software applications with potential for mathematics classroom use. Over the course of this very short time frame, there have been some significant shifts in relationship both between teachers and these machines, as well as between students and these machines, inside and outside of formal education. Consequently, there have also been some shifts in relationship between teachers and their students mediated or, in some cases, simply necessitated by the presence of such devices.

In 2003, an extensive government training programme for primary and secondary teachers in relation to information and communication technology (ICT) concluded after three years; it is discussed in detail in Chapter 10. Its intent was to bring all teachers (in terms of ICT knowledge and competence) to the level of recent newly qualified teachers in this arena, for whom ICT has played a growing part in their official preparation to become teachers. Nevertheless, and perhaps unsurprisingly, current Office for Standards in Education (Ofsted) inspection reports for England indicate a very wide variety of uptake and sophistication of pedagogic use of such technology in the service of the teaching and learning of mathematics. The question of how to ensure confident and well-qualified users of technology in mathematics classes remains both a significant and challenging one.

Electronic calculators and mathematics in schools

There has been a considerable history in education of technological 'solutions' being offered to various 'problems' of schools and schooling. Whether with the film strip, the overhead projector or, more recently, with electronic devices of various sorts, technological development is presumed simply placeable in a classroom. It is equally assumed that only good will come of it. The repeated facts of unintended and unforeseen turbulence, of the classroom and the curriculum being an ecology held together, only somewhat stable in a complex and fragile balance are often forgotten when the latest 'saviour' device is introduced. Portable, battery-operated calculators have repeatedly been heralded in this guise, first for arithmetic teaching and soon thereafter for much of mathematics.

The history of calculators in the UK is not so different from that of microcomputers, not least in terms of the inverse relationship over a relatively short space of time between cost and computational speed and power and the comparable direct relationship between cost and size. The first hand-held, battery-powered, four-function arithmetic calculators appeared in the UK between 1970 and 1972. (Clive Sinclair's initial electronic calculator in 1972 was the first that was, in his words, 'pocket-sized'.) The 'scientific' multi-function calculators (which included logarithmic, exponential and various trigonometric functions) became available very soon thereafter around 1972 (with the HP 35 and the HP 65, the latter being both hand-held and programmable). The first graphing (graphical, graphic) calculators emerged in 1985 (with the Casio fx-7000). The following year, Kenneth Ruthven, working at the University of Cambridge, started a school-based research project on 'graphic' calculators, involving this Casio machine. (For a detailed report on this project, see Ruthven (1990); for more on the history of calculators generally, see the archive with photographs at http://www.ernst.mulder.com/calculators.)

The arithmetic calculator undoubtedly perturbed the traditional number curriculum of the primary school. During the 1980s, there were a number of projects exploring what children could do when provided with unrestricted access to numerical calculators, as well as examining how the curriculum needed adjusting to their presence. The Calculator Aware Number (CAN) project was the most extensive and successful of these exploratory projects, running from 1986 until 1992 – see Shuard *et al.* (1991) or Duffin (1996).

A good example of unforeseen curricular turbulence occurred with regard to 'fractions versus decimals' in the presence of calculators. Calculators display decimal representations of numbers almost entirely, which markedly privileged this representation when calculators became widespread in classrooms. Consequently, students, who increasingly gained much of their arithmetic experience through interactions with calculators, needed greater emphasis on fraction work elsewhere. (More recently, some calculators have been developed which can handle arithmetic fractions as fractions: however, such calculators are substantially more expensive than the norm.)

Scientific and, subsequently, graphing calculators, which are of far greater relevance to secondary-school mathematics, have only seen somewhat limited usage, due to their relative exclusion from classrooms and examination halls. Some 20 years ago, a group of Her Majesty's Inspectors for Schools (Department of Education and Science (DES), 1982a) observed about then-current (scientific) school calculator usage in the sixth form:

> In A-level work there was a very widespread use of the pocket calculator as a substitute for mathematical tables. It was disappointing to find much less use being made of them in other examination courses in mathematics. The fact that some examination rubrics would not allow their use during the actual examination was often interpreted to mean that they cannot be used at any time during the course. Much valuable mathematical activity can be derived from the use of these devices beyond the more obvious purposes for which they are largely used at the present time.
>
> (p. 29)

These sentences, unfortunately, could equally well have been written very recently about the UK, whereas in Alberta, Canada, for example, a graphing calculator is a required element of the last three years of mathematics instruction in schools and an essential part of the province-wide public examinations taken at age 18. In an Ofsted report (2002a) written 20 years after the above HMI report, inspectors observed: 'Opportunities to use graphical calculators are taken increasingly with pupils in [Key Stage 4], but it is often only the higher-attaining classes that use them' (p. 2).

Currently, the mathematical capability of, say, a TI-92+ calculator far outstrips the expected performance of a successful A-level student. Its wide-ranging functionality also highlights the increasing blurring between the devices of calculator and microcomputer: what actually is the difference when you can run interactive geometry software (such as *Cabri-Géomètre* or *The Geometer's Sketchpad*), link up to the internet, program and much, much more on such hand-held devices?

Computers, software and the teaching of mathematics

One widespread experience of the past couple of decades is how changes in technology always seem to outpace pedagogy, not unlike the experi-ence of attempting to walk on a shale hillside. So while a particular teach-ing/learning approach can emerge either in conjunction with or in response to a particular computer program or application, shifting plat-forms or operating systems require either continued enhancement or transfer, or the program may simply be lost or left behind. Given this increasingly common pattern, it can, therefore, be interesting to reflect on three particular, partial counter-examples.

During the 1980s, as part of a curriculum development project based in London called Secondary Mathematics Individualised Learning Experi-ment (SMILE), teachers worked very hard to develop mathematical teach-ing software for the BBC 'B'/Master or RM 380Z/480Z. (These were the main microcomputers which were current in schools at the time.) These programs were extensively trialled and iteratively modified over time, in response to classroom experience.

The common school hardware in the UK evolved first into BBC Archimedes or RM Nimbus machines, then moved to generic PCs, before most recently incorporating hand-held 32K calculators with Flash tech-nology (which allows the downloading of small programs from the inter-net). Despite these significant platform changes, the SMILE programs are still widely available (see http://www.smilemathematics.co.uk) and, con-sequently, the pedagogic thinking that went into them is also still present. This educational thinking has thus been progressively built on rather than simply jettisoned due to the rapidly changing technology. This contrasts with the more recent development of many teaching CD-ROMs, where the pedagogy is relatively underdeveloped.

A second example comes from the work of David Tall (1985a, 1985b, 1985c, 1986a, 1986b, 1987), a professional mathematician based at the University of Warwick, who initially single-handedly developed an entirely graphical approach to the calculus, based on visualization, 'zooming in' on points and the notion of a graph being 'locally straight'. He developed a suite of programs written in BASIC, known as *Graphic Calculus*, to support his approach. These innovative programs and notions led to a subsequent generation of graph-plotting software which incorporated his ideas, insights and approach.

A third, more extensive example of a pedagogy continuing, deepening and modifying in conjunction with technological development can be seen in the case of the computer language *Logo*. Nearly 25 years ago, the book *Mindstorms: Children, Computers, and Powerful Ideas* appeared. In it, Seymour Papert (1980) presented a Piagetian-inspired educational philosophy involving children interacting with computers by means of programming in *Logo*. Students learned mathematics through programming rather than from 'example, exercise and test' methodologies that were incorporated into a traditional computer-aided instruction approach to computer software.

A common starting point in creating *Logo* programs involved directing and controlling a 'turtle' on the screen. This is an embodiment of what became known as 'turtle geometry', the original Papert *Logo* microworld (a notion we discuss further below). The software provided immediate screen feedback in the light of which students could modify their work. The available language was also *extensible*: that is, the student's own new procedures could be used as if they were simple system primitives (part of the original tool-kit of commands) within the language itself. (In passing, we note that the feature of extensibility is also available in the more recent interactive geometry packages such as *The Geometer's Sketchpad* and *Cabri-Géomètre*, which are discussed in Chapter 5.)

According to Paul Goldenberg (1982), a *microworld* is 'a well-defined, but limited environment in which interesting things happen and in which there are important ideas to be learned'. Students were set loose to explore interesting, mathematically rich environments. Examples of *Logo* school microworlds include *Newton* (modelling turtle motion with forces and masses), *3D-Logo* (which adds the primitives *pitch, yaw* and *roll*) and *LogoGrid* (which works with numerical grids and operations upon them). In the UK, books such as Ainley and Goldstein's (1988) *Making Logo Work* provided secondary mathematics teachers with a range of tasks and discussion of related classroom issues, as well as an introduction to the prevailing *Logo* educational philosophy. However, a tension remained concerning how overtly mathematical the task of programming the computer was.

This concern became especially fraught when subject-matter time was both limited and on the decrease (unlike in primary school, where subject-matter boundaries could be much more fluid). It also became of greater relevance in the UK when, as a consequence of the introduction of the national curriculum for mathematics in 1988, teacher flexibility with regard to content became more significantly constrained.

'Doing maths while learning *Logo*' was the title of an article written by Richard Noss (1983) and published in *Mathematics Teaching*, the professional journal of the Association of Teachers of Mathematics (ATM). It captures well some of the early beliefs about school students encountering significant mathematics in the course of learning to write computer programs. The first core educational arguments (see, for instance, Tall and Watson, 1987) emerged between those advocating the mathematical benefits of programming in *Logo* and those who adhered to the lower-level language *BASIC* (not so different in its intensity from the subsequent allegiance debates between Mac and PC users). Whether *Logo* or *BASIC*, this initial role for computers in the teaching of mathematics became known as 'mathematical programming' and it became common during the 1980s to see claims like 'mathematical programming should be a staple part of mathematics courses in the future' (1983, cited in Mann and Tall, 1992, p. xi)

The second main tension arose between those who advocated the mathematical benefit of programming computers and those who leaned more towards what were often termed 'short *BASIC* programs' (e.g. '132 short programs for the mathematics classroom': Higgo, 1985). These were initially often written either by the individual teacher or by students, in order to illustrate or provide practice in specific mathematical topics. However, the beginning of the separation between program writer and user, echoing the early nineteenth-century musical separation between piano composer and performer, had begun.

Over its 25-year life, *Logo* has seen various developments, including that of other, related programming media such as *Boxer*, an attempt to broaden the notion of programming into providing a 'medium of expression'. *Boxer* attempts to provide a challenging notion of computational literacy, one in which everyone (teachers and students alike) can both create their own educational products, as well as use those created by others.

Sometimes, more recently, dialects of *Logo* have appeared, for instance to support multiple agents operating in parallel. One such, *StarLogo*, allows students to control individual 'turtles' on a whole-class display through a wireless graphical calculator network. Another, *NetLogo* (short for 'Internet *Logo*') does not require the various 'agents' involved to be physically located in the same room. (Using the internet for mathematics is discussed extensively in Chapter 12.)

In order to illustrate how interconnected technology has become, we discuss this last development a bit further. *NetLogo* describes itself as 'a programmable modeling environment for simulating natural and social phenomena. It is particularly well-suited for modeling complex systems developing over time' (Wilensky, 2003, p. 1). Downloadable for free from the internet, *NetLogo* comes with a sizeable collection of pre-written simulations connected to a wide range of school content (in mathematics, mostly related to probability – see Chapter 6). Interestingly, what previously might have been seen as mathematical models or applications can now be seen directly as, say, geography (efficient traffic light flow) or biology (nutrient uptake in sunflowers or honeycombs). One consequence is that the mathematics becomes increasingly hidden within the program itself, apparently falling within the domain of an adult specialist.

When the models have been built, they can be saved as internet applets for use in web pages. One cutting-edge educational possibility is using *NetLogo* to run a participatory simulation in the classroom, with each student controlling part of the system using a device such as a TI-83+ graphical calculator. Consequently, it is possible now to think of graphical calculators as an interim technology (rather than a free-standing computational device), whose benefits include portability, accessibility and low relative cost. However, it seems more likely that the graphical calculator will metamorphose into a portable peripheral interface between a person in transit and a more fixed computer. It may also have a growing role as a virtual controller, as with *NetLogo*.

Even back in 1980, there were physical turtles programmable via the computer in *Logo*. Various subsequent developments in robotics (e.g. *Lego Mindstorms*) allow two-way flow of information between the computer and the 'robot', rather than the original turtle which was only able to receive and subsequently act on instructions. Currently, *Lego Mindstorms* is seen as being in the domain of ICT teachers rather than mathematics teachers (a professional distinction which, historically, as we discuss shortly, was not always so clear). The nature of the required programming (due to the image-based nature of the programming language) is perceived to be less mathematical in nature. (It is certainly true that it is more visual than algebraic, more iconic than symbolic.)

Thus, *Logo* continues to this day in various guises, but has not had the wide success that had been hoped for in secondary mathematics education. Nevertheless, it is still quite widely used in UK primary schools. Also, although reference to *Logo* has recently disappeared from the *mathematics* national curriculum specification, it is still present in the IT national curriculum.

Links between microcomputers and mathematics teachers in schools

At their very outset in the late 1970s, and although this changed fairly quickly, microcomputers initially had no screens and their only output

devices were teletype printers. Because no commercial software or applications were available, using computers (or 'computing' as it was often
termed) *meant* programming them. Even before microcomputers
appeared, programming was included, for instance, as a topic in the SMP
mathematics O-level syllabus in the early 1970s. The syllabus included
programming in *BASIC*. It was often mathematics teachers (whether or not
they were also teaching 'computer studies') who were most likely to have
the necessary skill and interest to learn how to program them.

It was these same mathematics teachers, therefore, who were interested
in students encountering the *mathematical* aspects of the task of programming *within* the formal school context, rather than seeing it as a topic
to be shared and explored among enthusiasts after school, perhaps in a
computing club. Mathematics teachers tended to pick up the computer
studies/computer science O-level teaching when the subject first appeared
in the mid-1970s (with an A level soon to follow). Being a new subject
meant that there were no specialist teachers readily available to teach it.

The distinction between computers as objects of school interest in their
own right (e.g. to physics teachers, to 'computer studies' teachers) and as
pedagogic tools for more traditional subject-matter teaching (such as
mathematics) is also a long-standing one. Not long after this time, in 1981,
one of us was teaching mathematics in a secondary school when the BBC
'B' microcomputer was first introduced to the school. For the first time in
the history of this school, these computers were placed directly in the
hands of maths, science and geography teachers rather than the computer
studies teacher, because the head specifically wanted them used to
enhance the teaching of non-computing subjects.

Yet, so close was this initial link between mathematics teachers and computers that, for instance, in 1984, the Computers in the Curriculum project
(emanating from Chelsea College in London) deliberately *excluded* mathematics teachers from consideration, in order to allow other subject-area
teachers access to computers to start developing curriculum materials. The
following year, in the editorial to the very first issue of *Micromath*, a new
ATM professional journal, John Wood and Derek Ball (1985, p. 2) asserted:

> We take it as axiomatic that computers and mathematics have a special
> relationship with one another. This relationship was played down by
> those who first introduced microcomputers into the school curriculum,
> because they thought it was important to try and ensure that computers
> are used relevantly across the whole curriculum. If computers had been
> shown to have a strong connection with mathematics from the start
> teachers of other subjects might well have felt inhibited about using
> computers.

A couple of years later, in the foreword to the report *Will Mathematics
Count? Computers in Mathematics Education*, its editors again commented on

the special relationship between computers and mathematics [which] is not to be found with other school subjects. This relationship is a consequence of the role which mathematics has played in the development of technology, and of computers in particular, and of the ways in which computers are used to help solve mathematical problems.

(Ball *et al.*, 1987, p. 3)

It is worth noting that, as we write this chapter two decades later (in the early years of the twenty-first century), this 'special relationship', under current ICT guidelines, has become all but lost. For instance, there are increasing numbers of IT departments and even more ICT co-ordinators for secondary schools who are not mathematics teachers. Mathematics teachers can now find it harder to get access to computers in school than they used to, when computers were far less common.

Technology and the mathematics curriculum

Twenty years ago, the authors of an HMI report on mathematics teaching in the sixth form (DES, 1982a) reflected on microcomputers and their potential for reshaping the mathematics curriculum based on what they had seen:

The influence that the microcomputer was having upon mathematics [teaching and learning] at the time of the survey was still in the early stages of development. ... As microcomputers become more readily available, they will be capable of changing significantly the way mathematics is presented visually in the classroom. Programming procedures will influence the methods used for solving problems and there will be a greater emphasis on numerical techniques. The microcomputer's capacity to store and rapidly reorganise data makes it an invaluable tool to carry out complex statistical and combinatorial investigations. The consequences for mathematics teaching are of the greatest significance and all concerned need to consider carefully how this expensive resource can be used to the best effect.

(p. 30)

It is not uncommon for subsequent reality to fail to match up – in whole or in part, in the short or even medium term – to past visionary statements. For example, if the above reference to changed visual presentation of mathematics was intended to signal some sort of 'electronic blackboard' approach, only relatively recently with the broader availability of data projectors and interactive whiteboards (see Chapter 9) has it really become feasible for the whole class to see what is on the computer screen at the same time. Although it is true that availability of computers has somewhat influenced the way mathematics is presented in a classroom setting, the issue of privileging whole-class teaching has led to a difficulty for teachers of mainstream classes. Whether the situation was one or two computers in a mathematics teacher's classroom or using a computer laboratory facility shared by the school as a whole, it was difficult to work with the whole class, so developments tended to take on an individual flavour.

However, *politically*, there has been a distinction drawn between data projectors running from a lap-top computer and the slightly more recent interactive whiteboard technology, in that there was no government initiative concerned with the former. While acceptable before, in the current era emphasizing whole-class teaching, the new availability of interactive whiteboard technology has reinforced this link between political will and technological means (see Chapters 9 and 10). Because interactive whiteboards are more technically demanding, it may mean computer classroom use will move back to the knowledgeable enthusiast rather than be something for all teachers of mathematics. Alternatively, it may require a reliance on technicians, where available, who have not previously been available to mathematics teachers. In some sense, the data projector is perhaps a more 'democratic' device in terms of its usage requirements.

Further, the HMI prediction of greater emphasis on numerical techniques has not manifested itself in the curriculum over the past 20 years. This is primarily due to an unresponsiveness to change in the centralized controllers of the mathematics curriculum, especially at A level which has remained relatively free of numerical techniques. Many students have voted with their feet, preferring to take statistics or business courses rather than pure mathematics, though even in statistics courses, the potential of ICT use is rarely fully drawn on. A decade after the above-mentioned HMI report, the editors of a Mathematical Association report (entitled *Computers in the Mathematics Curriculum*) once more claimed: 'Mathematics curricula should be able to respond flexibly to technological change' (Mann and Tall, 1992, p. xi). The reality over the subsequent decade has once more differed. In Chapters 3–6 of this book, the respective authors take the current school mathematics curriculum as given, whereas in Chapter 7, Douglas Butler looks at how the curriculum could, and perhaps should, be altered in order to reclaim mathematics for the majority in a technological era.

Finally, the comment in the HMI quotation about resources is still as significant today as it was then. The most expensive resource is, perhaps surprisingly, not the technology itself. It is the experience of teachers that it can take a good three years for a teacher to train to use technology well – one year to become personally familiar with its features, another year to work with the new device or software in a classroom setting and a third year to reflect on successes and learn from failures. We return to this topic briefly in the final section of this chapter.

Changing terminology, shifting purposes, fixed curricula

Over the past 30 years, there have been a couple of shifts in how developments in 'this area' of computer use in relation to teaching and learning mathematics in schools have been referred to and framed. Along with these shifts there have been a number of different ways of justifying school work using computers to teach mathematics.

The language of 'computers, computing and computer studies' was first used from the mid-1970s and referred to a separately timetabled school subject with its own syllabus and national examinations. Mathematics education documents referred to 'computers' in the 1980s – see, for example, Fletcher (1983) and Ball *et al*. (1987). In 1988, information technology first appeared as the name of a national curriculum subject, and it was also used in 1990 in the context of teaching mathematics in the ATM journal *Micromath*. However, two years later, in the Mathematical Association document already mentioned, the composite term 'computers/information technology' was used together with a definition for IT, as if it were a new or unfamiliar term:

> Information Technology (IT)   The storage, manipulation and transmission of data in electronic form. Use includes the use of computer software such as databases, spreadsheets, word-processors, graphic packages but has wider implications in television, radio, telecommunications, satellite transmissions and so on.
>
> (Mann and Tall, 1992, p. 161)

IT was still the term used in the School Curriculum and Assessment Authority (SCAA) report on mathematics in the national curriculum (SCAA, 1994) and up to 1998 in *Micromath* **14**(1). However, in issue **14**(3) later that same year, the term became 'information and communication technology' (ICT). ICT was also used in the government national curriculum document (Department for Education and Skills, 1999). Oldknow and Taylor (2000, p. 2) comment:

> Currently the term IT (Information Technology) is being increasingly replaced by the acronym ICT (Information and Communication Technology). In each case it is to emphasise that PCs, and other computers, are just one – albeit very important – element in the range of electronic devices that is revolutionising our society.

Part of the UK's under-documented recent history in this domain involves the question of who taught this emergent and changing subject, as well as what the various foci of the relevant syllabuses were. But equally interesting would be an exploration of the justifications and purposes that were proposed at the time.

One question to do with this evolving nomenclature in relation to mathematics is to what extent 'communicating mathematically' is intended to play a part, whether involving direct communication with an electronic device or with other individuals by means of such devices. The more general issue, concerning which – technology or mathematics – is to be subordinate to the other, was actually addressed in SCAA (1994), which among other things established the various key stages. The authors observed both that 'Pupils should be given opportunities to apply and develop their IT capability in their study of mathematics where appropriate' (p. 1) and that, 'Where appropriate, pupils should be given opportunities to use IT to support and enhance their learning of mathematics' (p. 7). Thus, we can see a decade ago an official perception of mutual interconnection and subordination one to the other.

One general question which has been around from the beginning is the connection between computers and the world of work and how this impinges on schools. In the 1970s, the work setting involved large mainframes requiring specialist programming and systems analysis. Even as late as 1982, the authors of the Cockcroft report into the teaching and learning of school mathematics were predicting that:

> Relatively few school leavers are likely to work directly with a computer. Their work will usually be at clerical or operator level dealing with the input and output of data, though some leavers with A-level qualifications obtain posts as junior programmers. . . . These tasks [related to data handling] demand little in the way of mathematical expertise apart from the need to feel 'at home' with the handling of numerical information. In some cases, it is also necessary to be able to carry out straightforward arithmetical calculations which may involve the use of decimals and percentages.
>
> (DES, 1982b, para. 144)

How gradually did the shift take place, from computers seen as devices comprising a source of interest to mathematics (and possibly physics) students to a far more pluralistic notion seen in terms of equipping students with tools necessary for employment (such as 'keyboarding', word-processing and spreadsheet familiarity and fluency)?

The final topic we wish simply to raise once more here is that of shifts that the existence and reframing (in relation to the tasks of schooling) of certain technology and applications require (or should require) in terms of school curricula. How sabre-toothed is the UK mathematics curriculum, for example (see Peddiwell, 1939)? Have recent developments in technology altered the nature of mathematics itself, not only how it is done, but what it actually is? How important is it for current secondary teachers to have a feel, for instance, for what might be called 'Sketchpad-maths' or 'Cabri-maths'?

The calculator fuelled considerable debate about the learning and automating of algorithms (particularly the one for long division – see Pimm, 1995). Where is the far bigger debate about the appropriate secondary maths curriculum in the face of computer algebra systems, interactive geometry software and sophisticated graphical calculators? What can we rely on computer tools to do for us, and at what gain and at what cost? What is conceptually important in the teaching of mathematics at school?

Teachers successfully teaching mathematics with technology

Clearly, new teachers are more aware of ICT in general, but there is still a strong need to learn about particular pieces of software or, for example, the use of various data capture/input devices, such as heat probes or other sensors. There used to be a rule of thumb in industry that computer users should only be expected to be familiar with two software packages (to master one, to be familiar with a second). The range of devices and programs described in this book clearly indicates the extent of the challenge for secondary mathematics teachers.

According to Ofsted (2002b), by 2002 only one-quarter of schools were putting ICT to good use in teaching mathematics. The authors further claimed that 'only a small proportion of departments has reached the point where they can evaluate critically their use of ICT and decide where it most benefits learning in mathematics' (p. 9). However, there has been a steep and rapid increase in home use of ICT. In addition, the needs of industry have been changing rapidly. This has resulted in a tension between student expectations and current mathematics lessons. There is a continuing need for professional development given the pace of change in ICT.

The impact of assessment constraints on the uptake of ICT in mathematics in England is still considerable, in contrast with Scotland where ICT is far more integrated into mainstream assessment practices. Assessment of ICT outcomes in England is proving challenging across many subject areas, so it has frequently fallen by default back onto the IT department, where the responsibility for assuring the current 'IT entitlement' customarily resides.

But the primary concern for mathematics teachers is related to the need to deploy the technology very carefully. We want to try to ensure that school students are learning *mathematics*, or at least gaining a good foundation for it, and not simply becoming fluent with the operation of the software itself. When working in *Excel* or with interactive geometry software, for instance, you are working in a mathematical environment. So it would be possible to think you are doing mathematics simply by using it (echoing the earlier debates about the inherent 'mathematicalness' of programming a computer in *Logo*). We return to the question of what students can gain by working in a mathematical environment in Chapter 2.

There is no space here to address the questions raised in this chapter to any extent (especially the key set of questions about the nature of mathematics and its relation to technology in the penultimate section). But to engage deeply with them seems significant in terms of coming to understand how we have reached the position we all currently find ourselves in.

References

Ainley, J. and Goldstein, R. (1988) *Making Logo Work: A Guide for Teachers*. Oxford: Basil Blackwell.

Ball, D., Higgo, J., Oldknow, A., Straker, A. and Wood, J. (1987) 'Foreword', in *Will Mathematics Count? Computers in Mathematics Education*. Hatfield: AUCBE, pp. 3–4.

Department of Education and Science (1982a) *Mathematics in the Sixth Form*. London: HMSO.

Department of Education and Science (1982b) *Mathematics Counts* (Cockcroft Report). London: HMSO.

Department for Education and Skills (1999) *Mathematics: The National Curriculum for England*. London: DfES/Qualifications and Curriculum Authority.

Duffin, J. (1996) *Calculators in the Classroom*. Liverpool: Manutius Press.

Fletcher, T. (1983) *Microcomputers and Mathematics in Schools*. London: Department of Education and Science.

Goldenberg, P. (1982) 'LOGO: a cultural glossary'. *Byte*, **2**(8), 210–29.

Higgo, J. (1985) *132 Short Programs for the Mathematics Classroom*. London: Nelson Thornes.

Mann, W. and Tall, D. (eds) (1992) *Computers in the Mathematics Curriculum*. Leicester: The Mathematical Association.

Noss, R. (1983) 'Doing maths while learning *Logo*'. *Mathematics Teaching*, **104**, 5–10.

Oldknow, A. and Taylor, R. (2000) *Teaching Mathematics with ICT*. London: Continuum.

Ofsted (2002a) *Secondary Subject Reports 2000/2001: Mathematics* (HMI 370). London: HMSO.

Ofsted (2002b) *Mathematics in Secondary Schools* (HMI 818). London: Ofsted.

Papert, S. (1980) *Mindstorms: Children, Computers, and Powerful Ideas*. New York: Basic Books.

Peddiwell, J. (1939) *The Saber-Tooth Curriculum*. New York: McGraw-Hill.

Pimm, D. (1995) *Symbols and Meanings in School Mathematics*. London: Routledge.

Ruthven, K. (1990) *Personal Technology in the Classroom: The NCET 'Graphic Calculators in Mathematics' Project*. Cambridge: University of Cambridge Department of Education/National Council for Educational Technology.

School Curriculum and Assessment Authority (1994) *Mathematics in the National Curriculum*. London: SCAA.

Shuard, H., Walsh, A., Goodwin, J. and Worcester, V. (1991) *Calculators, Children and Mathematics*. London: Simon and Schuster.

Tall, D. (1985a) 'Understanding the calculus'. *Mathematics Teaching*, **110**, 49–53.

Tall, D. (1985b) 'The gradient of a graph'. *Mathematics Teaching*, **111**, 48–52.

Tall, D. (1985c) 'Tangents and the Leibniz notation'. *Mathematics Teaching*, **112**, 48–53.

Tall, D. (1986a) 'A graphical approach to integration and the fundamental theorem'. *Mathematics Teaching*, **113**, 48–51.

Tall, D. (1986b) 'Lies, damn lies and differential equations'. *Mathematics Teaching*, **114**, 54–7.

Tall, D. (1987) 'Whither calculus?'. *Mathematics Teaching*, **117**, 50–4.

Tall, D. and Watson, F. (1987) 'Computing languages for the mathematics classroom'. *Mathematical Gazette*, **71**(4): 275–85.

Wood, J. and Ball, D. (1985) 'Editorial'. *Micromath*, **1**(1), 2.

Wilensky, U. (2003) 'What is NetLogo?'.
   (http://ccl.northwestern.edu/netlogo/docs/whatis.html).

2

SOME TECHNOLOGICAL TOOLS OF THE MATHEMATICS TEACHER'S TRADE

Sue Johnston-Wilder and David Pimm

Many ICT tools are available to support and enhance your teaching of mathematics. These tools are referred to in government-led literature on ICT and mathematics (see, for example, Teacher Training Agency, 2002; Department for Education and Skills, 2003; Ofsted, 2002). They include: the internet and CD-ROMs; spreadsheets; graph-plotting software; computer algebra systems; interactive or dynamic geometry packages; *Logo*; teaching software or 'small computer programs'.

Each of these tools is discussed in more detail in subsequent chapters in this book, but those chapters assume a basic familiarity with the relevant tool. The intention of this chapter is to give a relative beginner the opportunity to gain access to the rest of the book. If you are a more experienced user of ICT, you may wish to skip over the first two sections of the chapter. However, the third section contains discussion of some pedagogic issues that will be important for you to be aware of.

As you read about the various uses software may have, and as you yourself engage with particular forms of ICT, it is worth asking yourself whether it is taking the role of: an enabling *tool*, either for doing mathematics or for presenting ideas; a *tutor*, trying to teach and providing feedback; or a *tutee*, that is being taught. This tripartite distinction with regard to the software's interactive relation with the user is explored further in the second section of this chapter.

Different software tools offer widely varied experiences and access to differing aspects of a topic. Consequently, it can be important to offer variety for the purposes of enhancing inclusion. Simply to consider the range or number of applications (spreadsheets, interactive geometry software, etc.) which students are learning to use is generally not a good way to monitor the value of new technologies in the classroom. One student who only uses a single application may achieve far more in the same time than another student who uses several. Software applications are classroom resources, and it is more important to think about the nature of the students' experiences. This is the focus of the third section of this chapter.

Using software such as spreadsheets, interactive geometry or graphing programs in classroom settings can be invoked in two distinct ways. Sometimes it is appropriate to give the students a ready-made document or file which has been already created and invite them to *explore* it. At other times, it may be better for students to create their own from scratch, as they *express* themselves mathematically by means of a more open application or resource.

The chapter includes examples of tasks that involve students giving shape to their own ideas using technology in this latter 'expressive mode', as well as tasks in which students work with software in a more constrained, pre-planned 'exploratory mode'. This distinction is taken up in later chapters, for example, in Chapter 7 where simulations can be pre-built for students to explore or they can build their own simulation reflecting their particular way of looking at a situation.

It is also worth making a broad distinction between *generic* software tools, such as spreadsheets (which are used across the curriculum by teachers of many subjects), and more subject-specific tools, such as graph plotters and interactive geometry and statistics packages (which tend to be used by subject specialists for a particular job). The first section concerns itself with two generic tools, the internet and spreadsheets, while the second deals with a brief first look at a range of more specialist software available for teachers of mathematics.

In each instance, there is an initial list of what the software can contribute to mathematics teaching and learning, as well as examples of what it does. Also, there are resources to help you explore further on the website associated with this book: www.openup.co.uk/ict/johnston-wilder

Introducing two generic tools

Each tool takes time to learn and to become familiar with; sometimes it is worth 'cracking a nut with a hammer' (especially if you rarely eat nuts), as learning to use a more specialized tool generally takes longer than adapting a more familiar one. There are many generic tools that are available for all teachers. Presentation software, such as *PowerPoint*, word-processing tools, such as *MS Word*, and mind-mapping tools, such as *Inspiration*, have all been used to advantage by teachers of mathematics. Examples of the use of *PowerPoint* and of mind-mapping tools in connection with teaching mathematics are discussed further in Chapter 9. However, the generic tools most often used in teaching mathematics are the internet and spreadsheets.

The internet

The internet makes available a wide variety of information and resources to support mathematics teaching. Using the internet, you can: gather information, ideas and data; gain access to resources to download; engage directly with interactive material; and communicate mathematically with others. However, it is possible to use up a lot of time searching or browsing or simply *being* on the internet. Many people find it helpful to have a few recommended sites to visit first, so here are six sites that have strong links to secondary mathematics teaching. Each of these six recommended sites is directly linked from this book's website. (This theme is also the main focus of Chapter 12.)

If you are new to the internet, a good place to start is the NRICH website (http://nrich.maths.org.uk/). This site is part of the Millennium Mathematics Project hosted by Cambridge University and operates rather like an on-line maths magazine. New problems or puzzles are presented each month, which range from those suitable for primary pupils to very hard examples open to all. Everyone is encouraged to submit responses for publication on the site and solutions to challenges from previous months are available.

A good example of a resource site is St Andrews History of Mathematics site (http://www-groups.dcs.st-and.ac.uk/~history/), which offers a rich collection of historical material. In addition to short biographies of many important mathematicians, there are topic threads, as well as information about each salient date.

Brian Dye (head of a mathematics department in Norfolk) has put together a very informative website for secondary mathematics teachers called *MathsNet* (http://www.mathsnet.net/intro.html). His site includes an introduction to much of the software discussed in this book. The site includes software reviews, teaching ideas and links to software distributors from which you can often download demonstration versions of software, before you commit yourself to purchase. At the time of writing, Brian is the editor of *WebWatch*, a regular guide to mathematical websites featured in the Association of Teachers of Mathematics journal *Micromath* (http://www.atm.org.uk/journals/index.html).

A feature of the internet that students often find useful is that it is searchable. You might like to try out a search engine, such as the Yahoo! Mathematics site (http://www.yahoo.com/Science/Mathematics/), looking for items connected to a general topic such as the theorem of Pythagoras or possibly π, before trying a search for a poem about π. There are also search engines designed specially for students to use, such as Yahooligans! (http://www.yahooligans.com/School_Bell/Math/).

Finally, a relatively recent development is one from the Department for Education and Skills, making interactive teaching programs available, which can be linked from the national numeracy strategy website (http://www.standards.dfes.gov.uk/numeracy/publications/).

Spreadsheets

On the surface, a spreadsheet is a tool for operating systematically on tables of numbers by means of formulae that the user enters. Much of the power of a spreadsheet as a tool for *doing* mathematics derives from the algebraic potential of linking values in one column or row deterministically to those of another by means of formulae which make productive use of the possibility of naming cells. Using a spreadsheet, you can: perform many similar numerical calculations simultaneously; tabulate numerical data and statistics, represent them graphically and analyse them; explore number patterns; solve equations numerically and graphically; and locate optimum solutions, by homing in on the correct answer. In this subsection, we list some of the important facilities that spreadsheets offer to mathematics teaching. Some of these ideas are considered again in detail in later chapters, especially Chapters 4 and 6.

A spreadsheet as a function machine

In teaching mathematics, the image of a function machine is often invoked. The spreadsheet can be thought of as a real-life example. In Figure 2.1, the spreadsheet has only two active cells, input (cell A1) and output (cell B1), and as the input is changed, the output changes according to the function which has been 'hidden' in cell B1. This is a useful starting point for doing mathematics with learners new to spreadsheets.

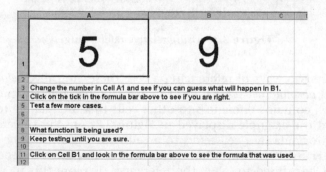

Figure 2.1 A spreadsheet as a function machine (Open University, 2003).

The construction of a table square on a spreadsheet is quite a good way to illustrate some of the underlying ideas. The numbers 1 to 12 can be entered manually in column A and row 1, as shown in Figure 2.2. Then in cell B2 the formula =A2 * B1 can be entered. (In *Excel*, every formula must start with '='; other spreadsheets do it differently.)

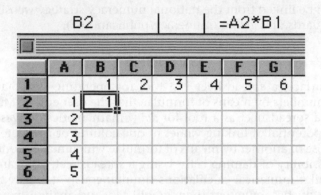

Figure 2.2   Beginning a table square.

The formula =A2*B1 can be 'filled down' (click and drag down) from cell B2 to B13, and then 'filled right' (click and drag right) from column B to column M. However, if this is done, strange things happen (Figure 2.3). Look at the resulting formula in cell C5 as an example.

	A	B	C	D	E	F	G
1			1	2	3	4	5
2	1		1	2	6	24	120	7
3	2		2	4	24	576	69120	497664
4	3		6	24	576	331776	2.2932E+10	1.1413E+
5	4		24	576	331776	1.1008E+11	2.5243E+21	2.8809E+
6	5		120	69120	2.2932E+10	2.5243E+21	6.372E+42	1.8357E+
7	6		720	49766400	1.1413E+18	2.8809E+39	1.8357E+82	3.37E+1
8	7		5040	2.5082E+11	2.8625E+29	8.2466E+68	1.514E+151	#NUM!

Figure 2.3   Using relative referencing.

There are two ways of referencing a cell: these are called *relative referencing* and *absolute referencing*. Relative referencing is when the formula in each cell contains references to other cells that are relative to its position, as in the example displayed in Figure 2.3. Absolute referencing is when the formula in a cell refers to a cell which is always the same, as shown in Figure 2.4. Think about the effect of absolute referencing. The $ sign has been used to 'glue' the references. Explore this in your own spreadsheet.

	C5		▼		=	=$A5*C$1			
	A	B	C	D	E	F	G	H	I	J
1		1	2	3	4	5	6	7	8	9
2	1	1	2	3	4	5	6	7	8	9
3	2	2	4	6	8	10	12	14	16	18
4	3	3	6	9	12	15	18	21	24	27
5	4	4	8	12	16	20	24	28	32	36
6	5	5	10	15	20	25	30	35	40	45
7	6	6	12	18	24	30	36	42	48	54
8	7	7	14	21	28	35	42	49	56	63
9	8	8	16	24	32	40	48	56	64	72
10	9	9	18	27	36	45	54	63	72	81
11	10	10	20	30	40	50	60	70	80	90
12	11	11	22	33	44	55	66	77	88	99
13	12	12	24	36	48	60	72	84	96	108
14										
15										

Figure 2.4   Using absolute referencing.

You might like to try the formulae =A$2*B1 or =$A$2*B1 in cell B2, and then fill down and fill right as above. Again, look at the resulting formula and think about the effect of putting in the $ sign. The facility to use either relative or absolute referencing in various ways enables the user to explore sequences in a spreadsheet, using sequences defined by either 'term to term' or a 'position of term' process.

Logical functions

The use of logical functions in a spreadsheet can provide a simple introduction to programming. One particularly useful example of a logical function is 'if–then–else'. The 'if–then–else' structure is a powerful idea in its own right, which can enable you and your students to explore some interesting ideas. Suppose, for example, you want to set up a simulation of an event that occurs with a probability of 0.3. You can use a formula to enter a random number between 0 and 1 in cell A1. Then, in cell B1, you can have 'IF cell A1 is greater than 0.7, THEN make B1 take the value 1, ELSE make B1 take the value 0'. The syntax for this conditional formula in *Excel* would be =IF(A1>0.7, 1, 0). Using 'fill down', you can generate as many random outcomes as you need.

Graphing with Excel

Excel provides the user with a wide range of graphs, including pie charts and line graphs (see Chapter 6 for much detailed discussion). The graphs are based on data, whether input by the user or generated by the computer from a function. However, most spreadsheets are not (yet) function graph plotters and need to be 'taught' how to plot graphs of functions by setting up a sheet that calculates some data first (see Figures 2.5 and 2.6). Data produced by using a function leads to a graph provided you are careful to

Figure 2.5   Table of values for $y = x^2$.

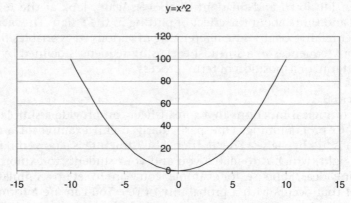

Figure 2.6   'Taught' how to plot the graph of $y = x^2$.

use the '*xy* scatter' option. This gives the user the possibility of exploring the built-in functions in the spreadsheet.

Spreadsheets are very good at handling large data sets, such as those provided by government agencies and charities. Researchers, publishers and others are making available sets of data which can be of interest to students of different ages. Sometimes such data are distributed on a CD-ROM, but many large data sets are now accessible on the internet (see Chapter 6).

Lastly, a spreadsheet can also be set up as a tutor on a particular topic. One of the best examples of this is the DISCUSS (Discovering Important Statistical Concepts Using SpreadSheets) material developed by Neville Hunt and Sidney Tyrrell of Coventry University (Hunt and Tyrrell, 2003).

Maths-specific tools and environments

As we have mentioned, spreadsheets can take on all of the roles of tool, tutor and tutee – and this is also true of much of the maths-specific software considered in this section. The first two subsections take a look at certain software seen primarily as tools, the third is concerned with instances of the computer acting as tutor, while in the last one the computer serves as tutee. As before, there is further information about each piece of software or application on the website that accompanies this book.

Any tool takes time to learn and to become familiar with. However, at times it is easier to use a tool designed specially for a particular purpose and so it is worth putting in the initial investment to learn a new one. As you look at each example in this section in turn, bear in mind that your circumstances will dictate which are the most useful ones for you to look at first. It is likely that you will become familiar with many ICT tools, but only confident with a few different ones. It is a common experience among teachers that some students quickly become expert at dealing with the specifics of a particular tool and are keen to share that expertise.

The best way to gain a sense of how software can help with mathematical thinking is to explore it yourself, provided the initial technical issues are well supported. You might also like to observe a student using the software – if you do, bear in mind an important maxim when using ICT, namely that all things are easy when you already know how. If people wish to teach you something about a new piece of software, ask them to demonstrate the new feature first. Then have them stand back to let you do it for yourself, without them taking back control of the mouse until you swap places again. This will help to build up your confidence.

Tools for exploring graphs of functions

As was mentioned in Chapter 1, the use the computer to provide an accessible graphing environment in which the user can 'zoom' in and out and investigate intersections and local gradients was largely due to the work of David Tall, who developed his computer graphing approach to teaching calculus in the early to mid-1980s. Software for plotting graphs of functions allows the user to: manipulate graphs; solve equations graphically, by estimating, then 'zooming in' on a point of intersection; and study relationships, by superimposing graphical representations and by changing scale.

Recent packages also include the means to study transformation geometry. There is a choice of graphing packages that offer such features: for example, *Omnigraph, Coypu* and *Autograph*. Some people have applied David Tall's approach to spreadsheets. These ideas have been reported in *Micromath* (see, for example, Jones and McLeay, 1996; Crawford, 1998;

Morrison, 1998). Some mathematics educators, such as Mike Quigley at SMILE, are writing spreadsheet macros (programs that run within *Excel*) to enable beginners to use *Excel* more easily as a function graph plotter. There are also function graph plotters available freely on the internet. One example is illustrated in Figure 2.7. If you are new to the idea of a graph plotter, but are familiar with the internet, this is an accessible example to start with. Otherwise you could ask a supplier for a demonstration copy of an example of your choice.

In some graph plotters (for example, in version 3 of *Omnigraph*), you are also able to drag a point on a curve and watch the equation change.

Once you have had a chance to explore plotting graphs with ICT, you might wish to extend the notion of exploring graphs to exploring mathematical diagrams of other kinds, especially geometric ones. It is to this tool that we now turn.

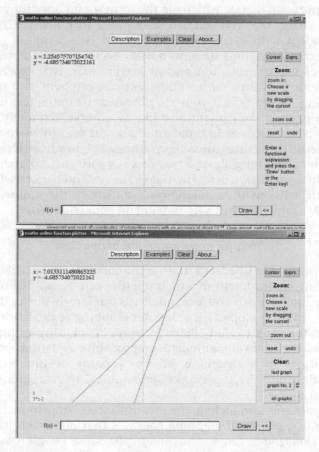

Figure 2.7a   A 'maths on-line function plotter'
(http://www.univie.ac.at/future.media/moe/onlinewerkzeuge.html).

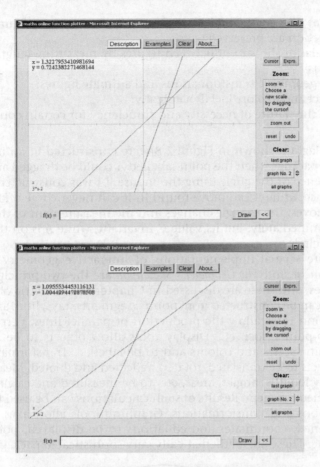

Figure 2.7b A 'maths on-line function plotter'
(http://www.univie.ac.at/future.media/moe/onlinewerkzeuge.html).

Tools for exploring diagrammatic representations

Imagine you are trying to convince a student that a particular angle formed at a point *A* remains the same when *A* is moved to a different position around the circle (an angle subtended by the same chord). You trace round the circle with your finger as you speak. If only the diagram would move with you too. The software that supports this fantasy of mathematics in motion, bringing it to life, has come to be known as interactive or dynamic geometry. Using interactive geometry software allows you to:

• make geometric constructions and, most importantly, change them by means of clicking and dragging on points or line segments, in such a way that the mathematical relations created by the figure's initial construction are preserved;

- study relationships in or between figures by measuring lengths, angles and areas;
- explore geometric transformations and animate figures;
- construct and explore loci dynamically;
- explore the nature of necessity and sufficiency for certain conditions to hold.

If the diagram shown in Figure 2.8 were constructed in an interactive geometry package, then the point labelled *A* could be dragged around the circumference of the circle using the mouse. (*A* was constructed to lie on the circle, so while it can move round it, it can never come off it.) As the point *A* moves, the triangle changes and the measurement of the angle is updated immediately. But its value is invariant, while *A* is on the 'major' arc of the circle.

There are several implementations of interactive geometry software: *Cabri-Géomètre* and *The Geometer's Sketchpad* are the two principal school alternatives, and these are discussed in Chapter 5. Geometric objects and diagrams can be constructed from points, segments, rays, lines and circles. Construction tools allow the production of parallel lines, perpendicular lines, mid-points, loci, etc. Display tools allow objects to be shown in different line styles and colours and to be labelled. Transformation tools allow objects to be translated, rotated, reflected and dilated. Measurement tools allow lengths, angles, areas, etc. to be measured and calculations to be performed on them. Results of such calculations can be used to control constructions and transformations. Graphing tools allow axes and grids to be defined, coordinates and equations to be displayed, points to be plotted, etc. These are mathematically very sophisticated packages.

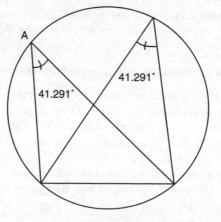

Figure 2.8 A demonstration of the theorem that angles subtended by the same chord are equal.

The main initial difference between *Cabri-Géomètre* and *The Geometer's Sketchpad* that you will notice if you try both is that when using *Cabri-Géomètre* you select a tool and then the objects to which it is to be applied, whereas using *The Geometer's Sketchpad* you select the objects first and then opt for the tool that you wish to use on them. If you have access to the internet, one of the easiest ways to try out the idea of interactive geometry is to visit the interactive geometry pages of Brian Dye's MathsNet site (http://www.mathsnet.net/dynamic/index.html). An example is shown in Figure 2.9.

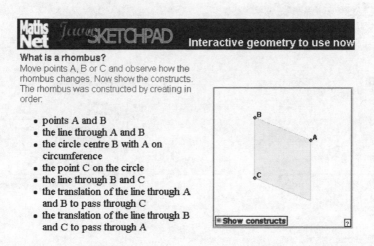

Figure 2.9 An example of a page from MathsNet interactive geometry.

Finally, when doing mathematics yourself, you may well work with algebraic representations. ICT can help turn algebraic symbols into graphical representations and vice versa. But sometimes the algebra itself is the focus of attention and it would be helpful to have access to a different kind of software, one which supports algebraic manipulation. Examples of such tools include *Mathematica, Maple* and *Derive*. These sophisticated tools can also provide a translation of algebra into graphs: algebra software is explored further in Chapter 4.

Computer as tutor

There has always been a vogue for using ICT to do some of the teaching. Some of this thinking is badly misplaced – the computer even now can frequently offer only a crude response. However, in the sense that ICT can offer feedback by implementing exactly what has been asked, it has great uses as a tutor. (There is an extensive discussion on the nature of computer 'feedback' at the end of Chapter 3.)

This feature has been implemented by software developers, such as SMILE, over many years of trial and development. For example, *Rhino* offers students a chance to enter coordinates in a 10 × 10 grid to locate a hidden rhino (Figure 2.10). The computer is programmed to respond by telling the student how far away they are from the rhino and leave the student to work out the next best response.

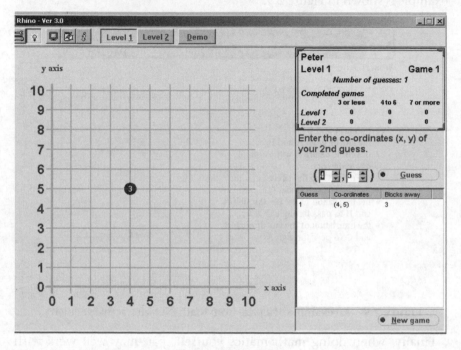

Figure 2.10   *Rhino.*

However, some of the currently available tutoring CD-ROMs have been developed with very little input from experienced teachers and the pedagogy is, at times, both suspect and occasionally dangerous – use with caution. A group of teachers have set up an evaluation programme called TEEM (http://www.teem.org.uk) which is a resource to help you make a first-time judgement about any piece of teaching software based on the experience of colleagues.

Computer as tutee

Historically, programming the computer has been a significant part of the role of ICT in mathematics, as you saw in Chapter 1. *Logo* is a programming language developed as an educational tool. It is also the name of an educational philosophy. Seymour Papert's (1980) book *Mindstorms* gives some background about the origins of *Logo*; it also contains some interesting ideas to explore. Although *Logo* is seen by many as being 'only' an educational language, it is in fact a very sophisticated computer language and can be used as a vehicle for exploring deep mathematical ideas (Abelson and diSessa, 1981). Using *Logo* allows you to: explore shape; develop the concept of function; develop programming skills and learn about the nature of algorithmic processes; and use *Logo* microworlds to study particular curriculum areas. The following program draws a square using *Logo*:

```
to square :side
repeat 4 [fd :side rt 90]
end
```

Once 'square' is saved, it becomes a procedure that can be called in another procedure. Thus, *Logo* is readily extensible.

The following is an example of a recursive procedure written in *Logo*, that is, a procedure which calls itself:

```
to inspi :side :angle :inc
forward :side
right :angle
inspi :side :angle+:inc :inc
end
```

It is possible to think of spreadsheets and interactive geometry tools as software to be extended or programmed in a similar way, even though it is more customary to think of these as software applications rather than programming languages *per se*. For example, you can 'teach' *Cabri-Géomètre* or *The Geometer's Sketchpad* how to construct an equilateral triangle from two points and then name and add that set procedure to the list of available constructions.

We now move from looking at particular ICT tools to looking at the range of opportunities involved for the student.

An entitlement to learning mathematics with ICT

Many teachers over recent years have found it helpful to try to identify a student's entitlement to the use of ICT in mathematics lessons. The term 'entitlement' relates to those opportunities offered by ICT to which all students can and should expect to gain access during their school mathematics course. Computers and calculators can be thought of as providing six major opportunities for students learning mathematics (BECTa, 2003):

Learning from feedback The computer often provides fast and reliable feedback which is non-judgemental and impartial. This can encourage students to make their own conjectures and to test out and modify their ideas.

Observing patterns   The speed of computers and calculators enables students to produce many examples when exploring mathematical problems. This supports their observation of patterns and the making and justifying of generalizations.

Seeing connections   The computer enables formulae, tables of numbers and graphs to be linked readily. Changing one representation and seeing changes in the others helps students to understand the connections between them.

Working with dynamic images   Students can use computers to manipulate diagrams dynamically. This encourages them to visualize the geometry as they generate their own mental images.

Exploring data   Computers enable students to work with real data which can be represented in a variety of ways. This supports its interpretation and analysis.

'Teaching' the computer   When students design an algorithm (a set of instructions) to make a computer achieve a particular result, they are compelled to express their commands unambiguously and in the correct order; they make their thinking explicit as they refine their ideas.

The rest of this section is organized by means of these six headings, each 'entitlement' being briefly illustrated by ICT classroom tasks.

Learning from feedback

One of the great advances that the technology offers is instant feedback. Imagine a student estimating that it is 100 cm from robot to tower, then programming the robot to move forward 100 cm, then trying it out.

One way to use a graph plotter is to pre-enter functions and invite the learners to guess what has been entered. The graph of the equation they type in will be superimposed on the existing graph (Figure 2.11). The software gives immediate visual feedback. Can they then use their

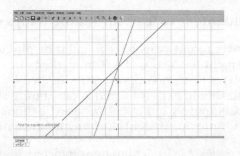

Figure 2.11   Find the equation of the line.

understanding about how properties of the symbolic form relate to visual features of the graph in order to meet your challenge mediated by the machine?

Observing patterns

The observation and justification of patterns lies close to the heart of mathematics: not just spatial patterns, but number patterns and patterns in data need to be recognized and understood. Computers and calculators can provide information very fast, and this often makes a pattern clear which might otherwise be missed.

Two children were using their calculators to explore patterns in the 11 times table:

$$12 \times 11 = 132$$
$$13 \times 11 = 143$$
$$14 \times 11 = 154$$
$$15 \times 11 = 165$$

'Oh look, the hundreds and the units always add up to the tens.'

The teacher asked whether this *always* works and the children used their calculators to continue the pattern.

$$17 \times 11 = 187$$
$$18 \times 11 = 198$$
$$19 \times 11 = 209$$

'This last one goes wrong . . .'.

The teacher wanted the children to understand the pattern and why it broke down. If the children had only been using pencil and paper, working out their answers by other means, they might never have seen a pattern in the first place. Some of the children would only have had three calculations to observe and, if two or even one of these were miscalculated, the pattern would have been far from obvious. If the aim of the lesson had been to practise conventional multiplication, the calculator's presence would have been worthless.

Seeing connections

One of the major advantages offered by ICT is that you can see more than one representation of an object at the same time and you can alter one and see the effect on the other. For example, when using the Code Book CD-ROM (Singh, 2003), the ICT makes exploration of affine shift ciphers relatively quick. It is also possible to move to exploring co-primes, thus making a link between codes and number theory which would be much more abstract without the ICT.

A common way to encode a piece of writing is to add the same secret number to each number, then translate that back into a letter of the alphabet. This is known as the Caesar shift code. Is it possible to multiply rather than add? Figure 2.12 shows what happens when you multiply by 2. This does not produce a useful code, as you cannot tell whether 0 is A or N. You can use 3 to produce a code. Try it and see.

Alphabet	A	B	C	D	E	F	G	H	I	J	K	L	M	N	O	P	Q	R	S	T	U	V	W	X	Y	Z
Numerical Equivalents	0	1	2	3	4	5	6	7	8	9	10	11	12	13	14	15	16	17	18	19	20	21	22	23	24	25
Transformed Numbers	0	2	4	6	8	10	12	14	16	18	20	22	24	0	2	4	6	8	10	12	14	16	18	20	22	24
Letter Equivalents	A	C	E	G	I	K	M	O	Q	S	U	W	Y	A	C	E	G	I	K	M	O	Q	S	U	W	Y

Figure 2.12 Table of results of multiplying letter number by 2 (mod 26).

Working with dynamic images

As we mentioned above, the whole of an interactive geometry software package is concerned with this theme, which is explored in Chapter 5.

Even with graph plotters such as *Omnigraph*, you can create an equation which includes parameters, for example, $y = ax + b$. Then you can control how those parameters change using an on-screen 'dynamic constant editor' (Figure 2.13). An example (using $y = mx + c$) is shown in Figure 2.14.

Figure 2.13 Dynamic constant editor in *Omnigraph*.

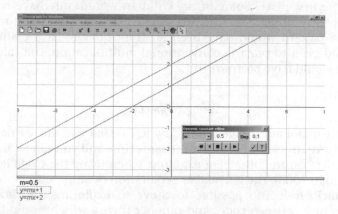

Figure 2.14 The 'animation' runs with decreasing values of *m*.

As you press the Forward button the value of m increases by the step size you have chosen, 0.1 in this case. If you press Fast Forward the value of m increases steadily as you watch. Similarly if you press Back the value of m decreases by 0.1, and if you press Fast Rewind, the 'animation' runs with decreasing values of m.

As you may have seen, MathsNet has implemented some of these ideas on its website (Figure 2.15). So as long as the machine you are using to connect to the internet is 'Java-enabled' (ask an ICT colleague to check), you will be able to explore these without needing directly to learn about any new software.

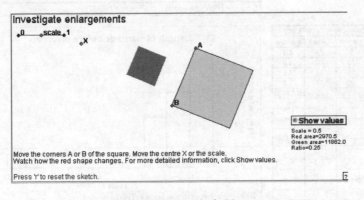

Figure 2.15   MathsNet.

Exploring data

ICT enables the exploration of data, both real and simulated. For example, a spreadsheet can be set up to generate first results from 30 dice being thrown at a time, then the average score of 5 at a time, then the average score of 20 at a time. A set of resulting distributions is summarized in Table 2.1.

Table 2.1 Simulated dice scores

	Minimum	Lower quartile	Median	Upper quartile	Maximum
Distribution of 30 dice scores	1	3	4	5	6
Distribution of average of 5 dice scores	2.2	3.2	3.8	4.2	5
Distribution of average of 20 dice scores	2.75	3.2	3.575	3.7825	4.55

Students can discuss differences between the distributions for several cases. Data can also be explored visually, thus also 'working with dynamic images'. These six categories of 'entitlement' are not intended to be mutually exclusive. An exploration of statistics software is discussed in detail in Chapter 6.

Figure 2.16 is taken from the template at http://home.ched.coventry. ac.uk/Volume/vol0/hist.htm; this template can be saved and used for students' own data.

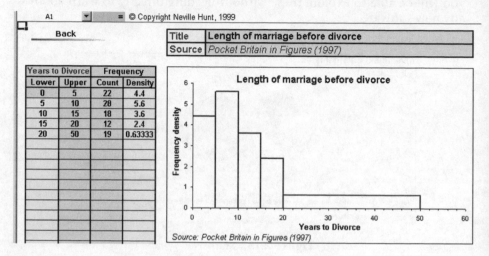

Figure 2.16   From the Volume template.

'Teaching' the computer

You saw an example of *Logo* being taught how to draw a square on page 31. In Figure 2.17, a student has taught the computer to 'spiral'. You saw on page 24 how you can extend this notion to think of teaching a spreadsheet how to draw graphs of functions. In the example in Figure 2.18, *Excel* has been set up to show graphs of the form $y = mx + k$ (c is used for other things in *Excel*) and m and k can be altered using the arrows.

The very nature of ICT means that teaching or 'programming' a machine to carry out some task that you know how to do yourself means that you learn from having to be precise and unambiguous at every stage. This is an essential ingredient in learning to think mathematically.

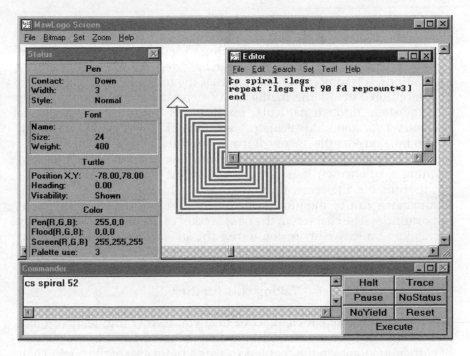

Figure 2.17   Teaching the computer to 'spiral'
(http://www.softronix.com/logoex.html).

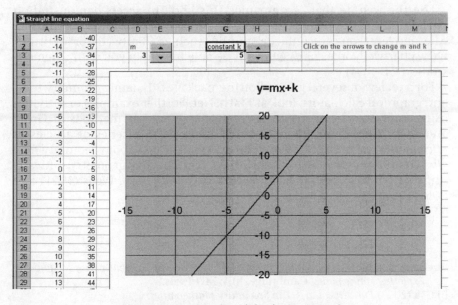

Figure 2.18   Graphs of the form $y = mx+k$.

Conclusion

The place of ICT in mathematics teaching varies across schools and from classroom to classroom. Access to resources varies, and so too do teachers' inclinations. It is important to ensure that the use of ICT is implemented and monitored across the mathematics department. Traditionally, this is to be done through particular applications: spreadsheet, interactive geometry, *Logo*, graphical calculators, etc. But ICT is increasingly prevalent. We do not consider the use of compasses or tracing paper when we make our decisions about the mathematics curriculum. In terms of teaching and learning mathematics, it is not the tools that should be the focus of monitoring, but the access to mathematics. The use of ICT in teaching mathematics can be monitored effectively by using the six entitlement opportunities. The chapters in the next section of the book are arranged by curriculum topic. We invite you to use the six entitlements to reflect on what ICT offers the teaching and learning of each topic.

Taking this further

The rest of the book has chapters to take you further into related topics and issues. The tools discussed in this chapter are revisited in the context of curriculum topics in the chapters in Part A of the rest of the book. Their use is further explored in the context of access in the classroom in chapters in Part B.

Use the website that accompanies this book to access demonstration copies of the software discussed here and to explore the ideas for yourself. Alternatively, you can contact a supplier such as Chartwell-Yorke (http://www.chartwellyorke.com/) who will be able to supply you with a demonstration CD-ROM.

For a review of several graph plotting packages, dynamic geometry tools and graphical calculators, look at MathsNet. Further examples of activities using interactive geometry to re-create the geometric methods of Greek and Arab mathematicians have been discussed in a series of articles in *Micromath* (Evans, 1996a, 1996b; Burns, 1996). Books about geometry may give you further ideas for exploration using interactive geometry software: some particularly fruitful examples are Coxeter (1961), Wells (1991) and Bold (1982).

References

Abelson, H. and diSessa, A. (1981) *Turtle Geometry: The Computer as a Medium for Exploring Mathematics*. Cambridge, MA: MIT Press.
BECTa (2003) *Entitlement to ICT in Secondary Mathematics*. (http://www.ictadvice.org.uk)

Bold, B. (1982) *Famous Problems of Geometry and How to Solve Them*. New York: Dover Publications.

Burns, S. (1996) 'Omar Khayyam and dynamic geometry'. *Micromath*, **12**(2), 29–30.

Coxeter, H. S. M. (1961) *Introduction to Geometry*. New York: Wiley.

Crawford, D. (1998) 'With a spreadsheet: introducing gradient functions and differentiation'. *Micromath*, **14**(1) pp. 34–9.
(http://www.atm.org.uk/journals/micromath/articles/mmarchivepdfs/mm141crawford.pdf)

Department for Education and Skills (2003) *Integrating ICT into Mathematics in Key Stage 3*.
(http://www.standards.dfes.gov.uk/keystage3/strands/publications/?template=down&pub id=2479&strand=maths)

Evans, W. (1996a) 'Rene Descartes and dynamic geometry'. *Micromath*, **12**(1), 30–1.

Evans, W. (1996b) 'Omar Khayyam's insight into the cubic equation'. *Micromath*, **12**(8), 28–9.

Hunt, N. and Tyrrell, S. (2003) *Discuss: Discovering Important Statistical Concepts Using SpreadSheets*.
(http://www.coventry.ac.uk/discuss)

Jones, P. M. J. and McLeay, H. (1996) 'Zooming spreadsheets: Putting functions under the microscope'. *Micromath*, **12**(1) pp. 35–8.
(http://www.atm.org.uk/journals/micromath/articles/mmarchivepdfs/mm121prysmorganjones.pdf)

Morrison, T. (1998) 'Using spreadsheets to teach differentiation'. *Micromath* **14**(1) pp. 30–3.
(http://www.atm.org.uk/journals/micromath/articles/mmarchivepdfs/mm141morrison.pdf)

Ofsted (2002) *ICT in Schools: Effect of Government Initiatives – Secondary Mathematics*. London. Ofsted.

Open University (2003) *Developing Mathematical Thinking at Key Stage 3: MEXR624 Course Materials*. Milton Keynes: Open University.

Papert, S. (1980) *Mindstorms: Children, Computers and Powerful Ideas*. New York: Basic Books.

Singh, S. (2003) *The Code Book on CD Rom*. London: Virtual Image and Simon Singh.

Teacher Training Agency (2002) *ICT and Mathematics: A Guide to Learning and Teaching Mathematics 11–19*, London: Teacher Training Agency/Mathematical Association (http://www.m-a.org.uk/).

Wells, D. (1991) *The Penguin Dictionary of Curious and Interesting Geometry*. London: Penguin Books.

— Part A —

ICT and the school mathematics curriculum

3

THINKING NUMERICALLY: STRUCTURED NUMBER

Dave Hewitt

This chapter presents a case study in the design of software, focusing on two programs in particular called *Numbers* and *Powers of 10*, from the package *Developing Numbe*r (Association of Teachers of Mathematics, 2004). My intention, however, is to bring out general issues and principles for you to consider when engaging critically with other software. Thus, although I attend to the pedagogic basis lying behind some aspects of these particular programs, my intention is for these to act as examples in highlighting general features and principles at work in most, if not all, educational software.

Numbers: an algebra *of* number names

Number lies at the heart of much mathematics, and if a student is not confident with number then that can have an effect on many areas of mathematics. Students aged 11–14 may exhibit many errors in reading and writing numbers. For example, responses to being asked to write down the number *six thousand, two hundred and fifty-one* included 600251, 620051, 600020051 and 60251 (Hewitt and Brown, 1998). It is worth being aware that such difficulties are not just an issue for primary school teachers.

The two programs I discuss here, *Numbers* and *Powers of 10*, are both based upon a chart created to highlight the structure within our number system or what I see as involving an algebra of number names (as I justify at the end of this chapter). This chart not only helps students to learn to say and write number names, but also provides a basis for work on place value, decimals, addition and subtraction, multiplication by powers of 10 and standard form. To begin considering the chart, say aloud the first few number names in English:

> one, two, three, four, five, six, seven, eight, nine, ten, eleven, twelve, thirteen, fourteen, fifteen, sixteen, seventeen, eighteen, nineteen, . . .

There is no noticeable structure (either of sound or written form) until into the -teens and even then the pattern is temporary and does not appear again for numbers up to 100. As Wigley (1997, p. 114) has pointed out: 'Significantly, the greatest irregularity is in the second decade, so that learning numbers in the natural counting sequence does not help understanding of place value at that crucial point where it is first used!' Furthermore, this structure is sometimes unhelpful, as with, for example, *sixteen*, where the first part of the word relates to the second symbol in its symbolic form:

six-teen

(See Fuson and Kwon, 1991, for a comparison with the Chinese number system.)

In fact, true regularity of English two-digit number names is only found when considering numbers above 59, the structure being based upon the number names for the digits 1 to 9:

> [digit name]-ty [digit name]
> six-ty, six-ty one, six-ty two, . . .
> seven-ty, seven-ty one, seven-ty two, . . .
> eigh(t)-ty, eigh(t)-ty one, eigh(t)-ty two, . . .
> nine-ty, nine-ty one, nine-ty two, . . .

If this structure were completely regular (something that is true of many Asian languages), then instead of having to learn 99 individual names for the numbers from 1 to 99, only the nine digit names would need to be memorized, along with the suffix -ty. The structure allows a considerable saving of effort on behalf of a student – a reduction from 99 names to only 10.

Of course, English is not this regular and there are plenty of exceptions. However, if the structure is presented first to students, then many numbers could be said correctly immediately and the exceptions (such as *fif-ty* rather than *five-ty*) can be gradually learnt. Gattegno (1988) identified that there were 18 number names required to learn how to say all the number names from 1 to 999. The structure is completely regular for *hundred, thou-*

sand, million and so only three more words are needed to learn to say all the names from 1 to 999,999,999.

Gattegno (1974, 1988) offered a visual image for this structure, which I will refer to here as 'the tens chart' (see Figure 3.1). Each column has a *digit name* associated with it (*one, two, three, . . ., nine*) and each row has a *value name* associated with it (*thousand, hundred, -ty,* [*nothing*]). Thus, a number name can be thought of as made up from *digit names* and *value names*. This brings the number names into a remarkably accessible structure and within this table are all numbers from 1 to 9999. The structure of the number names is thus brought to the fore and an algebra of number names is involved when students come to know, practise and then apply this structure in number tasks. This structure can be useful in working with secondary students (aged between 11 and 14) who have had considerable difficulties in mathematics, partly due to lack of confidence with number. The tens chart can help not only with reading and writing numbers, but also with addition and subtraction strategies (Hewitt and Brown, 1998).

1000	2000	3000	4000	5000	6000	7000	8000	9000
100	200	300	400	500	600	700	800	900
10	20	30	40	50	60	70	80	90
1	2	3	4	5	6	7	8	9

Figure 3.1 The tens chart.

Place value is often seen as a significant topic and it can become more of an issue when working with decimals. A number such as 384.87 is often read aloud as *three hundred and eighty-four point eight seven*. Here, the digits after the decimal point are not given value names, they are just said as *point eight seven*. A second issue is that, particularly within the context of money, students can become used to saying *point eighty seven*, thus having the same value name said for both the eights. The software *Numbers* has the possibility of having the value names extended into the decimals, with additional rows given names of *tenths, hundredths* and *thousandths*.

For instance, if 0.3 is clicked on, then feedback of either *nought point three* or *three tenths* can be given. The advantage of the latter is that the value name is present. Thus, practising saying *three tenths* and *three hundredths* for 0.3 and 0.03 allows students to have the value names present within the way they come to say the number. So 72.3 is said *seventy-two and three tenths*. Even a number like 72.364 (see Figure 3.2 overleaf) can be said as *seventy-two, three tenths, six hundredths and four thousandths*, with each digit name (except units) having a value name said after it. In this way, place value is also present within the number names of decimals as well as whole numbers.

If this sounds cumbersome, I suggest coming to say *four thousandths* for 0.004 is no more difficult than learning to say *four thousand* for 4000.

Numbers : Browse Mode								

File   Appearance   Written/Spoken   Tasks

100	200	300	400	500	600	700	800	900
10	20	30	40	50	60	70	80	90
1	2	3	4	5	6	7	8	9
0.1	0.2	0.3	0.4	0.5	0.6	0.7	0.8	0.9
0.01	0.02	0.03	0.04	0.05	0.06	0.07	0.08	0.09
0.001	0.002	0.003	0.004	0.005	0.006	0.007	0.008	0.009

Clear ▲ ▼ Random Number 1 Number 2 Number 3 ◄ ►

animation

C   v Write it
       Grid

72.364

seventy two, three tenths, six hundredths and four thousandths

Figure 3.2   Three forms of representation.

Saying *five, three tenths, six hundredths and four thousandths* for 5.364 is no more difficult than learning to say *four thousand, six hundred and thirty-five* for 4635. If decimals were regularly said aloud in this way in class, then place value for decimal digits would come with the language. It is relatively easy for students to learn that it is also possible to say *five point three six four* as well, as this way of reading is part of our everyday culture of speaking anyway. The structure of the tens chart leads to natural extensions of further rows above and below and thus encompasses the sense of the infinitely large (going upwards) and the infinitely small (going downwards). In this way, decimal places can be seen as conceptually similar to larger numbers, rather than a separate topic.

Features of the software

Ainley (1997) has offered a list of roles for software which is of the type where students can 'teach' the software to carry out certain tasks. Here, I offer a more general list of features which might be useful to consider when asking the following question. In what way, if at all, are each of these features utilized within a particular piece of software and, if so, how are they exploited for educational purposes?

(a) Presentation
(b) Accuracy
(c) Randomness

(d) Movement
(e) Ordering of events
(f) Speed
(g) Other time-dependent features, such as something only appearing on the screen for a certain time period
(h) Links between aural, visual and kinaesthetic senses
(i) Variability – choices in what appears on the screen
(j) Flexibility – the program changing what happens as a consequence of actions taken
(k) Feedback – offering potentially educational responses to actions taken
(l) Restricting the form and nature of what can be carried out and what can be entered – creating rules of interaction with the software

I will concentrate here on just three of these (variability, links and movement) in relation to the program *Numbers*. Later in this chapter, I will discuss two others: ordering of events in relation to the programs *Powers of 10* and *Tables*; and feedback in relation to *Numbers* and *Powers of 10*.

Having considered the structure of the number names, what does the software offer which is different from using, for example, a large printed version of the tens chart?

First, there is variability. The number of rows can be varied from one to seven (Figure 3.2 has six rows) and the range of numbers appearing can also be varied. So, for example, there could be one row which contained only the units or there could be three rows containing the tenths, hundredths and thousandths. This can be varied so that the visible chart on the screen can suit the needs of a particular class or student at that point in time. All tasks set by the software will be restricted to the numbers appearing within the chosen visible chart.

Also, the way in which certain forms of numbers are presented can be chosen: for example, 72.364 can be presented as either *seventy-two, three tenths, six hundredths and four thousandths* or *seventy-two point three six four*. This can be chosen through a drop-down menu to suit the focus of a lesson. Some people prefer the chart to be flipped, so that the higher numbers are at the bottom rather than the top. This is another choice from the menus.

Second, there are links among aural, visual and kinaesthetic senses. The chart offers both the kinaesthetic (through movement of the mouse and clicking on the chart) and visual imagery for the structure of the number names. This is linked with the symbolic and written forms of the numbers (both visual) and also the aural form of numbers, with the program able to 'say' the numbers as well. Thus, all the different forms of numbers are linked together (see Figure 3.3): the component form in the chart (the collection of component parts which make up a number, e.g. 70, 2, 0.3, 0.06 and 0.004); the symbolic form (e.g. 72.364) and the written form (e.g. *seventy-two, three tenths, six hundredths and four thousandths* or *seventy-two point three six four*). The program can also speak the number name, with

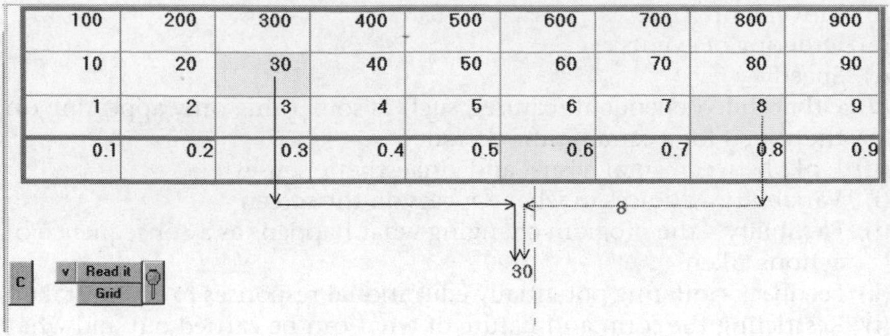

100	200	300	400	500	600	700	800	900
10	20	30	40	50	60	70	80	90
1	2	3	4	5	6	7	8	9
0.1	0.2	0.3	0.4	0.5	0.6	0.7	0.8	0.9

C　v Read it ○　30
　　Grid

Figure 3.3　First movements of component parts to form the number 38.6.

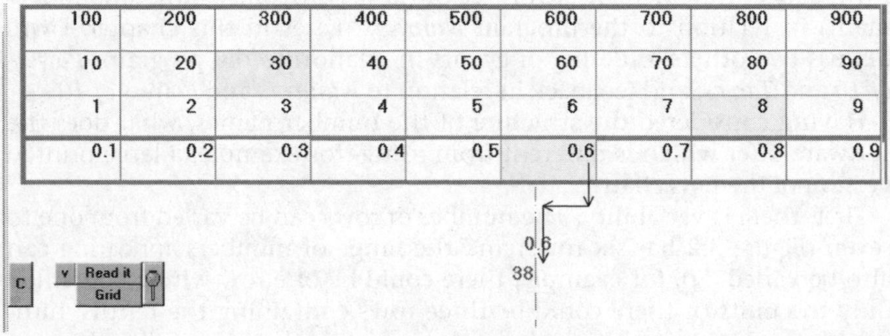

100	200	300	400	500	600	700	800	900
10	20	30	40	50	60	70	80	90
1	2	3	4	5	6	7	8	9
0.1	0.2	0.3	0.4	0.5	0.6	0.7	0.8	0.9

C　v Read it ○　0.6
　　Grid　　　38

Figure 3.4　The 0.6 drops into place to complete 38.6.

the relevant written parts being highlighted at the same time as those parts are being said.

Third, there is movement. The component parts of a number, such as 38.6 (see Figure 3.3), come together through each part in turn, starting from the one with highest value, dropping down to the bottom of the chart and then moving horizontally until it 'clicks' into place and slides down the vertical dotted line (coloured red in the software). In Figure 3.3, the '30' has already dropped into place (its journey is indicated by the arrows (which do not appear on the computer screen) and the '8' is part way towards the red dotted line and will drop down 'on top of' the '30' to make '38'. Lastly, the '0.6' will also drop down (see Figure 3.4) and complete the number 38.6.

Another role for movement is where a digit within the symbolic form of a number, such as the '6' in 72.364, can be clicked on and this will dynamically rise above the number (see Figure 3.5). Not only can the value of that digit be seen as '0.06', but also the program will write and speak the value of that digit. The 0.06 will then descend back into the number again to return it to 72.364.

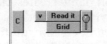

0.06
72.304

six hundredths

Figure 3.5   The digit 6 in 72.364 rises to show its value.

Powers of 10: an algebra on number names

So far, I have considered what might be available within the language of number names to help with students' understanding of place value and decimals, and, in particular, use has been made of the combination of digit and value names. Now I wish to shift from thinking of the value name as a *label* (indicating the value) to thinking of it as an *operation*. For example, take the number *two hundred*. I have been considering this name as being made of two parts: a digit name (*two*) and a value name (*hundred*). Now, I wish to view this as a digit name (*two*) and an operation name (*hundred* meaning *multiply by a hundred*). So instead of considering *two hundred* as a label for a particular number, it is now viewed as representing a dynamic movement (operation) starting with the *two* and performing the operation *multiply by a hundred* (see Figure 3.6).

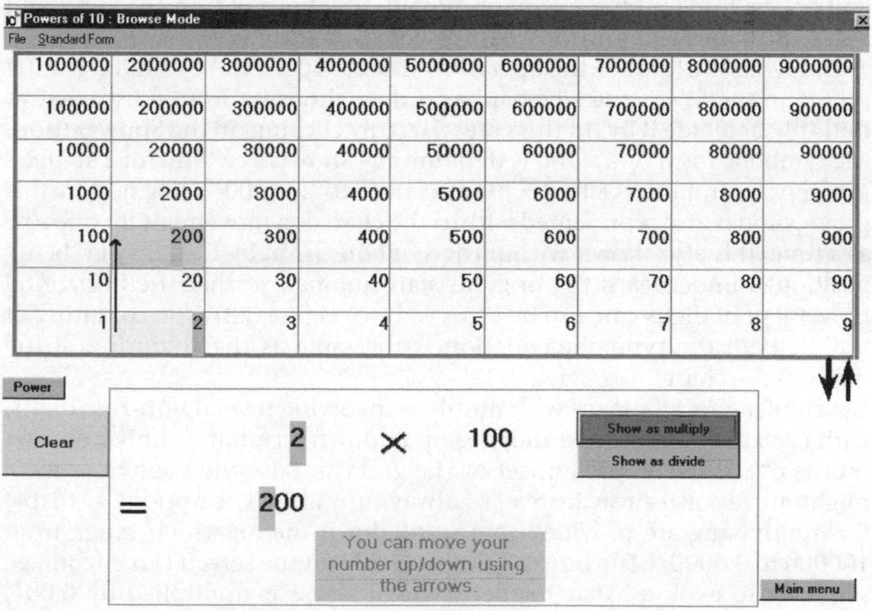

Figure 3.6   Seeing *hundred* as an operation.

Thus, this shift from value name to operation name creates a mathematical shift from describing a number to multiplying a number by a power of 10. The operation names *-ty, thousand, hundredths*, etc. are multiplying the digit name by 10, 10^3, 10^{-2}, respectively. The program *Powers of 10* uses the tens chart by allowing someone to shift a number up or down rows dynamically by clicking on an arrow (see the arrows at bottom right of the chart in Figure 3.6). This dynamic can then be expressed symbolically as $2 \times 100 = 200$. This symbolic statement can now be viewed as shown in Figure 3.7.

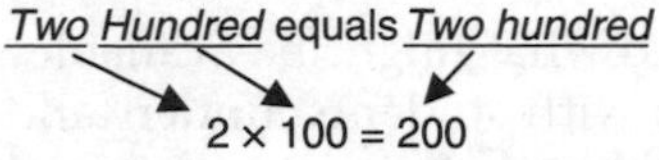

Two _Hundred_ equals _Two hundred_

$2 \times 100 = 200$

Figure 3.7 Symbolic representation of *two hundred*.

The first occurrence of the word *hundred* is viewed as an operation and the second is viewed as the value part of a number name. The operation of ×100 is quite accessible within the tens chart through moving vertically up the chart. So 200 can be seen through the language, as well as through the movement in the chart, as 2×100. However, in symbolic form there is a related movement of the digit horizontally. To assist with linking the two movements, vertical and horizontal, the '2' is highlighted; as the number is moved dynamically up the chart, attention can be placed on the digit and on the horizontal movement dynamically both within the chart and also within the symbolic form expressed below the chart.

The symbolic form of the operation (i.e. 2×100) can be entered first by typing in the '2' on the keyboard and then choosing from a list what to multiply or divide it by (in this case ×100). By clicking on the Show button, the symbolic form of 2×100 is dynamically shown as a 'film' of a stepped progression from 2×1 to 2×10 and then to 2×100. Each step in this progression is also represented within the chart as a movement up one row at a time. It is also shown within the symbolic form by the 'answer' being positioned underneath the original start number, so that the horizontal movement of digits can also be observed (see Figure 3.8). The colouring of the digits in the symbolic equation is the same as the colouring of the digits in the chart.

A similar effect happens with numbers involving several non-zero digits, with each component part moving up or down a certain number of rows on the chart. The visual impact of the grid can raise the issue of how '2' might move *down* a row instead of always upwards. The options available for multiplying are provided in a scroll-down menu, which range from 100000 to 0.00001. The possibilities available on the screen can encourage someone to explore what happens when, say, 2 is multiplied by 0.001. Again, if students are encouraged to say 0.001 as *one thousandth* then 2×0.001 can be naturally said as *two thousandths*, with this phrase

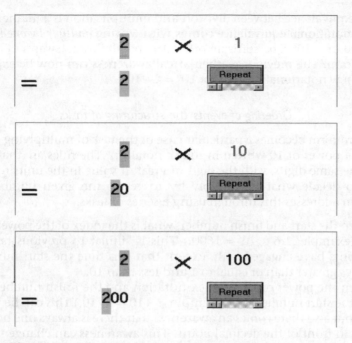

Figure 3.8 The staged horizontal movements of the digit '2'.

encompassing both the operation and the answer. If 0.1, 0.01, 0.001, etc. are seen as natural extensions of rows coming down from 1000, 100, 10, 1, etc. (see Figure 3.2), then multiplying by such numbers as 0.1 or 0.01 can feel a natural extension of multiplying by 100 or 10. Multiplying by decimals in this way can also help address the misconception that multiplying means 'getting bigger'.

The program also allows a number to be divided by a power of 10. Indeed after clicking on a number in the grid, such as 47, and clicking on an arrow to move it down the grid to 0.047, the process can be viewed symbolically as either a multiplication or a division. So the symbolic expression $47 \div 1000 = 0.047$ can shift to $47 \times 0.001 = 0.047$ and back again with the opportunity to work on the awareness of the equivalence of the two statements – exploring what changes and what stays the same. I suggest that having a variety of ways of viewing leads to variety in what mathematics can be done with what is viewed. Sometimes it is useful to see connections between 47 and 0.047 in terms of multiplication, and sometimes in terms of division. Awareness that $\times$ 100 and $\div$ 1/100 are equivalent, and more generally $\times n$ and $\div 1/n$ are equivalent, is useful when working with fractions:

$$\frac{a}{b} \div \frac{1}{n} = \frac{a}{b} \times n.$$

The equivalence between division and multiplication is a mathematical one. A notational equivalence comes with writing *multiply by one hundred* as $\times 100$ or $\times 10^2$. The software offers the possibility to swap notation to index form. The previous mathematical awareness can now be expressed in the new notational form of $x \times 10^n = x \div 10^{-n}$.

Ordering of events: the structuring of tasks

Standard form becomes a particular case of the task of multiplying a number by a power of 10 written in index notation. The rules are that I start with the same digits, with the digit of greatest value in the units row, and have to decide what to multiply by to get to the given number. The program addresses this through using a series of tasks.

1. Given the start and finish number, what is the index of the power of 10? (For example, $1.6 \times 10^? = 1600$.) This is similar to previous tasks the students have engaged with, except that this time the start number is always greater than or equal to 1 and less than 10.
2. Given the power of 10 in index notation and the finish number, what was the start number? (For example, $? \times 10^3 = 1710$.) This can be worked out, but also there comes an awareness that there is always one non-zero digit in front of the decimal point. This awareness can change the task into a routine one with little calculation taking place. However, this is useful as it reinforces what is an arbitrary convention for the form of the start number when writing standard form.
3. A mixture of the above two tasks.
4. Only the finish number is given and so the start number and the index for the power of 10 need to be provided. (For example, $? \times 10^? = 1124$.) Of course, without the convention already being established, there are an infinite number of solutions. So this is a test of knowing the convention of the start number having a single digit before the decimal point, as well as the mathematics involved in finding the index of the power of 10.

Computers can offer help with structuring the types of tasks offered and when they are offered. Within *Developing Number*, there is a progression mode where the tasks are structured so that a level of success has to be demonstrated with certain types of tasks before other tasks become available. My understanding of one individualized learning package is that the questions offered try to maintain a success rate of about 70%. So the judged difficulty of questions is varied in order to maintain that level of success.

The structuring might not only be about levels of difficulty. Another program in the *Developing Number* suite is *Tables*, which approaches the learning and practice of multiplication tables through the use of doubling and halving. The assumption is that most students working on their tables can double and multiply by 10 (if they cannot, then I suggest there are more fruitful areas of mathematics for them to work on rather than trying to learn the times tables). From the 2 times table another doubling produces the 4 times table and a further doubling produces the 8 times table. This is shown by the connecting straight lines in Figure 3.9, where continuous lines indicate doubling or halving. For example, there is a continuous line from the 10 to the 5 times table (halving). The dotted lines indicate how a table is obtained from another table through either adding or subtracting one number. Thus the 9 times table is obtained from subtracting the number being multiplied from the 10 times table.

This approach to working out the multiplication tables tries to avoid repeated addition, which often leads to mistakes through the need for double counting (Gray and Tall, 1993), while trying to rely upon as little student prior knowledge/skills as possible. As an aside here, the 7 times table does not have any links with others. It is developed through the idea that it is always 7 times something else, and so use the *something else* times table to work it out! (Of course, 7×7 needs to be known as a special case.) The desirable aim of knowing tables quickly is developed within the program through challenges to beat previous personal best times.

More generally, the strategies developed are also applied to other multiplications by the numbers 1 to 9, such as 38 × 4 or 63 × 9. Learning to multiply by (say) 9, as opposed to rote-learning the 9 times table, can be applied to many calculations, and the program utilizes this fact by requiring success with 'bigger' calculations in order to progress, as well as beating personal best times with the times tables.

The structuring of progression through a series of tasks for individual students is based not so much on level of difficulty as on the way in which the tables are related to each other through doubling/halving, etc. Initially, only the ×2 and ×10 tables are offered, and only with success will the next row of tables become available: ×4, ×3, ×5, ×9 (see Figure 3.9). Success with these leads in turn to the bottom row of tables: ×8, ×6 and ×7.

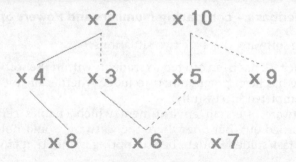

Figure 3.9   Seeing how tables are linked through doubling/halving and addition/subtraction.

Within a given times table, there are also stages of challenges. The first stage begins with a chart where there is visual help as to what is required to be done to work out, for example, 7×8 (see Figure 3.10). At this stage, someone would be required to enter each stage of the doubling process.

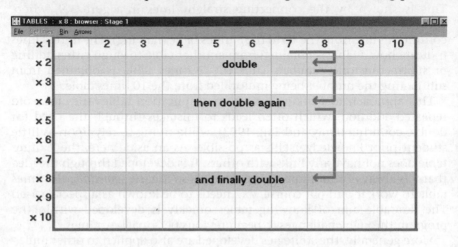

Figure 3.10   Visual help for the 8 times table.

Then, gradually, further stages involve entering the final answer without visual support and also introducing the inverse process of division (e.g. ? = 5/68). The computer offers the possibility of structuring an approach to the learning of a particular topic. This has its strengths, but there are also weaknesses. For example, there are other ways in which the 8 times table might be approached, such as knowing ×10 and subtracting ×2. The design of the program is based upon a certain pedagogic approach which might have advantages, but the price that is paid for such a strong approach is that a certain flexibility is lost.

Feedback – comparing *Numbers* and *Powers of 10*

When using software, there are two situations:

(a) a specific task has been offered to students within the software and the software has been programmed to judge whether or not the task has been completed successfully;
(b) the software offers an environment which enables certain actions to be carried out, but one where the software would not know what specific task students might be attempting within that environment.

Examples of the second situation include *Excel, Logo*, interactive geometry software such as *The Geometer's Sketchpad* and *Cabri-Géomètre*, as well as graph-drawing packages such as *Autograph* and *Omnigraph*. These enable certain actions to be carried out within the set of rules governing the software. As long as a student works within these rules, then the software obediently carries out the instructions without offering any value judgement. Thus, if a student is attempting to draw an equilateral triangle in *Logo* and enters:

repeat 3 [forward 100 right 60]

then, provided the rules governing the software are met, such as correctly entered syntax, the software will do as it has been told without making any judgement on what has been produced (see Figure 3.11). Such feedback I describe as *seeing the consequences of your actions*. Through being fed back the (geometrical) consequence of what was entered, students can not only judge whether they achieved what they were trying to achieve, but are also given useful information if any corrections are required. This information is not just a report of what the student entered (in this case, the command repeat 3 [forward 100 right 60]); it provides an additional consequence to what was entered, in this case the geometrical image. This can help students realize that there is an issue with the angle involved. An analogy for this is when I set myself the task of throwing some waste paper into a bin, I watch what happens after throwing the paper. If it does not go in the bin, then I can observe, for example, that it fell short and was slightly to the right of the bin. Such feedback is valuable in how I decide to adjust my throw next time.

The situation can be quite different with the first situation, where the software sets a task and is able to judge success. What about feedback now? What options exist? I propose the following categorization of possible feedback when software is capable of making value judgements about actions taken by students:

1. *None*: no feedback additional to actions carried out by students is offered at all.
2. *Stressing and ignoring*: certain aspects are highlighted either through them being stressed or through others being ignored – it is left to the students to decide the relevance of the highlighting.

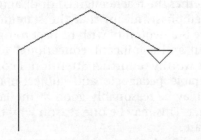

Figure 3.11 *Logo* gives the result of: repeat 3 [forward 100 right 60].

3. *Consequences*: non-judgemental consequences additional to actions carried out by students are fed back – it is up to the students to make judgements, from observing the consequences, about whether what they did was correct or not.
4. *Explicit yes/no*: the students are explicitly told whether they are correct.
   (a) In addition, to this, there are particular possibilities if students are told explicitly *no*:
      (i) no other information is offered;
      (ii) a penalty is provided;
      (iii) an explicit hint is offered as to how they might proceed successfully;
      (iv) an explanation is offered as to how to proceed successfully (this includes the possibility of being told the correct answer).
   (b) In addition, there are particular possibilities if students are told explicitly *yes*:
      (i) no other information is offered;
      (ii) a reward is given.
5. *Implicit yes/no*: the students can deduce whether they are correct or not, even though they are not told explicitly. For example, progression to other parts of the program may be dependent upon a correct response and students may find that they now either can or cannot progress.

A combination of feedback types is possible in some circumstances, and it is quite possible for any particular piece of software to be used in such a way that different types of feedback occur in different situations. For example, a worksheet in *Excel* can be created which has ten arithmetic questions set out and cells to enter the answers to each question. One version of such a file will just accept any answer entered by a student, whether correct or not. Another version of the software might have a macro created so a 'Yes' or 'No' appears, according to what is entered.

These categories of feedback have not come from, and are not particular to, computer software. For example, Loska (1998) has talked about a German philosopher, Leonard Nelson, restructuring the Socratic dialogue (e.g. Plato's *Meno*) between teacher and students, where 'students got no information on whether the teacher agreed or disagreed. They could only conclude that the emphasis meant that the statement should be examined' (p. 239). There is a neutrality with respect to right and wrong; however, there is skilful and significant educational feedback by stressing something which is worthy of further attention. I consider such feedback to require considerable pedagogic and subject-matter awareness, and although software may be reasonably good at the latter, it is often sadly lacking in the former. This may be one reason why this form of feedback within software is rare.

I will offer examples of some of these categories and compare the two programs *Numbers* and *Powers of 10*. *Numbers* makes use of *implicit yes/no* within its tasks linking the written, symbolic and chart representations of numbers. When a student enters the program in what is called *Browse tasks* mode, the number name *three hundredths*, for example, appears and a student is asked to click on this number in the tens chart. If a different number is clicked on, then nothing happens at all. The student can only progress to the next question by clicking on the correct number.

One attribute of this type of feedback is that students are allowed to learn what *three hundredths* is in symbolic form, rather than there being an expectation that they get it right on their first attempt. Learning the names can indeed come from finding out which symbolic form is accepted for the given number name. However, when a student enters *Progression* mode, their progress through structured tasks is noted by the computer and can be available for the student and teacher to see. In this instance, the computer notes any incorrect clicking on the grid. Consequently, there is feedback of *explicit no* given to a student, so that the student knows that the program has registered an incorrect response. The structure of the program is such that a student cannot progress to the next stage of challenges unless they complete correctly all of a set of questions at a current stage. The emphasis now changes from the student exploring to the student testing themselves and being challenged to see if they can answer correctly first time.

Within part of the tasks for *Powers of 10*, the feedback gives *consequences* of what is entered. For example, when asked to enter the result of 8000×0.001, a student might enter incorrectly 0.8. The student is fed back the fact that this is not correct through the appearance of a sad face. However, if this were the only feedback, then the student would have little information to inform their next attempt. The *consequences* feedback reflects back to the student which scenario could have resulted in the answer they entered. So, the incorrect 0.8 remains visible and instead the question is adapted to show which question would have resulted in an answer of 0.8, in this case 8000×0.0001 (see Figure 3.12).

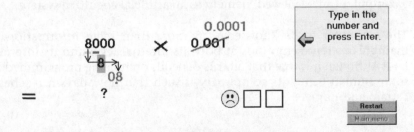

Figure 3.12 A frozen screen-shot of dynamic feedback for an incorrect answer of 0.8. (Note: arrows are drawn to demonstrate the movement of the digit 8. They are not present on the screen.)

Additionally, a copy of the digit involved in the original number 8000 (i.e. the '8') moves as indicated by the arrows (which are not present on the computer screen, but are added here to indicate the dynamic movement), where the number of places the digit moves horizontally is indicated through the presence of red markers. The frozen screen shot captured in Figure 3.12 has the digit '8' caught in mid-journey. The student now has information which can help their awareness of what question would have resulted in the answer entered and how the question originally asked differs from this question.

The choice of these two different types of feedback for *Numbers* and *Powers of 10* is consistent with the notion that number names are essentially arbitrary, while arithmetic calculations are necessary (Hewitt, 1999). I describe as arbitrary those things where there exists a choice. In this case, the choice of number names is a social convention. There is nothing about 0.03 which says it *must* be called *three hundredths*; after all, in other languages it is said differently. Students need to be informed of names and conventions and the use of the tens chart tries to do this in as efficient a manner as possible.

However, there is something necessary about 8000×0.0001. There is only one single number which is the result of this calculation. This is not choice, not a social convention; it is something which has to be the case and something which students (for whom this is an appropriate task) can work out using their awareness of mathematics. So, whereas it is appropriate for feedback for number names to be *yes/no* in nature, mathematical calculations require different feedback. In this case, feedback assists students in continuing to use their awareness of the mathematics involved and does not either simply say *yes/no*, nor does it attempt to do the mathematics of the original question for the student.

Conclusion

Sutherland and Balacheff (1999) report a relatively recent way in which the computer can be viewed, namely as an artificial cognitive system.

> The computer treats knowledge as more than mere information, it manipulates representations at both its internal level and its interface [. . .] Although it is true that all this depends on it being programmed by some human being, its complexity is such that nowadays it reaches a certain autonomy.

> (p. 6)

The key issue I highlight here is not to underplay the human programming and the pedagogic significance this can have on the learning opportunities for students. The way in which a computer internally manipulates information is programmed along with the way in which the student and computer relate (the interface). *How* the computer internally manipulates information and *how* the interface is designed are fundamentally pedagogic decisions when it comes to educational software. All educational software, I suggest, has pedagogy embodied within its design.

The pedagogy appears in three main areas:

1. The images and approaches which form the *content* of the program (such as the tens chart).
2. The rules of interaction with the software which form the *engagement* with the program. This interaction consists of:
   (a) ways in which a student is allowed and not allowed to act to input and affect what happens within the program (such as choosing from a list of multipliers – ... × 0.01, × 0.1, ×1, ×10, ×100, ... – rather than typing in a multiplication from the keyboard). These form the allowable *actions* on the program.
   (b) ways in which the software responds to such actions (on choosing a multiplier from the list, the software responds with a 'film' of the original number moving up or down the chart one row at a time while simultaneously an equivalent horizontal dynamic movement takes place with the digits in the written symbolic form). These form the *feedback* from the program.
3. The hidden internal dynamics which form the *workings* of the program (such as the carrying out of calculations, or the in-built structure determining which tasks are presented in what order).

However, the pedagogic possibilities which software offers are only possibilities. The most significant factor of all remains the pedagogic skills and awareness of the teacher and the quality of interactions between teacher and students. It is what the teacher or student makes of a program and how it is incorporated within the teacher–student dynamic which will make a program, just like any other resource, a significant factor in learning mathematics or whether it simply ends up being another distraction from more productive activities.

Postscript: the use of the word 'algebra' within the context of number names

Algebra is often associated with arithmetic by means of such work as writing, manipulating and solving general arithmetic equations such as $7(x + 3) + x = 23$, or considering graphs such as $y = mx + c$. The essence of such work is threefold:

(a) To bring to the fore the inherent structure of arithmetic operations. For example, an image for addition might be as shown in Figure 3.13.

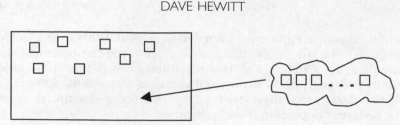

Figure 3.13   Image for addition.

(b) To articulate what can be said about the generality of arithmetic operations, irrespective of the particular numbers involved. For example, subtraction might be viewed as shown in Figure 3.14 (and seen as the inverse of addition).

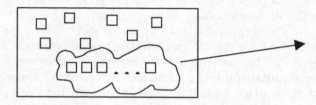

Figure 3.14   Image for subtraction.

(c) To apply awareness gained from (b) to give new insights into arithmetic problems. For example, if $7(x + 3) + x = 23$ then $7(x + 3) = 23 - x$ would also be true.

By taking out the explicit reference to arithmetic, these can be rephrased as:

(a′) To bring to the fore the inherent structure to be found within a topic.
(b′) To articulate what can be said about the generality of the structure irrespective of any particular circumstances.
(c′) To apply awareness gained from (b′) to give new insights into the original topic.

Thus, these three statements (a′), (b′) and (c′) have been obtained from carrying out the processes identified within the original (a) and (b) on the three parts (a), (b) and (c) to get more general statements about the essence of algebra. By applying this notion of algebra to the topic of number names (i.e. carrying out (c′)), I considered an algebra *of* number names where the inherent structure was stressed and articulated to find generalities which could then be applied to number names which might not have been previously considered.

   An algebra *on* number names comes from imposing a new structure upon the (by now established) number names. This structure looks at the dynamic between number names such as *two* and *two hundred*. The structural difference comes in the value word *hundred* and this is used not just as a statement of the value difference between the two numbers, but as an operation to move from one number to the other. Thus, number names are operated on to arrive at other number names and a new structure, or algebra, is constructed by moving between number names.

References

Ainley, J. (1997) 'Roles for teachers, and computers', in E. Pehkonen (ed.), *Proceedings of the 21st Conference of the International Group for the Psychology of Mathematics Education*. Helsinki: Lahti Research and Training Centre, University of Helsinki, Vol. 1, pp. 90–98.

Association of Teachers of Mathematics (2004) *Developing Number (version 2)*. Derby: ATM.

Fuson, K. and Kwon, Y. (1991) 'Chinese-based regular and European irregular systems of number words: the disadvantages for English-speaking children', in K. Durkin and B. Shire (eds), *Language in Mathematical Education: Research and Practice*. Buckingham: Open University Press, pp. 211–26.

Gattegno, C. (1974) *The Common Sense of Teaching Mathematics*. New York: Educational Solutions.

Gattegno, C. (1988) *The Science of Education, Part 2B: the Awareness of Mathematization*. New York: Educational Solutions.

Gray, E. and Tall, D. (1993) 'Success and failure in mathematics: the flexible meaning of symbols as process and concept'. *Mathematics Teaching*, **142**, 6–10.

Hewitt, D. (1999) 'Arbitrary and necessary, Part 1: a way of viewing the mathematics curriculum'. *For the Learning of Mathematics*, **19**(3), 2–9.

Hewitt, D. and Brown, E. (1998) 'On teaching early number through language', in A. Olivier and K. Newstead (eds), *Proceedings of the 22nd Conference of the International Group for the Psychology of Mathematics Education*. Stellenbosch, South Africa: University of Stellenbosch, Vol. 3, pp. 41–8.

Loska, R. (1998) 'Teaching without instruction: the neo-Socratic method', in H. Steinbring, M. Bartolini Bussi and A. Sierpinska (eds), *Language and Communication in the Mathematics Classroom*. Reston, VA: National Council of Teachers of Mathematics, pp. 235–46.

Sutherland, R. and Balacheff, N. (1999) 'Didactical complexity of computational environments for the learning of mathematics'. *International Journal of Computers for Mathematical Learning*, **4**(1), 1–26.

Wigley, A. (1997) 'Approaching number through language', in I. Thompson (ed.), *Teaching and Learning Early Number*. Buckingham: Open University Press, pp. 113–22.

4

THINKING ALGEBRAICALLY: MANIPULATIVE ALGEBRA

John Monaghan

This or that piece of software might provide students with useful experiences for this or that aspect of algebra, but we should not expect any single system to help with all aspects of algebra *per se*. The first section of this chapter briefly examines different views of what constitutes school algebra. The second section looks at examples of the use of ICT in teaching algebra, while the third identifies various advantages and disadvantages of the varied notational formats different pieces of software use. The fourth and fifth sections deal with the challenge of incorporating algebra-related ICT into school teaching and learning respectively, and the chapter finishes with a discussion of aspects of student learning in this area.

What is school algebra?

School algebra can be viewed in many ways: as using letters for numbers, as solving equations, as generalized arithmetic, as generalization and abstraction or as a codified and systematic approach to problem-solving. An exclusive focus on any one of these (especially the first) can be detrimental to student learning of algebra. Bednarz *et al.* (1996) provide a useful collection of essays on aspects of school algebra from a diverse range of authors. This North American book considers four general approaches to algebra: generalization, problem solving, modelling and functional representation.

Generalization

Generalization involves seeing specific examples as instances of general features. Among other things, algebra can provide a language both for expressing and subsequently manipulating such generalizations. John Mason (1996, p. 65) speaks of 'seeing a generality in the particular and seeing the particular in the general', and these sophisticated perceptions can initially be hard to develop in students. Pattern spotting arising from exploring a range of related situations is a stage on the way to seeing generality, but being able to express what has been seen is an additional and sometimes challenging step.

Consider the example of factorizations of $x^n - 1$, in the cases where n is prime. Use of a computer algebra system such as *Derive* can present particular factorizations of the same form as the general case, for unspecified values of n. Having the output that is shown in Figure 4.12 (page 73) in front of them, students may be able to see the commonality of form/structure and be able to reason why this form must result for $x^{prime} - 1$.

Problem-solving

Problem solving is far from easy to categorize. For some, it involves resolving verbally-posed problems, while for others the nature of the problem is supposed to be more 'problematic' and for which the would-be solver has few or no algorithmic resources available to hand. A common format to many such problems at Key Stage 3 involves unequal sharing, such as the following chocolate problem.

100 chocolates were distributed among three groups of children. The second group received four times as many chocolates as the first group. The third group received ten chocolates more than the second group. How many chocolates did each group receive?

There are many ways to solve this problem, certainly not all of which deserve to be called 'algebraic'.

For instance, one essentially non-algebraic approach would be to start with knowns and work towards unknowns. This could mean giving each group $100 \div 3$ chocolates in the first instance and then proceeding by trial and improvement, subject to the problem's criteria and constraints. A spreadsheet would seem to encourage such an approach and help a student move towards a solution.

One essentially algebraic approach would involve working in the opposite direction, from unknowns to knowns. Assigning a particular unknown quantity the label x (here the number of chocolates the first group has), an equation can be generated which reflects the problem's inner relationships: $x + 4x + (4x + 10) = 100$.

Teresa Rojano (1996) found that, although students working with a spreadsheet started with a non-algebraic approach, many students moved to a structured, algebraic approach in terms of the unknown and drawing out the mathematical relationships in the problems: e.g. =A5*4, =A9+10, =A5+A9+A11. Interestingly, she noted that students who already had efficient informal strategies for solving word problems were the least motivated to learn spreadsheet solution methods.

The same is often true of students for whom such verbal problems are not really 'problematic' with regard to an initial introduction of algebra by means of such problems. In order that the sophistication of the required algebra does not interfere with students being able to follow algebraic manipulation, textbooks often provide problems that do not actually require the resources of manipulative algebra.

Modelling

Modelling is important, but hard to characterize. According to Mason and Sutherland (2002), its critical features are: the resolution of 'real-world' questions and moving from a specific situation into a world of mathematical models and symbols and then returning to the original setting once a mathematical solution has been obtained.

Nemirovsky (1996) characterizes modelling as the construction of mathematical narratives. He uses examples which readers familiar with the Shell Centre 'Red Box' (Swan, 1985) will recognize: interpreting real-world graphs. Graph plotters set up to receive input from motion sensors can provide students with rich experience of real-world graphs: e.g. 'distance–time' graphs of students walking towards and away from a motion sensor. The real 'plus' for the student and teacher of such graphs is that they are graphs of the students' actions themselves and the feedback is almost immediate.

Nemirovsky notes four implications of such work for student learning:

- a shift from the usual focus on internal relationships between variables (e.g. distance/time) to describing connections between narratives, graphs and symbolic expressions;
- variables are situated in real actions;
- there are many possible narratives for the same situation;
- narrative accounts interrelate many aspects of mathematics, e.g. distance, direction, velocity and acceleration.

(p. 215)

Functions

Functional approaches to algebra centre on developing student experience with functions and families of functions, often through 'real-world' situations. This approach has found favour in 'reform' mathematics in the USA and is often accompanied by the representational 'trinity': numerical (tabular), graphical and symbolic. A good understanding of a phenomenon or situation can be said to be present if a student can successfully link across these three types of representation, as each can reveal different aspects of the situation under examination. The use of ICT is particularly appropriate for this approach to algebra, as spreadsheets, graph plotters and computer algebra systems all allow links among representations.

ICT can be used in each of these four approaches. However, this categorization does not explicitly include algebra as solving equations at the top level, despite this still being the most common perception of algebraic activity in school mathematics. In addition, these four categories are not mutually exclusive: for example, modelling often involves the use of functions, problem-solving often involves generalization, etc.

Examples of use of ICT

In this section, I focus on four (of many) uses of software of interest in the teaching and learning of algebra: spreadsheets, graph plotters, programming and computer algebra systems. For instance, the recent document *Integrating ICT into Mathematics in Key Stage 3* (Department for Education and Skills, 2003, p. 6) offers a number of potential examples of student ICT use in algebra:

- a Year 9 student deploying a computer algebra system to solve a cubic equation by trial and improvement;
- a Year 8 student working on a spreadsheet for a numerical investigation of decimal multiplication, which includes 'programming' the spreadsheet by means of formulae;
- a Year 7 student using a graph plotter to investigate changing a value of the parameter m in the one-parameter family of lines $y = mx$.

Spreadsheets

Spreadsheets were invented for adult finance and accountancy, not as a pedagogic tool for teaching and learning mathematics. In consequence, mathematics teachers often have to be quite devious in how they appropriate them for use in mathematics lessons. They can be used for many sorts of graphs (though graphs of functions are usually much better displayed on a graph plotter) and statistics (see Chapter 6). Another way of thinking about algebra is as a language for communicating with your spreadsheet. Figures 4.1–4.4 illustrate some algebraic uses of spreadsheets.

Figure 4.1 shows how 'iterative refinement' may be used for solving equations. The layout as shown here is largely for the present reader's benefit. If I were doing this example with a class, I would probably do everything in the same x and x^3 columns, to illustrate 'zooming in' more clearly.

	A	B	C	D	E	F	G	H
1	x	x^3		x	x^3		x	x^3
2	3	27		4.25	76.76563		4.55	97.336
3	4	64		4.5	91.125		4.6	100.5446
4	5	125		4.75	107.1719		4.65	103.823
5	6	216					4.7	0

Figure 4.1 Using a spreadsheet to solve $x^3 = 100$ by successive refinement.

Figure 4.2 shows the 'max box' problem. This has many slight variations, e.g. the box could have an open top. Max box is probably the most widely used mini-investigation in secondary mathematics classes. It is an example of an optimization problem, classically the preserve of calculus. No calculus is needed here, but a certain algebraic formulation is required before the spreadsheet can help. As in the previous example, iterative refinement is used (here, to confirm the dimensions which produce the maximum volume; but in other variations of the max box, iterative refinement may be used to find the specific dimensions giving rise to the maximum).

Figure 4.3 shows a spreadsheet being used to generate number sequences (the triangular numbers in this case). Are columns B and C identical? They have the same numbers in them, but column B was produced using an iterative formula, e.g. B2=B1+A2, whereas column C was produced using the formula for the nth term, e.g. C2=A2*(A2+1)/2. Just as with dynamic geometry diagrams (see Chapter 5), spreadsheet columns are specified and calculated dynamically, which means they carry their structural history and definition with them.

Figure 4.4 shows how a spreadsheet may be used to investigate algebraic properties and justify claims. The 2×2 rectangles were created using the following template (where the blank cell is A1).

	=A1+6
=A1+2	=A1+8

All of these examples could be done without a spreadsheet or with other software, but a spreadsheet is a suitable tool to tackle them.

A closed rectangular box is made by cutting the shaded portions from a 12 cm square card as shown below. Find the dimensions (h, l and w) which give the maximum volume.

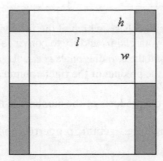

	A	B
1	h	V=h(12-2h)(6-h)
2	1	50
3	2	64
4	3	54
5	4	32
6	5	10
7		
8	1.8	63.504
9	1.9	63.878
10	2	64
11	2.1	63.882
12	2.2	63.536

Figure 4.2 The max box problem and a spreadsheet solution.

	A	B	C
1	1	1	1
2	2	3	3
3	3	6	6
4	4	10	10
5	5	15	15
6	6	21	21
7	7	28	28
8	8	36	36

Figure 4.3 Triangular numbers in a spreadsheet.

Examine the two rectangles below.

3	9
5	11

7	13
9	15

If you build more rectangles like these, which of the following properties will hold for all these rectangles? Justify your claims and try to convince others.

♦ The sum of the numbers in the two diagonals is equal.
♦ The difference between the product of the right column and twice the product of the left column equals 69.
♦ The difference between the products of the numbers in the diagonals equals 12.

Figure 4.4   Investigating algebraic properties and justifying claims.

Graph plotters

Graph plotters are often simple to use and their purpose is clear – they plot graphs. They plot all sorts of graphs: Cartesian, parametric and polar (see Figure 4.5). Depending on the particular system, you may also be able to plot polar parametric graphs, implicit functions, three-dimensional surfaces and inequalities (see Chapter 7). Both novice and experienced teachers using them for the first time often generate tasks that merely imitate traditional paper-and-pencil tasks, for example, plot this family of curves. This can certainly speed up the process of producing graphs.

However, some computer-based tasks can go considerably beyond equivalent paper-and-pencil ones. I present two such tasks below, a linear functions game and a task that requires reflecting quadratic functions. Both could be extended to other types of functions.

Present students with graph paper or a screen with lots of dots on it (see Figure 4.6). The aim is to plot straight lines which go through the dots. Students can play in pairs, getting a point for each dot they 'hit'. Get the students to plot some quadratic functions (see Figure 4.7). Then ask them to reflect these graphs in the x-axis by keying in the equation (but not by using a *Reflect* command). With paper-and-pencil only, this is a fairly low-level drawing exercise, but with a graph plotter the students need to think quite hard about the equation of the reflected curve.

Programming

There are many debates in mathematics teaching circles about programming: should it be taught at all as a part of the mathematics curriculum? If so, then is this language better than that and why? This chapter is not the place for this debate (which was also mentioned in Chapter 1). I will merely indicate very briefly what can be done in an 'imperative language' (such as *BASIC*) and what in a 'functional language' (such as *Logo*).

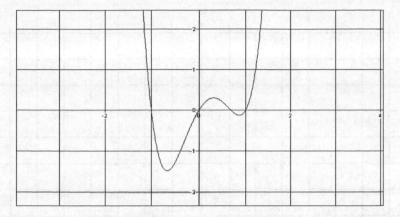

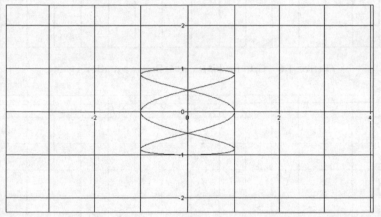

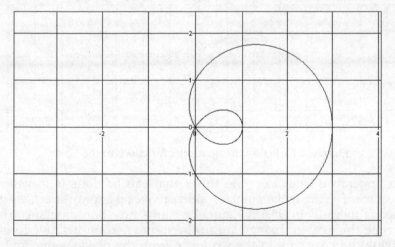

Figure 4.5 Graphs of $y = 3x^4 - 2x^3 - 3x^2 + 2x$; $x = \sin(3t)$, $y = \cos(t)$, for $t = 0$ to 2π; and $r = 1 + 2\cos\theta$, for $\theta = 0$ to 2π.

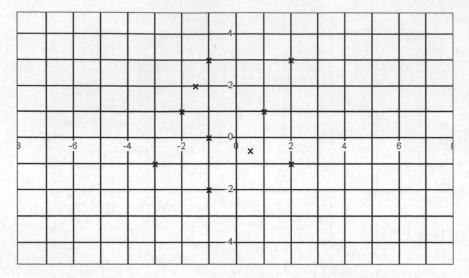

Figure 4.6 Grid for *hit the dots* linear equations game.

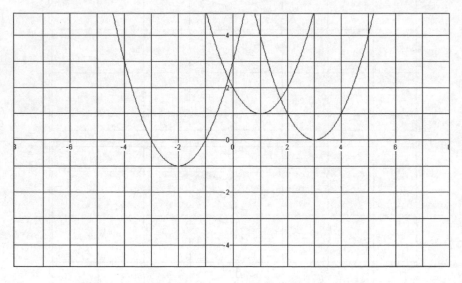

Figure 4.7 Reflect the quadratic functions in the *x*-axis.

In imperative languages, one thing that can be done is to generate sequences. The triangular numbers, done above on a spreadsheet, are generated fairly easily in *QBasic*. Figure 4.8 shows two short programs which generate the first ten triangular numbers: one uses an iterative formula deriving the next term in the sequence from the previous one and the other uses a general formula.

Let n=1	For i=1 to 10
For i=2 to 11	Print i/2*(i+1)
Print n	Next i
Let n=n+i	
Next i	

Figure 4.8 Two *Qbasic* programs to generate the first 10 triangular numbers.

Logo can be used without using variables, but variables add so much to what can be done. *Logo* distinguishes between the name (indicated by a double quotation mark) and the value (indicated by a colon) of a variable (a key distinction in algebra and one that is not marked in conventional algebraic notation). Variables may be used in place of constants in, say, generating regular polygons. Figure 4.9 shows a program for an equilateral triangle of variable side length. It also shows how, by use of variables, a program can be written that will generate *any* regular polygon. Once the procedures are written, the triangles and polygons in this figure are created by the commands tri 100, tri 150, poly 3 100, poly 4 100 and poly 5 100.

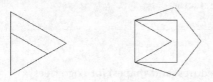

To tri :side	to poly :sides :length
repeat 3[fd :side rt 120]	repeat :sides[fd :length rt 360/:sides]
end	end

Figure 4.9 *Logo* procedures (and shapes) for generating an equilateral triangle of variable side and for generating any regular polygon with variable side.

Recursion, the process whereby a procedure calls itself, is a powerful feature of *Logo* and makes essential use of variables. Figure 4.10 overleaf shows the code and the graphics of *Logo* trees. This tree was produced by the command branch 100 30 0.75. The development and proving of algorithms is a valuable algebraic activity in its own right.

Computer algebra systems

Software that allows the user to carry out algebraic manipulations in a manner akin to work with paper-and-pencil is now common: for computers there are *Derive, Maple, Mathematica* and others, while on calculators, there is a similar functionality on the TI-89, the Casio fx 2.0 and others. As with all software suitable for algebra use, we need to attend

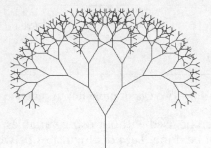

```
to branch :side :angle :factor
if :side<10 [stop]
fd :side
lt :angle
branch :side*:factor :angle :factor
rt :angle*2
branch :side*:factor :angle :factor
lt :angle
bk :side
End
```

Figure 4.10 *Logo* procedures (and shapes) for Logo trees.

to the issue of suitable classroom tasks that make necessary use of the possibilities such devices afford.

For example, ask a computer algebra system to factorize $x^2 - x - 12$ and it will produce $(x + 3)(x - 4)$, but the educational value of this task by itself may be questioned (just as having a calculator compute $4 \times 9 = 36$ may). I give two examples of factorizing tasks which are more substantial than simply getting the system to produce a result below. (These are aimed at the 14–16 and the 16–18 age levels, respectively.)

Figure 4.11 shows how algebraic and graphical facilities (windows) can be drawn on to provide students with tasks which link together factorization, solutions to equations and the x-axis intercepts of quadratics.

Figure 4.12 shows an investigation of factorizations of $x^n - 1$, for natural numbers n. The standard factorization of this polynomial expression is $(x - 1)(x^{n-1} + x^{n-2} + \ldots + x + 1)$, but many interesting sub-patterns emerge when you put in specific values of n. This second task allows for differentiation by outcome in that some sub-patterns are straightforward, while others are more complex and the full solution is likely to tax even the teacher.

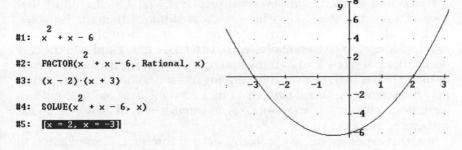

$$\#1: \quad x^2 + x - 6$$

$$\#2: \quad \text{FACTOR}(x^2 + x - 6, \text{ Rational}, x)$$

$$\#3: \quad (x - 2) \cdot (x + 3)$$

$$\#4: \quad \text{SOLVE}(x^2 + x - 6, x)$$

$$\#5: \quad [x = 2, \ x = -3]$$

Figure 4.11 Using *Derive*'s algebra and graph windows to relate factors and zeros of quadratic functions/equations.

$$\#1: \quad x^2 - 1$$

$$\#2: \quad (x + 1) \cdot (x - 1)$$

$$\#3: \quad x^3 - 1$$

$$\#4: \quad (x - 1) \cdot (x^2 + x + 1)$$

$$\#5: \quad x^4 - 1$$

$$\#6: \quad (x + 1) \cdot (x - 1) \cdot (x^2 + 1)$$

$$\#7: \quad x^5 - 1$$

$$\#8: \quad (x - 1) \cdot (x^4 + x^3 + x^2 + x + 1)$$

$$\#9: \quad x^6 - 1$$

$$\#10: \quad (x + 1) \cdot (x - 1) \cdot (x^2 + x + 1) \cdot (x^2 - x + 1)$$

Figure 4.12 *Derive*'s output for factorizations of $x^n - 1$, for $n \in \{2, 3, 4, 5, 6\}$.

Some peculiarities of ICT algebra

This section focuses on the sometimes vexed question of notational systems used in algebraic ICT packages and discusses how different ICT systems implement aspects of algebraic notation. I begin with a consideration of the multitude of uses of letters in paper-and-pencil mathematics (see Heck, 2001, for further considerations of these issues).

Letters may be used as *abbreviations* such as $A = \{2, 4, 6, 8\}$. I think that even in cases like $A = l \times b$ where teachers think of them as variables, students often see these letters as abbreviations. A here also serves as a *computable number*. Letters may refer to *constants*, e.g. π, g and e. In the case of equations like $2x + 3 = 17$ I think that many teachers regard x as a *specific unknown* rather than as a variable. Moving to a more complex level, letters may be seen as *generalized numbers* as in $a + b = b + a$, as *indeterminates* in identities such as $x^2 - 16 \equiv (x + 4)(x - 4)$, as *parameters* as in $y = mx + c$, and as *variables* as in $f(x) = 2x + 3$.

Students experience many problems in their interpretations of letters in algebra (see Küchemann, 1981, or Usiskin, 1988, for discussions of some of these problems). I do not wish to dwell on these problems here but, rather, introduce other potential problems (and enablements) that ICT notational systems may introduce.

Spreadsheet algebra, that is, using 'formulae' like =2*A1+3, has both similarities to and differences from paper-and-pencil algebra, namely equations like $y = 2x + 3$. Dettori *et al.* (1995) point out some discrepancies between these two forms of algebraic notation. The equals sign, '=', is used as a command to compute a new cell in a spreadsheet, but it serves as a relation in 'normal' algebra. Equations, such as $2x + 3 = 17$, are solved by manipulation in conventional algebra, but are solved by successive refinement in spreadsheets. Only cell assignments, not true variables, can be used in spreadsheets. Spreadsheets operate from knowns to unknowns instead of from unknowns to knowns.

In imperative programming languages, letters are again assignments. Indeed, when we speak of 'the value of a variable' in statements such as $A + B = C$, we should really say 'the value contained in a variable'. This subtle difference means that statements such as $A + 1 = A$ make sense in these languages, whereas $a + 1 = a$ does not make sense in 'normal' algebra. These remarks also apply to functional languages such as *Logo*, for example, MAKE "SIDE :SIDE + 1, but the necessary marking of the distinction between the name and value of a variable in *Logo* adds a layer of complexity.

Different computer algebra systems also have subtle differences in their notational systems. In my next example, I refer to *Derive*. Figure 4.13 shows that $2x + 3$ was entered, then *Derive* was asked to solve this and subsequently graph it. From the point of view of pure mathematics, three types of mathematical object are being confused here: expressions, equations and functions. I clearly remember being concerned, when I first used this system with school students, that this ambiguity would confuse some of them. In practice, however, I have rarely found that students notice and, when they do, they easily shrug this off as simply being 'how the system works'.

Earlier in this chapter, I claimed that computer algebra systems 'do algebraic manipulations in a manner akin to paper-and-pencil manipulations'. Although there is a sense in which this is true, the reality is not so simple. Recio (1997) details attempts to get *Maple* to do manipulations

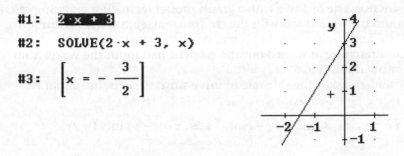

Figure 4.13 *Derive* solving and plotting an expression.

which are fairly straightforward on paper, e.g. if $e + f = 8$, then $e + f + g =$ . . .?; if $P = R + S - T$, then $S - T = $ . . .? He could not get *Maple* to do the first manipulation and only succeeded in getting it to do the second by using some very advanced mathematics and programming.

I have merely skimmed the surface of notational differences between ICT algebra and paper-and-pencil algebra (and also differences within ICT systems). It is, however, enough to appreciate that we should not go into classrooms expecting automatic or easy 'transfer' from ICT algebra to paper-and-pencil algebra.

Teaching

Using ICT in the teaching of algebra can be exciting and rewarding, but it comes with a number of potential problems. Teachers, moreover, are essential in this endeavour. This short section focuses on problems in the positive spirit that *forewarned is forearmed*. I focus on three issues: time, subject knowledge and use of resources.

Incorporating ICT into lessons involves becoming competent with the software, finding suitable topics and tasks, planning lessons in greater detail than is usual and often writing and testing worksheets. This extra work usually tails off as teachers become used to using ICT. The software considered here is not uniform with regard to this time commitment. In my experience, the extremes are graph plotters (usually fairly easy to learn to use and to see where to use them) and computer algebra systems (which can take a long time to master and it is often hard to see where to use them, because they can do so much). Another related issue is the time required to get a 'feel' for how to use it – not just what topics but what aspects of these topics and what features of the software to exploit.

Sometimes using ICT in algebra lessons can create situations where it is possible to get stuck on the mathematics, on the technology or on both. Depending on the confidence of the teacher, this can be amusing or frightening. Here are two examples with which I have first-hand experience. The first was with a graph plotter (actually a graphing calculator) and the second was with the computer algebra system *Derive*.

A student input sin(x) but a graph of $y = -\sin(x)$ appeared. After much head-scratching, it turned out the student had input the y-axis from 5 to −5 rather than −5 to 5.

A student asked the software to solve sin $x = 2$, and the output is:

$$\left[x = \frac{\pi}{2} + i \ln(\sqrt{3} + 2), \; x = \frac{\pi}{2} - i \ln(\sqrt{3} + 2), \; x = -\frac{\pi}{2} + i \ln(\sqrt{3} + 2) \right].$$

In a report on teachers' beliefs about the development of algebraic reasoning, Nathan and Koedinger (2000, p. 181) state that 'textbooks have been identified as a primary resource – and often the *only* source – of the content planning performed by high school mathematics teachers'. Their study, moreover, showed a highly significant correlation between teachers' ranking of algebra item difficulty and the curricular sequencing of the textbook they used. In a study (Monaghan, 2000) of 13 upper secondary teachers who used ICT in their lessons (which invariably had an algebra focus), all of the teachers made considerable use of a textbook in non-ICT lessons and all but two of the teachers initially felt that textbook work was inappropriate in ICT-based lessons.

Learning

Much of the above has directly or indirectly concerned student learning, but in this section I make learning the explicit focus. In some sense, an obvious question to ask is whether using ICT helps students to learn more or better mathematics. I think the question is either misplaced or unanswerable. I can, however, provide some details about what students learn in specific areas. I go through the different systems described above and provide snapshots of learning opportunities and some potential problems.

Spreadsheets can be used to help students understand what it means to solve an equation by finding cell values that make another cell equal to a given number. Such an understanding is unlikely to be tested, but is nevertheless crucially important. By means of iterative refinement, spreadsheets can provide a means to solve equations and tackle optimization tasks which are beyond students' paper-and-pencil technical ability. Spreadsheets can help students to develop algebraic approaches to solving word problems.

For instance, Dettori *et al.* (1995, p. 269) discuss how the use of relative and absolute cell references can help students appreciate the difference between parameters and variables. Even the algebraic peculiarities of spreadsheets, particularly the 'equals' sign used as a command and variables designating cell assignments, can be used as learning opportunities to highlight the nature of the equals sign and variables in paper-and-pencil algebra.

With graph plotters, students can draw lots of graphs and use these to focus on commonalities and differences in families of functions, for example, $f(x) = x(x - a)$ This can, if you plan for it, turn classroom exposition on its head, for example with regard to families of functions. Instead of you explaining to the whole class, they can see what happens and explain things to you or the rest of the class. 'Hard' mathematics can become accessible to a wider number of students. For example, students who cannot see that $y = 1 - x^2$ is a possible candidate for the curve in Figure 4.14 without assistance may get to an answer by another route: It's quadratic, try $y = x^2$. Oh, I need a minus, try $y = -x^2$. Oh, I need to move it up 1, try $y = 1 - x^2$ – that's it.

However, in terms of what students do when they sketch a graph by hand and when they plot it with a graph plotter, the two tasks can be seen as having little in common. When working by hand, students are likely to be engaged in calculating, tabulating, scaling, plotting, interpolating and sketching. With a graph plotter, they basically key in the function and zoom in or out to view it properly. My point is simply that we should not expect graph plotting on its own to help students with graphing by hand.

There is little evidence that learning programming *per se* has a beneficial effect on learning algebra, and even its effect on problem-solving is disputed. (See Noss and Hoyles, 1996, pp. 167–78, for a discussion of one dispute over this topic with regard to *Logo* programming.) However, since the heyday of teaching programming in school some 20 years ago, the focus of mathematics educators who have attended to programming has been on small amounts of programming.

Tall and Thomas (1991), for example, used simple *BASIC* programming

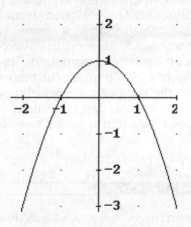

Figure 4.14 Write down a possible function for this curve.

to introduce algebraic symbolism. The problem this was designed to overcome was students viewing expressions such as $2x + 6$ as a 'process' instead of both a process and a 'product'. In other words, $2(x+3)$ may be viewed as not equivalent to $2x + 6$ as it is a different process, even though they agree numerically no matter what value is provided for x. The computer can perform the process, leaving the student free to concentrate on the product, with the student hopefully seeing that the two expressions are equivalent to each other but not equivalent to, say, $2x + 3$.

Sutherland (1990) argues that it is not easy in 'traditional' algebra to find introductory problems which require variables as problem-solving tools, but that this is not the case with *Logo*. I think the variable triangle and polygon examples above provide some evidence for the second part of her statement. She goes on to argue that students accept that *Logo* variables represent a range of numbers, that students can accept expressions such as $x + 5$ as objects and that they can create and use functions to explore relationships. Using *Logo* does not automatically ensure these educational outcomes, but they are surely important algebraic learning experiences to aim for.

Mayes (1997) reviews computer algebra system education research and concludes that there is compelling evidence that integrating computer algebra systems into the curriculum can have positive affects on mathematics learning. He claims an improved understanding of mathematical concepts, improved retention of computational skills, improved attitudes towards mathematics and an ability to resequence computation skills and conceptual understanding. He adds, however, that if a computer algebra system is appended to the curriculum, or used primarily as a computational aid, then learning may not be as dramatically affected.

This is positive, but Artigue (2002) suggests the reality of integrating computer algebra systems into the classroom is much more complex than earlier studies suggest. Her integration combines paper-and-pencil and software-specific 'techniques'. These different techniques focus on subtly different aspects of mathematics and, of course, the educational value attached to different techniques is not equal. Use of a computer algebra system forces a focus on equivalent expressions. To appreciate this, consider the output in Figure 4.15. Changing the place of '$-x$' in the original expression resulted in the computer algebra system, on a TI-92 in this instance, returning two different but equivalent expressions. This is a fairly trivial point from a 'pure mathematics' viewpoint but, in classroom

$$\blacksquare\ 1 - (1 - x)\cdot(3 + 2\cdot x) - x \qquad\qquad 2\cdot x^2 - 2$$
$$\blacksquare\ 1 - x - (1 - x)\cdot(3 + 2\cdot x) \qquad 2\cdot(x - 1)\cdot(x + 1)$$
$$\boxed{1-x-(1-x)(3+2x)}$$

Figure 4.15 Different but equivalent outputs resulting from different but equivalent inputs to a computer algebra system (TI-92).

settings, examples like this require discussion so that students can organize their thoughts or their learning may be minimal.

In the foregoing we have viewed 'learning' in a narrow cognitive manner, but learning involves more than just mental activity: it involves the whole person acting in a social situation. Use of ICT can be a great motivator, an important factor to keep in mind in an education system dominated by measurement of learning. One of the problems with teaching algebra is that many students see algebra as dry and of little or no practical use. (If it is just learning rules, it is dry. When was the last time you used algebra in an out-of-school setting?) One very positive aspect of doing mathematics with the software described above is that it really does require a form of algebraic input.

Conclusion

Incorporating ICT into the teaching and learning of algebra can be exciting, rewarding and can have great educational outcomes. There are potential problems, which it is a good idea to be aware of, but many of these diminish as we get used to new ways of working.

The two important themes in the discussion above are: first, the design of suitable tasks for algebraic activities with ICT; and second, the way in which different ICT systems 'do' algebra in different ways, none of which automatically assist with paper-and-pencil algebra. Designing tasks involves thinking creatively about what specific software does well. It also involves being critical of tasks others put forward – as well as actively stealing good ideas when they appear. Two books which take the ideas presented in this chapter further are French (2002) and Oldknow and Taylor (2000). Two publications which address wider aspects of school algebra are Mason and Sutherland (2002) and Sutherland (2002).

One boon of ICT is that it forces us to consider what exactly algebra is, and such considerations are very important for any mathematics teacher's continued professional development.

References

Artigue, M. (2002) 'Learning mathematics in a CAS environment: the genesis of a reflection about instrumentation and the dialectics between technical and conceptual work'. *International Journal of Computers for Mathematical Learning*, **7**(3), 245–74.

Bednarz, N., Kieran, C. and Lee, L. (eds) (1996) *Approaches to Algebra: Perspectives for Research and Teaching*. Dordrecht: Kluwer Academic.

Department for Education and Skills (2003) *Integrating ICT into Mathematics in Key Stage 3*. (http://www.standards.dfes.gov.uk/keystage3/strands/publications/?template=down&pub_id=2479&strand=maths)

Dettori, G., Garuti, R., Lemut, E. and Netchitailova, L. (1995) 'An analysis of the relationship between spreadsheet and algebra', in L. Burton and B. Jaworski (eds), *Technology in Mathematics Teaching: A Bridge between Teaching and Learning*. Bromley: Chartwell-Bratt, pp. 261–74.

French, D. (2002) *Teaching and Learning Algebra*. London: Continuum.

Heck, A. (2001) 'Variables in computer algebra, mathematics and science'. *International Journal of Computer Algebra in Mathematics Education*, **8**(3), 195–221.

Küchemann, D. (1981) 'Algebra', in K. Hart (ed.), *Children's Understanding of Mathematics: 11–16*. London: John Murray, pp. 102–19.

Mason, J. (1996) 'Expressing generality and roots of algebra', in N. Bednarz, C. Kieran and L. Lee (eds), *Approaches to Algebra: Perspectives for Research and Teaching*. Dordrecht: Kluwer Academic, pp. 65–86.

Mason, J. and Sutherland, R. (2002) *Key Aspects of Teaching Algebra in Schools*. London: Qualifications and Curriculum Authority.

Mayes, R. (1997) 'Current state of research into CAS in mathematics education', in J. Berry, M. Kronfellner, B. Kutzler and J. Monaghan (eds), *The State of Computer Algebra in Mathematics Education*. Bromley: Chartwell-Bratt, pp. 171–89.

Monaghan, J. (2000) *End of Award Report: Moving from Occasional to Regular Use of ICT in Secondary Mathematics classes*. (http://www.regard.ac.uk/regard/home/index_html) (search on Monaghan).

Nathan, M. and Koedinger, K. (2000) 'Teachers' and researchers' beliefs about the development of algebraic reasoning'. *Journal for Research in Mathematics Education*, **31**(2), 168–90.

Nemirovsky, R. (1996) 'Mathematical narratives, modeling, and algebra', in N. Bednarz, C. Kieran and L. Lee (eds), *Approaches to Algebra: Perspectives for Research and Teaching*. Dordrecht: Kluwer Academic, pp. 197–220.

Noss, R. and Hoyles, C. (1996) *Windows on Mathematical Meanings: Learning Cultures and Computers*. Dordrecht: Kluwer Academic.

Oldknow, A. and Taylor, R. (2000) *Teaching Mathematics with ICT*. London: Continuum.

Recio, T. (1997) 'Didactical relevance of meaningless mathematics'. *International Journal of Computer Algebra in Mathematics Education*, **5**(1), 15–27.

Rojano, T. (1996) 'Developing algebraic aspects of problem solving within a spreadsheet environment', in N. Bednarz, C. Kieran and L. Lee (eds), *Approaches to Algebra: Perspectives for Research and Teaching*. Dordrecht: Kluwer Academic, pp. 137–45.

Sutherland, R. (1990) 'The changing role of algebra in school mathematics: the potential of computer-based environments', in P. Dowling and R. Noss (eds), *Mathematics versus the National Curriculum*. London: Falmer, pp. 154–75.

Sutherland, R. (2002) *A Comparative Study of Algebra Curricula*. London: Qualifications and Curriculum Authority.

Swan, M. (1985) *The Language of Functions and Graphs*. Nottingham: Shell Centre for Mathematical Education, University of Nottingham.

Tall, D. and Thomas, M. (1991) 'Encouraging versatile thinking in algebra using the computer'. *Educational Studies in Mathematics*, **22**(2), 125–47.

Usiskin, Z. (1988) 'Conceptions of school algebra and uses of variables', in A. Coxford (ed.), *The Ideas of Algebra: K-12*. Reston, VA, National Council for Teachers of Mathematics, pp. 8–19.

5

THINKING GEOMETRICALLY: DYNAMIC IMAGERY

Kate Mackrell and Peter Johnston-Wilder

Mathematics, especially geometry, is most often done in the imagination. Northrop Frye observed that mathematics is one of the languages of the imagination and the geometer Jean Pedersen has commented that 'geometry is a skill of the eyes and the hands as well as of the mind'. The very word 'theorem' has the Greek word meaning 'vision' at its root, as well as linking to the word 'theatre': both are concerned with show, with display; both have a touch of revelatory magic about them.

Imagine, then, that you had access to a piece of software with which you could create and continuously transform diagrams and other mathematical configurations the way you can in your mind. But unlike human mental imagery, the computer screen can also hold still particular images for scrutiny and contemplation. Additionally, the computer screen is a public place, rendering your dynamic imaginings visible to all who can see them, perhaps in a laboratory or classroom setting.

In this chapter, to avoid repetition, we will use the term *interactive geometry* for such sophisticated interactive packages; *Cabri-Géomètre* and *The Geometer's Sketchpad* will be the primary exemplars. These two packages have been available in various growing incarnations since the late 1980s. Their common essence lies in the way users can interact directly with geometric figures they have constructed (or that have been preconstructed for them). This interaction occurs in a continuous and dynamic way, by means of the direct control of your hand on the mouse.

It is also possible to 'animate' a construction, so that the screen images move 'on their own'. But, for us, the most striking and powerful impact comes when, in pursuit of a mathematical question or goal, students directly explore a geometric realm informed by hand and eye, focused by their minds.

We are pragmatically assuming that you have read the brief introduction given in Chapter 2 and we strongly encourage you to try out one of these packages yourself, if you have not seen such 'mouse' mathematics before. One of the ironies of trying to describe motion and its effects in text is that one necessarily has to miss out on *all* of the essential ingredients. Not least among these is the sense of surprise and wonder that animating mathematical diagrams and images can bring, externalizing and setting back in motion images that have been held static within the pages of textbooks for over 2000 years.

Unquestionably, such geometry software is a powerful tool for facilitating mathematical learning, exploration and problem-solving. There are many accounts in the literature (e.g. Jones, 2000; Weeden, 2002) of teachers and researchers working productively with their students on significant mathematical work. Arising from its dramatic richness and scope, there are, perhaps unsurprisingly, significant pedagogic issues to be addressed in order to use geometry software effectively in secondary classrooms. This chapter indicates the potential for interactive geometry to support teaching and learning of mathematics, as well as considering how learners can be introduced to the considerable possibilities afforded by the software.

The first section begins with a discussion of some secondary teachers' experiences when using interactive geometry in a class for the first time. In order to present these in a concise way, we have compressed a great deal of actual experience into certain vignettes, designed to highlight more general pedagogic issues which we then explore.

Recall from Chapter 2 the separating out of *exploratory* versus *expressive* approaches to using ICT. One place where this distinction arises in relation to interactive geometry is with the question of offering students preconstructed files to explore, rather than having them construct figures of their own. (A similar distinction arose almost a generation ago, with regard to *Logo* procedures – see Ainley and Goldstein, 1988.) And, as always, there is the general pedagogic question of what kinds of questions and tasks can help students to focus their attention on the mathematically important aspects of the situations presented to them by others or generated by themselves.

One particular issue we consider towards the end of this chapter is how to evoke the need for students to prove or otherwise explain and justify general claims or results that the software seems to show them directly. As you saw in Chapter 2, a dynamic demonstration can be very compelling. Recall the demonstration in Figure 2.8 (page 28) of the result that angles subtended by a given chord in the same segment of a circle must be equal. This may leave little or no need for proof in the mind of the student.

Historically, geometry has usually been the part of the curriculum where students first encounter issues of mathematical conviction and proof. The role of seeing in relation to the apparent particularity of mathematical diagrams has often been at the heart of the challenge. How can a geometric diagram which is always and necessarily particular be used to argue convincingly about what *must* happen in general? With interactive geometry, most often seeing *is* believing, especially given the sense of generality evoked by the plurality of linked instances of a given configuration.

First encounters

In the scenarios presented in this section, teachers start to use interactive geometry in exploring the properties of quadrilaterals. In each vignette, the teacher approaches the use of the software in a somewhat different way. Inevitably when a new piece of software is used in a lesson for the first time, some things do not go quite as expected or hoped. We have chosen these examples to illustrate some of the issues involved in making effective use of the software. The section ends with some concluding remarks that lead into the discussion in the next section about whether and when to use preconstructed files.

Scenario 1
The teacher asks students to construct their own quadrilaterals and then to explore their properties. Having seen demonstrations of the software in which constructions are made effortlessly, the teacher assumes that the students will find this unproblematic. He finds quite quickly, however, that the task seems beyond some students' capabilities. The complexity of the task has been underestimated and he has been unaware of how much he knows about the general way in which the software operates as well as the way in which his own prior geometric understanding comes into play.

As with any new software, there is a learning curve involved in acquiring a certain facility with it. A task that looks simple when demonstrated by an informed individual might involve steps that are not so easily discovered by a novice. Interactive geometry software is very open, offering a wide variety of tools and facilities. Some students thrive in such an open-search setting, exploring at length and at will. Others can become somewhat overwhelmed initially by the variety of options in the menus and by the fact that each tool *does* something mathematical to the image on the screen and is related to a geometrical concept. However, with a structured introduction to certain of the available tools, and with perhaps some introduction to the experience of dragging dynamic constructions, students can acquire confidence and build valuable insights.

The interactive geometry pages on Bryan Dye's MathsNet site, which we hope you explored for yourself having read Chapter 2 (see Figure 2.9, page 29), can also provide a useful introduction to interactive geometry for students. These accessible tasks use Java versions of *Cabri* and *The Geometer's Sketchpad* for interactive use on the internet. Through working with these tasks, students can gain experience of interacting with a construction and have a limited introduction to the processes involved in making a construction themselves.

Scenario 2

This teacher recognizes that the process of constructing the quadrilaterals is not straightforward and hence prepares worksheets with instructions. Figure 5.1 shows an excerpt from one of her worksheets.

To draw a square using interactive geometry:

1. Construct two points and label them A and B.
2. Now construct a line segment joining A and B.
3. Construct lines through both points perpendicular to this segment.
4. Draw a circle with centre A and radius point B and label the point of intersection between the perpendicular line through A and the circle D.
5. Draw a circle with centre B and radius point A and label the point of intersection between the perpendicular line through B and the circle C.
6. Join up the points ABCD to form the square.

Figure 5.1   Excerpt from teacher's worksheet.

When the worksheet is presented to the class, some students have problems following the instructions, even when diagrams accompany them. A couple of the instructions are insufficient, while others involve using features of the software that really need a careful introduction. Some students are able to resolve these problems for themselves or by working collaboratively with peers around them (some certainly have more experience with software environments than their teacher). Others have difficulties finding the appropriate tools or menus in the software.

Predictably, a few students feel the worksheet instructions are more complicated than the shapes they are trying to create. Some try the 'shortcut' of creating a quadrilateral and then dragging the vertices into the shape of a square. These students are confused when their teacher insists that these are not *constructed* squares and drags the vertices to demonstrate.

In using interactive geometry software, students need to come to distinguish between a *drawing* and a *figure* (Laborde, 1995). The student's quadrilateral that looks like a square may simply be a *drawing* of a square.

However, this square will 'mess up' when any of its vertices are dragged: it is not the figure of a square.

The worksheet instructions are designed to give rise to the figure of a square, one which may be moved around or enlarged by dragging, but one that will always remain a square. The properties programmed into this square via the sequence of commands and their relation to geometric relationships ensure that the image will always be a square, no matter how it is interfered with.

This can actually give rise to engaging classroom challenges, with students creating figures and then seeing whether someone else can 'mess' them up. Pragmatically, those diagrams that resist, those that remain what they started as, are figures rather than simply drawings. As often happens when students are engaged and challenged in technological environments, knowledge and expertise become commodities freely offered and traded: an innovation is quickly identified, its creator temporarily lauded and the 'trick' or 'device' rapidly transmitted to interested others.

Once again, there is an echo of a challenge that *Logo* users encountered: the distinction between a drawing that 'looked right' and a construction that 'is right' mathematically. With interactive geometry, the distinction is clearer to make, in terms of whether or not a given screen configuration retains its geometric identity and properties (e.g. as a square, a rectangle or a parallelogram) when dragged.

Part of the confusion may lie in how words are used. We often use the word *draw* to mean both simply 'draw' and 'construct', thereby failing to distinguish precisely what is at issue here. (Perhaps the word 'make' could be used, when 'construct' is the intent?) For students who are used to geometry in terms of look (of semblance) alone, there is a significant conceptual issue to be addressed. Explicit class attention needs to be drawn repeatedly and at length to this significant interactive geometry idea. Is this simply a screen drawing of a geometric figure or does it have mathematical 'glue', namely specified properties and relationships bred into it that it will retain no matter what?

A useful mathematics education framework for describing the development of students' geometrical understanding was introduced by Pierre and Dina van Hiele (1959/85, 1986). At level 1, shapes are recognized by their visual appearance – looking is enough to identify them and naming shapes based on visual recognition alone is a key school task initially. At level 2, the properties of a shape are isolated and recognized, they can be listed perhaps, but are not related to one another. At level 3, the necessary relationships that hold among the various properties of a shape are understood, and definition by means of these properties is a possibility.

Students who operate primarily at van Hiele level 1 may have particular difficulty with the distinction made in interactive geometry software between 'figure' and 'drawing'. For example, some hold that a square and a diamond (the same square rotated by 45°) are different shapes. In consequence, such students may not see any fundamental difference between changes in a figure arising from a rotation and changes in their drawing when dragged. Work with interactive geometry can bring this fact into prominence and focus and so can be very informative for a teacher about her students and their geometric world-views.

Michael de Villiers (2003) has conjectured that, for the process of geometric construction in an interactive geometry environment to be meaningful, students need be able to work at van Hiele level 3. The worksheet instructions shown in Figure 5.1 rely on the properties of parallel lines. They do not use the familiar definition of a square as a regular right-angled quadrilateral. Students working primarily at level 2 may not recognize the relationship between the instructions and the properties of a square as they know them. But they may also be excited about making connections, and about using circles as rulers to create points at a known distance along a line, as well as developing a growing mastery of a small part of this package.

Scenario 3 is presented in two parts, scenario 3a and scenario 3b, in order to allow for discussion of two distinct issues.

Scenario 3a

The teacher decides to give the students time to familiarize themselves with the software before attempting any constructions.

There are two different but related kinds of learning involved in using software, which we call *instrumental* and *conceptual*. Instrumental learning is about how to *do* things in the specific software: how to create points or lines or circles, how to operate with menu items (like 'rotate' or 'construct perpendicular bisector'), how to perform calculations (like measuring lengths, areas or angles). It reflects the decisions made by the software designer. For example, in order to be an effective user of the software, the student may need to find and use the tool to construct a mid-point. Such learning is not intrinsically mathematical and can be developed in a context in which students are not deliberately extending their mathematical understanding. Tasks that develop instrumental understanding may involve the creation of images or the use of features such as reflection or animation.

One striking thing about interactive geometry is that instrumental learning is also frequently conceptual. Teachers report that the mathematical language of the interface both provides and seeds the preferred vocabulary for subsequent mathematical discussion. An understanding of some or many of these terms is gained in the software environment and the words act as both labels for that experience as well as the commands to make that action occur. Thus, the words can serve as both verbs and nouns. This is a common process in mathematics, where verbs are turned into nouns.

However, effective use of the software also requires conceptual learning. For example, the worksheet instructions for the square require the student to understand that a circle can be used to create line segments of equal length.

A student in the class wrote in her mathematics journal:

> Some tools are quite hard to utilise. For example I needed to set points equidistant along a line. Finding the tool was easy, but I wasn't initially able to use it.

Although the student saw her problem as an instrumental one of how to use the tool, the task requires conceptual understanding to solve a geometrical problem. One solution is to use a series of intersecting circles of equal radius and centres on a line (Figure 5.2); other solutions might involve repeated translation or reflection of a point.

A task that for one user requires only instrumental learning may require conceptual learning by another, geometrically inexperienced, user. For example, a student who is familiar with the idea of a perpendicular bisector knows that, to create one, they just need to use the general construction principles of interactive geometry and locate the appropriate menu or tool-box items. In contrast, a student who is not familiar with the notion perhaps needs first to learn more about the concept of 'perpendicular bisector'. Or possibly they can learn about both at the same time, the one reinforcing the other. And certainly some students will simply explore, asking 'what does this do?' and 'why can't I use this tool on this object?'.

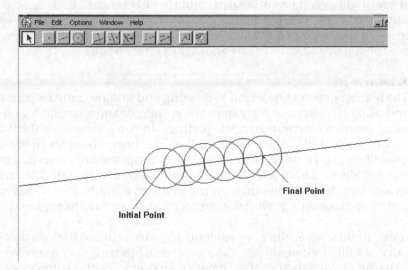

Figure 5.2 Equidistant points.

In general, a mathematically experienced teacher interacts with the software in a different way from a student who is still coming to grips with the underlying mathematics (Hoyles and Healy, 1997). A teacher must recognize that the way in which he or she learns to use the software may not be appropriate for all students.

Conceptual learning develops gradually, through deepening experience with both geometry and the software, both on and off the computer. A student drawing circles with a compass may experience the way in which points on the circumference are all at the same distance from the centre more directly than a student drawing circles using interactive geometry. Folding a paper triangle so that two vertices come together may initially be more meaningful than constructing the perpendicular bisector of one side of the triangle using interactive geometry. But then the screen experience can also deepen their understanding of what can be *done* with geometric constructions – they can actually be used to *make* something.

Some necessary conceptual learning in interactive geometry is not part of the identified mathematics curriculum. For example, it is necessary to distinguish between three possible types of point: a basic point, which can be freely dragged; a point on an object, such as a circle or a line, which can only move along the object; and a point of intersection, which does not move (relative to the objects upon which it depends) when dragged. A common misconception is that intersection points are the 'glue' which hold objects together, as if they were rivets or screws (Jones, 1999). Students need also to come to understand the idea of functional dependency (Jones, 1996); in other words, they need to realize that certain parts of a figure will depend on other parts and that figures need to be created in a particular sequence. For example, there will always be the student who starts with four segments of equal length and then tries without success to make them perpendicular to one another to create a square.

Scenario 3b

The teacher devotes one lesson to creating and folding compass patterns and using visualization away from the computer and a second lesson to using geometry software to create pictures. In consequence, by the third lesson, most students are able to follow the instructions to create the quadrilaterals. However, when exploring properties of quadrilaterals, some students cannot tell what they should pay attention to. They tend to focus on details rather than on the figure as a whole. Sometimes, the action of dragging a point results in incomprehensible changes.

It can be difficult at times for students to make sense of the visual complexity of a filled, changeable computer screen. Students may be unable to see the quadrilaterals that they have created among the complexity of circles and lines used in the construction. A more experienced user learns to 'hide' objects used in a construction and to construct visible line segments where they need to be visible.

The questions posed to students need to be worded carefully, in order to direct their attention productively and to encourage them in their exploration. It may be useful to focus attention on which properties stay the same and which change. This may require first teaching students to measure lengths or angles. But it also may involve them reasoning geometrically about what *must* be true about their figure from the way it was constructed.

Time and again, teachers report students engaged and motivated when working on such geometry software. There is animation not only on the screen but also in the classroom. Although the example we have chosen here was relatively straightforward, the scope of these programs allows them to be an expressive companion as students work on many varied mathematical tasks. The names of the programs are informative and similar – a geometer's sketchpad, a **ca**hier **br**ouillon **i**nformatique (the origin of the name *Cabri*, meaning 'a computer drafting sketchbook') – both suggest a mathematical place to work, to explore, to think.

Alternative approaches

The vignettes presented are all based on a common assumption when using ICT in mathematics education: meaningful interaction with the learning situation depends upon students individually constructing their own figures from a blank screen (the expressive option, to use the language of Chapter 2). Certainly, many if not all of the most compelling documented examples of such geometry software's impact on students' mathematics involves student-constructed sketches. Nevertheless, this is not the only option.

This was a similar situation to that with students working freely with *Logo*, where the same tension arose. And there, as now, we wish simply to indicate that there are alternatives (this is discussed more fully in Chapter 14). Here are two further possibilities.

One way to develop meaningful interaction is to run a teacher-centred lesson using a single lap-top with a data projector and an interactive whiteboard (as exemplified and discussed in Chapter 9). The problem of constructing different types of quadrilateral could have been the focus of a discussion, with different student ideas being tried out and the consequences explored.

A second possibility is to provide the students with preconstructed files. In such files, students could manipulate the figures that appear before them: many of the initial access problems can be somewhat bypassed. But, as ever, there are trade-offs and sacrifices in both approaches. The next section considers the use of preconstructed files in more detail.

Working with preconstructed files

There is growing interest in the use of preconstructed files (see Gawlick, 2002 for further discussion), and there are increasingly sophisticated files available. The complexity of such files varies widely. They range from a simple figure, such as a triangle with its circumcentre created by the teacher, to files such as the *Active Geometry* files publishes by the Association of Teachers of Mathematics (ATM, 2001). There are also sample files, versioned for both *Cabri* and *Sketchpad*, some of which have taken many hours to construct and which, in fact, form their own microworlds. Such files can contain preconstructed figures or can be blank screens with special macros or custom tools provided.

A major feature of such files is that it is possible to modify or add to them. While the purposes they serve may be similar to those of a piece of commercial software, they do not suffer from the same inflexibility. For the lessons in the scenarios at the start of the chapter, it would be possible to create a file for each of the required quadrilaterals. An alternative would be to use the *Active Geometry* file *Quadinc*, which displays all the names applicable to each quadrilateral and varies the displayed names according to the position of the vertices (see Figure 5.3).

The use of preconstructed files involves students working in 'exploratory mode', to explore within the constraints set by the creator of the files. This is in contrast to students engaging in making constructions of their own, which can be seen as working in 'expressive mode'. Table 5.1 summarizes some advantages and disadvantages of using preconstructed files.

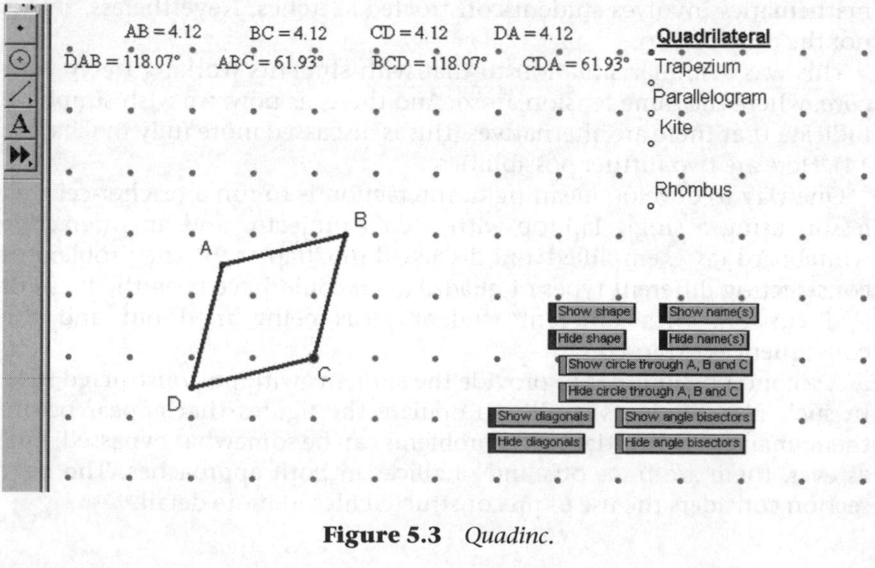

Figure 5.3 *Quadinc.*

Table 5.1 Advantages and disadvantages of preconstructed files

Advantages	Disadvantages
Students (and teacher) only need to be able to manipulate: no initial knowledge of the software is needed.	Teacher resources to either acquire (cost), find (time) or create (time).
Less time-consuming for students, as object does not need to be constructed.	
Can focus immediately on desired learning outcomes without the distraction of needing to construct the required figures.	May restrict student exploration.
Files can be modified or added to, unlike commercial small software.	Files can be drastically messed up: be sure that the version on the network is read-only!
Such files may lead to questions such as 'how did they do that?', which may motivate students (and teachers) to begin to create their own files.	Some students (and teachers) need to know how a file works before they can be comfortable using it, and hence get little out of using it.

Although learning to use a new tool takes time, there are advantages for students in making constructions of their own. Construction offers considerable scope for students to be creative, to be challenged and to engage in open-ended problem-posing and problem-solving. They can work at their own mathematics. The process can give the student ownership of what they create and can lead to a deeper understanding of the figure. Of course, it is possible that some tasks may be too challenging for certain students, leaving them frustrated and not knowing where to begin, but with support these issues can be overcome.

To end this section, Table 5.2 overleaf offers some suggestions as to when to use a preconstructed file and when to construct.

Focusing attention when exploring geometry

Whether constructing from a blank screen (expressing) or exploring a preconstructed file (exploring), many students will benefit from having some fundamental questions to ask themselves as they investigate. This section looks at some fundamental questions to address while working geometrically, both with and without preconstructed files. In it, we discuss what might be involved in helping students deal meaningfully with these questions.

Table 5.2 When to use a preconstructed file and when to construct

When to use a preconstructed file	When to construct
In the early stages of learning to use the software (by either teacher or student).	When students have sufficient confidence with the software (or the geometry).
In the early stages of geometry learning when shapes can be identified visually, but the idea of properties of the shape is not understood.	When students have some idea of the relationship of the properties of a shape to the construction of a shape.
When the learning objectives are unrelated to the way in which the file was constructed.	When the process of construction is intrinsic to learning objectives, such as exploring ways to create a rhombus or constructing a figure in order to explain its properties.
When a useful preconstructed file is more complex than a student could reasonably be expected to create.	When the complexity of construction is an appropriate challenge to the student.
When instructions to create a figure are more complex than the resulting figure (as with the worksheet instructions to create a square).	In open-ended tasks or when using the software to solve a particular problem or when looking for an explanation of why something is happening.

What's happening?

This is the fundamental question that all students must ask when confronted with an interactive geometry file. It is not always a straightforward question to answer, as it is not always easy to make sense of a confusion of changing geometric figures.

One way of beginning to make sense of what's happening is to start with the question of *What stays the same and what changes?* This question focuses attention on the hunt for invariance, a fundamental issue in geometrical thinking. Interactive geometry software is particularly useful for exploring this question in various contexts.

In Figure 5.4 the circumcentre of a triangle has been constructed and construction lines have been hidden. In exploring this situation, students might:

- drag the vertices of the triangle and conjecture the type of relationship that the circumcentre has to the vertices;
- measure distances from the circumcentre to the vertices or to the sides;
- construct segments joining the circumcentre and the vertices;
- construct the (obvious) circle.

What is significant in such an exploration is the ability to recognize aspects of the figure that remain invariant. Although the circumcentre will

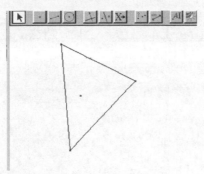

Figure 5.4 The circumcentre of a triangle.

not always remain within the triangle when the vertices are dragged, or at the same distance from any particular vertex, all the distances from the vertices to the circumcentre will always be equal. The question 'what stays the same and what changes?' is key.

However, while a teacher may find interesting the fact that three lines meet at a point, or that the diagonals of a rectangle bisect each other, such results may be taken for granted by students. Hölzl (2001) noted that students neither noticed by themselves nor found surprising when pointed out that the perpendicular bisectors of the sides of a triangle intersect at a point. A task that motivates students to want to explore further might involve surprising connections to other knowledge, such as exploring the area of circle via progressive polygons or enable students to create a visually pleasing pattern, such as a ring of pentagons. These expressive challenges can arise naturally from a preconstructed setting.

Another aspect to the question of what's happening is to ask about the way in which change is occurring. The following example of a situation to explore is discussed further below.

The *orthocentre* of a triangle is the point where its altitudes meet. The triangle [in Figure 5.5 overleaf] has been created so that its vertices all lie on a circle. How does the position of the orthocentre change as one of the triangle vertices is moved around the circle?

An important issue in such explorations is to clarify that the results of exploration are often a conjecture to work on further rather than a conclusion (see, for example, Hadas *et al.*, 2000).

What if . . .?

'What if . . .?' questions provide a variation on the theme of looking for invariance. The process is now one of asking 'if I change this, what else changes?' and, by implication, 'what stays the same?'. 'What if . . .?'

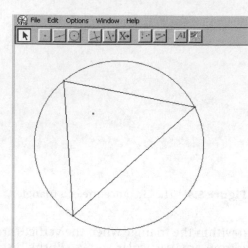

Figure 5.5   The orthocentre of a triangle.

questions are particularly important in whole-class discussion around a single screen. At every stage, students can be asked to predict what will happen if the teacher changes something. It is also an important question in independent exploration, where the question can lead to changing initial aspects of the situation to extend a task. It is always questions that drive exploration and investigation.

As an example of a 'what if . . .?' question arising from another situation, consider the following situation.

> In the triangle and orthocentre situation given above, what if one of the triangle vertices is moved slightly away from the circle? Make a prediction before you try this out.

Can I make . . . happen?

Challenges to make something happen can arise from situations posed by an outside source or they can arise within the minds of students as they explore a situation. The question might be quite simple ('can I create a triangle of a certain area?') or it might involve complex problem-solving ('can I create a file to depict a rotating icosahedron?'). Sometimes the question is not overtly mathematical: kaleidoscopes are created for their visual properties, but their creation involves mathematical problem-solving. The answer to the question may turn out to be 'no', but the process of exploration still may well be valuable. For example, an attempt to create a triangle with two right angles may lead to an understanding of why this is not possible.

Problems and puzzles can come from a variety of sources. For example, Peter Ransom (2002) has created a good locus problem from the story of Daniel in the lion's den. Heather McLeay (2002) created a puzzle based on the use of geostrips. A particularly challenging problem is: given the centroid and circumcentre of a triangle, construct the triangle. Extending the properties of a shape can also be a source of challenges. The perpendicular bisectors of a triangle all meet at a point – is it possible to construct a quadrilateral (other than a square) in which this will happen?

This focusing question is also important in working with many preconstructed files. For example, the ATM's *Active Geometry* files contain a number of challenges, ranging from predicting the image of a shape under reflection or rotation to attempting to create a shape which overlaps with its image in a particular way.

Why is this happening?

This question, more than some others in the previous section, suggests the student is seeking to explain and, perhaps, to prove. There is a certain tension between interactive geometry and proof. Students learn about empirical 'proof' in science. Dragging the vertices of a triangle and finding that the angle sum is always 180° is likely to lead to a conviction that the angle sum is 180° for all triangles. The activity of 'proving' in a formal sense that this is always true may well be seen as rather pointless. Michael de Villiers (2003) has pointed out that proof actually serves a number of functions apart from demonstrating that something is true and that it may be more useful to consider proof in the non-formal sense when dealing with dynamic images.

The traditionally understood role of proof is as a means of verification or conviction. De Villiers claims that in fact most mathematicians attain conviction before attempting to find a proof of a result. Hence, the conviction by experimentation that something is true may, in fact, be a useful first stage towards proof, rather than an impediment to it. A student may not want to attempt to explain *why* the angles in a triangle always add to 180°, if they are not convinced that this will always be the case.

The most immediately meaningful role of proof to the student is proof as a means of explanation. No amount of manipulation of differently sized and shaped triangles will explain why the angle sum remains constant. (The result actually has two components: the fact that the angle sum is a constant and the numerical value of that constant.) The issue here is whether or not the student cares *why* the result is true.

There are several approaches to enhancing students' desire to explain why something happens. One is to offer situations whose results contradict the students' expectations. The task with the orthocentre introduced above can provoke in students a need to explain why it happens that way. This figure was showed to a 10-year-old: she was unsurprised that the three altitudes met at a point, mildly interested in the locus of the orthocentre when all vertices were on the circle – and extremely surprised by what happened when one was moved off the circle. She demanded to know why this was happening and would not let go until she was satisfied that she had understood.

It is also possible to create surprise by asking students to commit themselves to conjectures that are then contradicted. Hadas *et al.* (2000) asked students to explore the sum of the interior angles of polygons and then to make a conjecture about the sum of the exterior angles. Most students conjectured that this would increase with the number of sides. When tested, this conjecture led to surprise and the desire to find out why the conjecture was not correct. Explanations may also be socially motivated. Weeden (2002) reports some successful work on explaining the angle sum of a triangle, which was motivated by different groups competing to create the best possible presentation.

Both construction and preconstructed files have a role in provoking a desire for explanation. Many results can be demonstrated visually using a preconstructed demonstration file (for example, both *Cabri* and *Sketchpad* come with a file called 'Pythagoras'), with discussion of why the demonstration works the way it does.

However, construction is particularly valuable for generating a desire for as well as supporting the process of proof. This is partly because students have greater insight into the properties of a figure that they have themselves designed and created, but also because the process of construction involves making purposeful decisions and hence continually engages the student with the question 'why?'. Healy and Hoyles (2001) found that, 'while constructing on the computer, some (although not all) students spontaneously provide justifications of their actions' (p. 237). Jones (1996) has also found construction to be important in promoting mathematical reasoning.

Traditional, formal proof fits within de Villiers' category of proof as a means of systematization. For this type of proof to be meaningful, students must be able to function at van Hiele level 4, in which students develop sequences of statements and begin to understand the significance of axioms and definitions in relation to proof as a general process. This is the level at which interactive geometry should probably not play an explicit role (apart from possibly as a demonstration), as it involves abstraction beyond specific screen figures. However, extensive experience with such figures and with informal explanations will help students to build the conceptual structures which are necessary to be able to engage in proof at this level. And careful observation of the dynamic interplay may also suggest an approach to the proof.

For further discussion and tasks, we strongly recommend de Villiers (2003). Although written for *The Geometer's Sketchpad*, most tasks can readily be adapted to *Cabri-Géomètre*.

Images beyond geometry

By now, you should be aware of some of the issues and alternatives that a teacher might consider in planning a suite of lessons using interactive geometry. Many other applications of such software are possible, but there is not space here to consider them all. Fundamentally, interactive geometry can be used in any mathematical situation involving working dynamically with visual images. But although such software's initial core is Euclidean geometry, it also works extremely well with challenges from analytic geometry, calculus, algebra and arithmetic.

For example, more recent versions of the software can plot functions given by algebraic specifications. However, an explicit algebraic relationship between variables is not needed in order to create a graph. Figure 5.6 shows a graph created simply from measurements. A circle was created, with variable radius, and the radius and area were both measured. These measurements were then used to plot a point and draw the graph of radius against area. The relationship between the two can then be explored directly: 'the student is not distanced from the meaning of the situation by the need to manipulate symbols' (Arcavi and Hadas, 2000, p. 34). Algebraic graph plotting can then be used to attempt to fit a curve to the

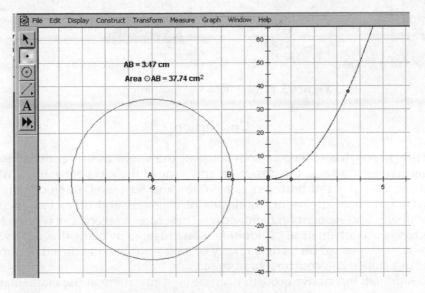

Figure 5.6 Plotting the area of a circle.

graph: this may enhance understanding both of the initial situation and of the graph. When symbols are finally introduced, the 'algebraic expression comes alive' (Noss and Hoyles, 1996, p. 245).

Finally, these graphs can be manipulated more directly than in many graph-plotting programs. Graphs can be defined with parameters that can be dragged. It is even possible to set up graphs such as the one in Figure 5.7, in which the position and shape of the quadratic graph are altered by manipulating points on the graph. Point B determines the position of the stationary point on the curve, and point A determines the shape of the curve.

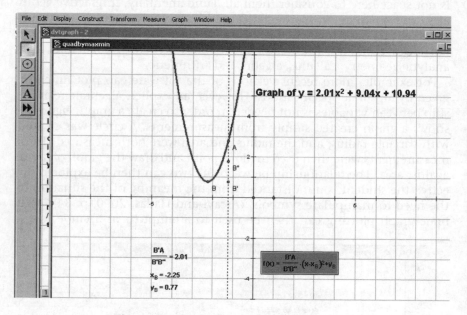

Figure 5.7   An interactive quadratic graph.

Conclusion

This chapter has looked at both some of the issues in using interactive geometry software in the classroom and some of the ways of dealing with them. The hearts of both programs, *Cabri* and *Sketchpad*, lie in dynamic visualization of situations, by means of diagrams and other bearers of mathematical elements and properties. These screen objects can be used as a basis for mathematical exploration – interrogated by being dragged by a mouse or operated on using a variety of tools – either constructed personally or guided and contributed from outside.

Although interactive geometry can be used anywhere in the mathematics curriculum where a visual approach is appropriate, it is geometry and geometric thinking that underlie all such models. Preconstructed files can be created for students to manipulate – but if the geometry is neglected, students will not be able to represent mathematical situations expressively for themselves. The ultimate aim should be to equip students so that they are able to choose to use such software in support of their mathematical thinking whenever and wherever it is useful.

References

Ainley, J. and Goldstein, R. (1988) *Making Logo Work: a Guide for Teachers*. Oxford: Basil Blackwell.

Arcavi, A. and Hadas, N. (2000) 'Computer-mediated learning: an example of an approach'. *International Journal of Computers for Mathematical Learning*, **5**(1), 25–45.

Association of Teachers of Mathematics (2001) *Active Geometry*. Derby: ATM.

de Villiers, M. (2003) *Rethinking Proof with The Geometer's Sketchpad*. Emeryville, CA: Key Curriculum Press.

Gawlick, T. (2002) 'On dynamic geometry software in the regular classroom'. *International Reviews on Mathematical Education*, **34**(3), 85–92.

Hadas, N., Hershkowitz, R. and Schwarz, B. (2000) 'The role of contradiction and uncertainty in promoting the need to prove in dynamic geometry environments'. *Educational Studies in Mathematics*, **44**(1–2), 127–50.

Healy, L. and Hoyles, C. (2001) 'Software tools for geometrical problem solving: potential and pitfalls'. *International Journal of Computers for Mathematical Learning*, **6**(3), 235–56.

Hölzl, R. (2001) 'Using DGS to add contrast to geometric situations: a case study'. *International Journal of Computers for Mathematical Learning*, **6**(1), 63–86.

Hoyles, C. and Healy, L. (1997) 'Unfolding meanings for reflective symmetry'. *International Journal of Computers for Mathematical Learning*, **2**(1), 27–59.

Jones, K. (1996) 'Coming to know about "dependency" within a dynamic geometry environment', in L. Puig and A. Gutiérrez (eds), *Proceedings of the 20th Conference of the International Group for the Psychology of Mathematics Education*. Valencia, University of Valencia, Vol. 3, pp. 145–52.

Jones, K. (1999) 'Student interpretations of a dynamic geometry environment', in I. Schwank (ed.), *Proceedings of the First Conference of the European Society for Research in Mathematics Education*, Osnabrück: Forschungsinstitut für Mathematikdidaktik, Vol. 1, pp. 245–58 (http://www.crme.soton.ac.uk/publications/kjpubs/JonesERME.pdf).

Jones, K. (2000) 'Providing a foundation for deductive reasoning: students' interpretation when using dynamic geometry software and their evolving mathematical explanations'. *Educational Studies in Mathematics*, **44**(1–2), 55–85.

Laborde, C. (1995) 'Designing tasks for learning geometry in a computer-based environment', in L. Burton and B. Jaworski (eds), *Technology in Mathematics Teaching: A Bridge Between Teaching and Learning*. Bromley: Chartwell-Bratt, pp. 35–68.

McLeay, H. (2002) 'Geostrips or dynamic geometry'. *Micromath*, **18**(3), 7–10.

Noss, R. and Hoyles, C. (1996) *Windows on Mathematical Meanings: Learning Cultures and Computers*. Dordrecht: Kluwer Academic.

Ransom, P. (2002) 'Bart's parts'. *Micromath* **18**(3), 21–5.

van Hiele, P.M. (1959/1985) 'The child's thought and geometry', in D. Fuys, D. Geddes, and R. Tischler (Eds) *English translation of selected writings of Dina van Hiele-Geldof and Pierre M. van Hiele*, pp. 243–52. Brooklyn, NY: Brooklyn College, School of Education.

van Hiele, P. (1986) *Structure and Insight: A Theory of Mathematics Education*. Orlando, FL: Academic Press.

Weeden, M. (2002) 'Proof, proof and more proof'. *Micromath*, **18**(3), 29–32.

6

THINKING
STATISTICALLY:
INTERACTIVE STATISTICS

Peter Johnston-Wilder

Statistical thinking in the widest sense has been transformed by the avail-ability of computer technology. First, the development of the internet has made data widely available in ways that were never possible before. Specif-ically within education, schoolchildren using the internet can gain access to real data about matters that interest them. Then, with the use of appropriate software, a variety of displays and statistical summaries are readily accessible, with several different analyses able to be undertaken in a short time. Consequently, using appropriate software tools, it is now much easier to explore a large data set.

An important concept in statistical thinking is variability. Variability is present everywhere, in any context that gives rise to data. Individuals vary and even repeated measurements of any one individual will vary. The discipline of statistics provides ways of thinking about data that take account of the presence of variability, using graphical displays or statistical measures to gain insight, to build arguments and to draw conclusions. Sometimes the task may be to detect underlying systematic effects against a background of variation, while at other times it will be to identify unusual individuals in a large set of data. By means of working on carefully designed tasks and using appropriate statistical software, students can develop their intuitions about variability.

In a modern democracy, the availability of data about a variety of issues, and of tools for their effective analysis, provides material for the potential empowerment of individuals. The variety of different ways of representing and summarizing data is reflected in the kinds of graphical displays and statistical summaries that appear in the media. Statistical literacy – having the skill required to interpret the results of various calculated statistics, to read various displays and to follow a statistical argument – has become ever more important to enable individuals to play a fuller and more active part in a democratic society. Students need to become familiar with a variety of displays and statistical summaries and learn how to interpret them. At a more advanced level, students need to use statistical reasoning to make inferences and to draw statistically valid conclusions, but such work is beyond the scope of this chapter.

This chapter discusses some specific examples of computer use to facilitate statistical thinking, especially in the secondary school. These examples show how computer technology can have a significant impact on the development of statistical concepts, as well as facilitate thinking about and interaction with data. In particular, the possibility of interacting with different representations of data can enable the user to receive feedback from the visual display and build a sense of how to set up such displays to communicate most effectively. Such interactivity can help to enable users to see statistical displays as dynamic and general, rather than static and particular.

After a brief look at software, this chapter is structured in two parts. The first deals with statistical displays, which represent characteristics of a whole data set. The second deals with using simulations to represent random processes and to explore associated emergent phenomena, such as the notion of distribution.

Software for learning statistical thinking

I mainly consider two widely used packages in this chapter – *Fathom* (Finzer *et al.*, 2000) and *Excel*. These two represent, respectively, two major categories of software relevant to the teaching and learning of statistics: statistical data-analysis packages and spreadsheets.

General-purpose spreadsheets, such as *Excel*, are readily available in any school and offer many facilities for developing statistical thinking. The ability to perform the same calculation many times makes them good for statistical calculation and for simulation. Also, because most teachers and students have acquired some skill in using the software already, examples that use *Excel* will be discussed in the next two sections.

However, *Excel* was not primarily designed as a tool for data analysis, and some forms of statistical display are not readily available. In addition, certain kinds of analysis are more difficult in *Excel* than they would be in a dedicated software package for statistics. The statistical tools in *Excel* are not structured for developing either confidence or understanding in a novice. Specialist statistical software, such as *SPSS* or *Minitab*, can help, but such packages are usually much more sophisticated than is required for statistics education at ages 11–18.

Few dedicated statistical packages have been designed specifically for teaching and learning at school level. A particularly interesting development, which is becoming more widely used in secondary schools in the UK, is *Fathom*. *Fathom* accurately describes itself as dynamic statistics software, in the same sense that *The Geometer's Sketchpad* is dynamic geometry software (see Chapter 5).

Fathom has been developed specifically as an environment for learning to think statistically. Its design has drawn upon research evidence about learners' difficulties with statistical concepts, but it essentially presents the user with standard statistical tools. Examples of what *Fathom* can offer will be discussed in the next section, especially its interactive facilities, in order to demonstrate what is possible. Although *Fathom* is not discussed in the section on simulation, it is important to note that it also has powerful facilities for simulation of randomness.

Most statistical software has been designed primarily for use by professional statisticians or to support business contexts. Tools available for use by young students are often effectively simplified professional tools. As such, they may be unsuitable for younger learners who, according to Biehler (1995, p. 3), 'need a tool that is designed from their bottom-up perspective of statistical novices and can develop in various ways into a full professional tool (not vice versa)'. Relatively little attempt has been made to design statistical software for learners 'from the bottom up'. An important instance which has is *Tinkerplots* (Konold and Miller, 2001). This is a data-analysis tool, under development for middle-school use, within which school students are enabled to construct non-standard graphical representations of data that make sense to them. *Tinkerplots* is designed for use by children who have not yet acquired much knowledge of conventional graphs or different types of data. It allows students to construct a wide variety of graphs, including novel ones of their own, and is discussed later in this chapter.

Another software package offering the possibility to teach some statistical concepts at school level is *Autograph* (Hatsell, 2000). This software is basically a mathematically sophisticated graph plotter, but it includes the possibility of plotting various graphs of data or of probability distributions, as well as exhibiting some facility for simulation. (*Autograph* is further discussed in Chapter 7.)

Finally, an excellent internet resource for ideas about teaching statistics with ICT, particularly if you use *Excel*, as well as providing many links to other useful sites, is Sydney Tyrrell's website (http://www.mis.coventry. ac.uk/~styrrell/index.php). In addition to giving many links to good sources of data, the site has links to instances of small software designed to illustrate a specific concept or to allow the user to explore a particular kind of example. Some of these small software developments are readily illustrated by applets that are available on the internet (see Chapter 12). Many of these take the form of small simulations through which the user can gain experience of random variation and of the emergence of a clear underlying probability distribution in the long run. I refer to some of these when I discuss simulation later in this chapter.

Representing data

The development of computer technology has radically changed how people interact with data. The applications of ICT described in this section facilitate what the statistics curriculum always did. But, because the computer's response is essentially immediate, and because of the possibility of using multiple linked representations, these applications enable the user (learner) to interact with the data to a much greater degree. Interaction with the data promotes an exploratory approach to data analysis, an essential element of statistical thinking.

Secondary data sources – large data sets

The opportunity to analyse real data and to discuss issues highlighted in the analysis is important in the development of statistical literacy in students. The Census at School project (http://www.censusatschool.ntu. ac.uk/; see Figure 6.1), based at the Centre for Statistical Education at Nottingham Trent University in the UK, takes advantage of the capacity of computer technology to enhance communication. Schools register to conduct a census of their students and collect a variety of data. The project has gathered large data sets from participating schools in the UK, in South Africa and in Queensland, Australia. Over the lifetime of the project, UK schools have participated in several different phases, each of which has involved collecting new data by means of a different questionnaire.

Data collected from the UK in phases 1 and 2 have been analysed by the project team, and some of their analyses can be viewed on the website: for example, one question in phase 1 asked whether the respondent owned a mobile phone. Tables are available on the web for each region of the UK, showing the proportions of primary and secondary school students owning a mobile phone. If students have been involved in collecting data from their own school on this question, they may have a genuine interest in seeing how the proportions vary across different regions of the UK and so may be strongly motivated to interpret the differences they see. Students can download a random sample from the data base of raw data. The sample is provided in CSV (comma separated variable) format for the student to import into their own software for analysis.

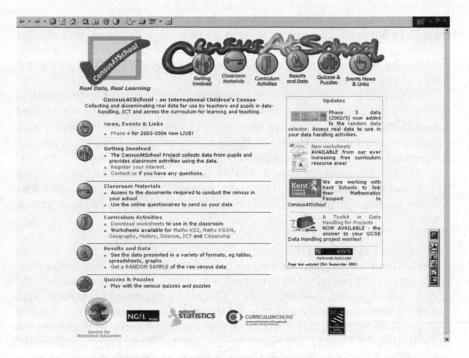

Figure 6.1 Screen dump of the Census at School home page.

For illustration, I have downloaded a sample of 200 records from the UK data base from phase 3. I have used this data set to illustrate the data analysis possibilities of *Fathom* and *Excel* in the remainder of this section. UK phase 3 data provide sampled information about each respondent, such as gender, age, height, foot length and pulse rate, as well as information about leisure activities and diet.

Graphical display of data

Computer software has the potential to enable users to generate graphical displays of data more easily. It may also increase the range of graphical displays that are available and accessible to the user.

To generate and display by hand a histogram of a data set of 200 values of a continuous variable, such as the height of an individual, requires the user to make some critical decisions before undertaking the lengthy process of sorting the data and constructing the graph. The user has to select a suitable method of grouping the data, before sorting the 200 individual values into groups, selecting an appropriate pair of scales for the horizontal and vertical axes of graph, then plotting the bars, before seeing the overall shape of the distribution 'revealed' by the histogram. Any misjudgement in these decision points – selecting the groups or deciding on the scales for the axes – can result in significant extra work, as the data may need to be sorted again into a different set of groups or the graph redrawn on new axes. Because of the time involved, it is unusual for a student working by hand to explore the benefits of displaying the data in several different ways based on different groups.

By contrast, computer software can enable the user to produce such a graph quickly and, at the same time, may reveal relationships with other variables by allowing the user to construct and view other graphs and calculations in parallel. However, there are significant differences among the possibilities and their accessibility in various software environments. Although many tools are now available that are better suited to learning to use and interpret graphical displays, I pragmatically begin with a discussion of the spreadsheet *Excel*, because it is widely available in UK schools.

Working with a spreadsheet (*Excel*)

A spreadsheet such as *Excel* offers many useful 'affordances' for doing statistics, but it was nonetheless written for a professional business clientele and is not intended specifically as a piece of educational software. The statistical facilities are not structured for developing a novice's confidence and understanding: indeed, some of the statistical tools in *Excel* can be unhelpful or misleading. For example, among the many graphical displays available in *Excel* is a pie chart. Novice users who nonetheless think they understand what a pie chart is rapidly get into difficulties when they attempt to use this tool to display many observations of a single variable. This is because *Excel* will display a pie chart with a single slice for each different value, a representation that is uninformative to the novice and offers no guidance to help the user progress.

This problem arises from the fact that *Excel* first requires the user to aggregate the data into a frequency table. Many different graphs require similar aggregation, but some graphs are only appropriate for certain types of data. For example, a dot plot can be used to display the frequencies of different categories in a categorical variable (such as hair colour) and it can display the frequencies of an ordered discrete variable such as the score when a single die is thrown. When the data are of a continuous variable, such as height, a histogram may be appropriate, but this particular representation is not easily produced in *Excel*.

Unfortunately, even when *Excel* can be used to produce statistical images that are pedagogically valuable, it is often difficult to arrange the software to produce them. Consider plotting a graph to show the distribution of the number of portions of fruit eaten daily by each of 200 individuals in the data set sampled from Census at School. The variable in this case is discrete, so the distribution is shown in a bar chart. However, before the graph can be plotted in *Excel*, you first need to use the FREQUENCY function to create a frequency table. The FREQUENCY function is an array function: it takes arrays of cells for input and produces output into a range of cells at once. This makes it more difficult to use than the standard *Excel* functions. Figure 6.2 shows the frequency table produced in *Excel*.

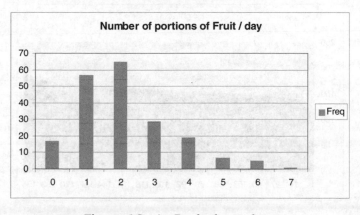

L	M	N	O	P	Q
	Fruit portions	Freq			
	0	17			
	1	57			
	2	65			
	3	29			
	4	19			
	5	7			
	6	5			
	7	1			
	total	200			

Figure 6.2 An *Excel* frequency table.

A graph of the frequency table needs to be plotted as a column chart (see Figure 6.3). Again, the process of creating such a graph is not intuitively obvious to students.

Number of portions of Fruit / day

Figure 6.3 An *Excel* column chart.

Some types of graph are even more difficult to produce in *Excel*. Consider, for example, the task of displaying a histogram of the heights of 200 individuals in the data set sampled from Census at School. A naive user might hope to highlight the column of the spreadsheet showing the 'height' variable and then select the appropriate graphing tool from the toolbar. Unfortunately, this only produces the simplistic bar chart, shown in Figure 6.4 overleaf, with a separate bar for each value. This kind of bar graph is often chosen by students when they are learning to select appropriate graphs for data, but it is more useful when the data have first been sorted into ascending order, a straightforward operation in *Excel*. The graph in Figure 6.5 overleaf is similar to the 'value' bars produced in

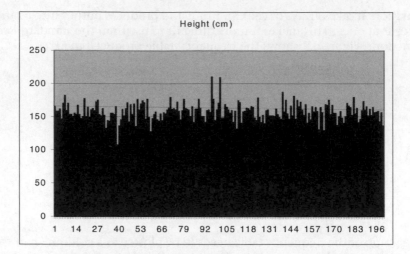

Figure 6.4   An *Excel* column chart of height data.

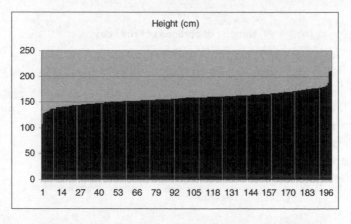

Figure 6.5   An *Excel* ordered column chart of height.

Tinkerplots (see Figure 6.17, page 115) and this kind of graph can provide a visual model for medians, quartiles and percentiles.

Producing what passes for a histogram in *Excel* is easier if you have first installed the appropriate tools, which are optional when installing *Excel*. Even then, the process is not simple and does not provide much in the way of interactivity. Indeed, the result is not even a true histogram, but rather a bar graph, which is mathematically incorrect as a histogram. A histogram should show bars whose area is proportional to the frequency of the interval to which they relate. Moreover, the bars should be drawn on the value scale so that they cover the entire scale, leaving no gaps between bars.

Having produced a bar graph, such as shown in Figure 6.6, it is possible to amend aspects of the graph, such as the scales or the format. However, this is difficult and rather messy, involving various dialogue boxes. In contrast, the same task in a dedicated statistical software tool, such as *Fathom*, is much more accessible and the result is considerably more interactive.

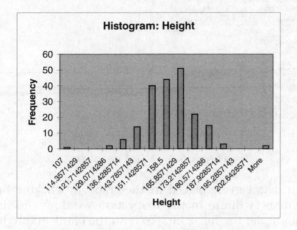

Figure 6.6   An *Excel* 'histogram' of heights.

Many 'add-ins' are available for *Excel* to provide improved statistical facilities (see, for example, http://www.mathtools.net/Excel/Statistics/) and some are being created specifically for use in schools (for example, SMILE, 2003).

Working with a statistical package (*Fathom*)

A particular strength of *Fathom* is that, once created, a graph is completely interactive. Initially, the software creates a dot plot of the variable, but this is readily changed to a histogram by using a pull-down menu on the graph window. The user can then interact with the histogram via the mouse to change the class widths and get feedback about what appears to be 'best'. Thus, the class widths and the scales become 'dimensions of variation' of a graph, rather than something fixed at the outset. You can display the mean, median, spread and inter-quartile range on the same graph. The entire graph is dynamically linked to the data, so the user can manipulate a particular data point and see the effect of this change both on these statistics and on the chosen representations.

For example, the data set sampled from Census at School can be loaded directly into *Fathom* in CSV format. In the screen dump shown in Figure 6.7 overleaf, the box icon at the top left is the data set. Double clicking on this opens the Inspection window below it. A blank graph can be created on the screen using the graph icon on the tool bar.

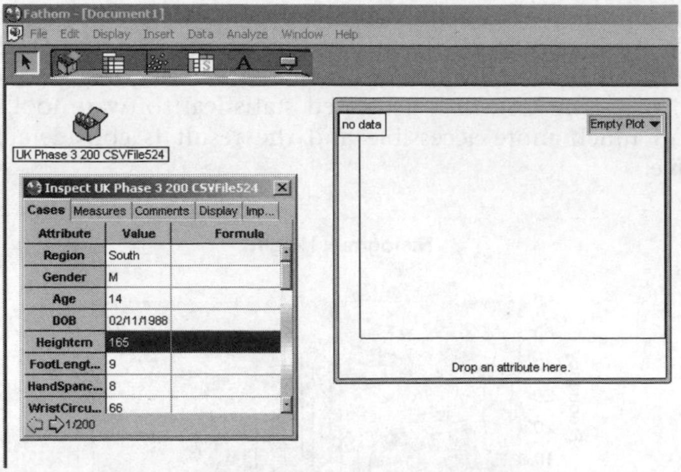

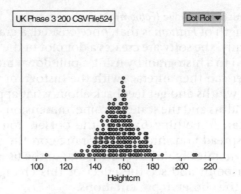

Figure 6.7   A *Fathom* screen.

The height data can be placed in the graph by clicking on the name of the Heightcm attribute in the Inspection window and dragging this into the space under the horizontal axis on the blank graph. Initially, this creates a dot plot (see Figure 6.8), but using the pull-down menu at the top right, it can subsequently be represented as a box plot (see Figure 6.9) or a histogram (see Figure 6.10). Dragging the boundary of a class interval changes the class interval width and the frequencies of the intervals update as you drag. Similarly, the scales can be changed by dragging the scale to be changed (see Figure 6.11).

Figure 6.8   A *Fathom* dot plot.

The idea of being able to treat a table or a graph as an object, like a triangle or a circle in *The Geometer's Sketchpad*, and then click and drag the data into the appropriate object, is highly intuitive and extends naturally.

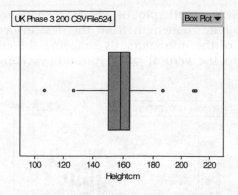

Figure 6.9 A *Fathom* box plot.

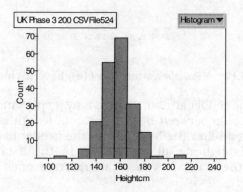

Figure 6.10 A *Fathom* histogram (original scales).

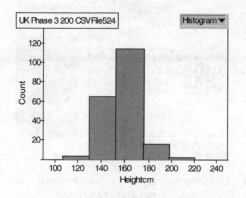

Figure 6.11 The histogram of Figure 6.10 with scales changed.

For example, to create a scatterplot of, say, foot length against height, you can drag the attribute Footlength from the data inspection window to the vertical axis of the histogram. By dragging the attribute from the horizontal axis to the vertical one, you can exchange the axes (see Figure 6.12).

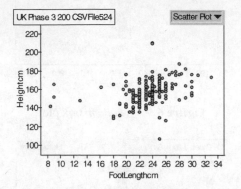

Figure 6.12 A *Fathom* scatterplot of height versus foot length.

By dragging the gender attribute into a new graph window, you can see how the relationship between height and foot length is associated with gender. When you select the Male bar of the gender bar graph, this has the effect of highlighting all individuals in the data with the Male attibute, so all the males in your scatterplot become highlighted (see Figure 6.13).

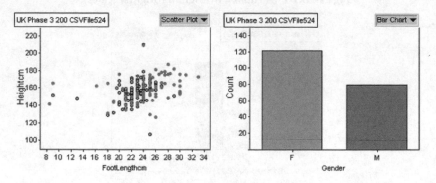

Figure 6.13 A *Fathom* scatterplot of height versus foot length (males highlighted).

It is also possible to explore the effects of moving a single data point. In Figure 6.14, the first image shows the dot plot of a sample of 20 individuals from the original data, as well as the positions of the mean and the

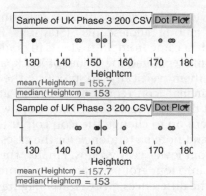

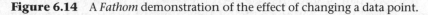

Figure 6.14 A *Fathom* demonstration of the effect of changing a data point.

median. In the second image, the highlighted data point on the left has been dragged towards the centre, with a substantial effect on the position of the mean, but no impact whatsoever on the median. Dragging it a little further to the right has an interesting effect on the median, but little effect on the mean. By exploring in this way, students can build intuitions about the resistance of various statistical measures to errors or change in the data.

Through the use of such interactive tools, students can build a sense of variability in the data and of how the variability is affected by other attributes, such as gender. The interactivity that is built into *Fathom* offers a powerful means whereby learners can build their understanding, giving them a degree of control over the representations produced. Future developments are set to carry this further, as illustrated in the next subsection about *Tinkerplots*.

Development of pedagogical software (Tinkerplots)

The plot windows in *Tinkerplots* (Konold and Miller, 2001) have been designed to support children's reasoning about data. Any plot shows data icons, each of which represent an individual case in the data set. When a data set is first opened, the data icons are arranged randomly on the screen to represent unsorted data. Users are able to organize the data progressively into a variety of graphical representations using basic intuitive operators – stack, order and separate. As well as using position along an axis to portray variability, students can also use colour gradations, variations in the size of the plot icon and sound.

Examples of work by North American students in seventh grade (aged 12–13) using *Tinkerplots* to explore a data set are shown on the *Tinkerplots* website (http://www.umass.edu/srri/serg/projects/tp/tpmain.html). The students worked on data they had collected relating to a suggestion that

'Some doctors believe that heavy backpacks are responsible for an increase in back problems among adolescents' (Statistics Education Research Group, 2002). The data came from 55 students in grades 1, 3, 5 and 7.

One pair of students separated the values of 'backpack weight' horizontally and stacked them vertically to produce the 'graph' shown in Figure 6.15. Each circular icon represents one case and the colour gradation of the icons at this stage represented backpack weight.

These students went on to change the icon colour to represent the year group of each case and noted a tendency for the cases at the lower end of their graph to be from lower year groups. Finally, the students separated 'grade' (year group) into four groups to produce a representation that they thought displayed the differences more clearly (Figure 6.16).

A second pair of students displayed the backpack weights as 'value' bars and ordered them, before changing the colour of the icons to represent 'grade' and then separating the value bars by 'grade' (Figure 6.17).

Graphical representations of similar kinds have also been used successfully with students by Cobb *et al.* (2003) in their work on 'statistical minitools'. Various research studies indicate that many people have difficulty judging covariation from standard representations such as scatterplots or contingency tables (see, for example, Batanero *et al.*, 1997). Representations such as those shown in Figures 6.15–6.17, which are

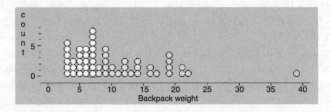

Figure 6.15   A *Tinkerplot* graph of backpack weight.

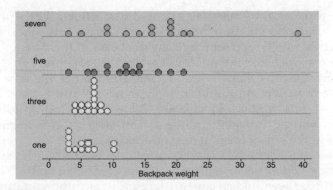

Figure 6.16   A *Tinkerplot* graph of grouped backpack weight.

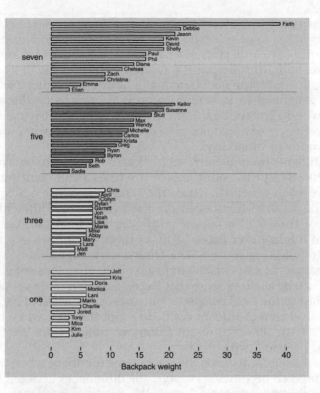

Figure 6.17 A *Tinkerplot* graph of ordered value bars.

made possible in *Tinkerplots* and are chosen by students working on real data within this software, may be important stepping stones towards using more abstract scatterplots (Noss *et al.*, 1999; Konold, 2002; Cobb *et al.*, 2003).

Simulation – using the computer to generate the data

Two different approaches can be taken to using simulations of random processes and events in teaching statistics. One is for students to use a simulation that has been constructed for them and to explore the under-lying nature of the phenomenon as already represented in the simulation. Starting with the given simulation, students can be asked to adjust it to implement their own changes. The alternative, which is rather more chal-lenging and time-consuming, is for students to build their own simulation of a situation or phenomenon.

There are significant gains possible from using computer-based simula-tions of random phenomena. An important gain arises from the possibility of fusing two distinct views of randomness. One approach to randomness, which is familiar to people who have played games of chance involving throwing dice or casting jacks, is what I call the *micro-level* view or the *local* perspective. From this perspective, randomness gives rise to a sequence of outcomes, in which the next outcome is always unpredictable. Thus, the sequence generated by a random process is seen to be disordered and without pattern. The student working from this perspective pays attention to short sequences of outcomes or to predicting subsequent outcomes and is mostly aware of variability.

As the students become more sophisticated in their analysis of the data, they might attempt to count how many of each different possible outcome have been observed. Thus, they might produce a frequency bar graph to display the number of occurrences of each different face in a sequence of throws of a fair die. However, the total number of throws considered might never exceed 100, as there are immense practical difficulties in collecting reliable data from a very large number of throws. Thus, although the students might begin to discern a sense of distribution, there will still be a strong sense that the data remain quite variable.

In contrast to the local perspective is what I call the *global* perspective or the *macro-level* view. A student is able to adopt this view when he or she is able to relate the observed results from, say, rolling a die 100 times to an underlying probability distribution.

A central idea in statistics is the law of large numbers: when the number of trials observed becomes very large, the differences between the underlying probability distribution and the relative frequencies observed become vanishingly small. It is difficult fully to appreciate and experience the power and importance of this idea in practice if it is not possible to look at very large numbers.

Computer-based simulations make it possible to experience this idea many times and in many different contexts. Thus, it is possible to collect and record data from complex experiments and still collate the results from a very large number of outcomes. This might involve displaying a bar graph to show the observed relative frequencies of the different faces when a die is thrown 10,000 times, or 100,000 times, or comparing the relative frequencies of getting a 6 followed by a low number (a 1, 2 or 3) and getting a 6 followed by a high number.

In the past, the local perspective was the main concern when working with empirical data, as it was difficult to collect aggregate data from very large numbers of outcomes. The concept of distribution was introduced as a theoretical idea and the relationship between the theoretical distribution and the observed frequencies from large numbers of trials was never really experienced. For some students, these two perspectives of randomness are contradictory: the local perspective is disordered and without patterns, while the global perspective of statistical distribution carries with it a sense of long-run pattern and order. Older students are taught that the underlying distribution can be seen in the outcomes of a large number of trials, but they do not often experience how the empirical distribution varies from the theoretical distribution in the course of relatively small numbers of trials.

The underpinning pattern of *distribution*, which emerges from the aggregation of very large numbers of observations, exposes an underlying order, but students rarely experience how many results they need before the pattern of the distribution can be trusted to emerge. Working with computer-based simulations of random phenomena can enable students to experience thinking with both these two perspectives and to move between them. Within a sophisticated software environment such as *NetLogo* (see below), it becomes possible to experience distributional phenomena emerging in a variety of probabilistic situations.

In order to illustrate these ideas, I first describe and discuss a simple simulation of a dice-throwing experiment in *Excel*. Then I give a brief description of the 'emergent phenomenon' of distribution. (It is important for readers to be aware that *Fathom* offers pedagogically powerful tools for simulation, distinguishing clearly among the population, the sample and the measures collected, even though, for reasons of space and *Fathom*'s lesser availability in the UK, they are not discussed in this chapter.)

Simulation using Excel

One of the fundamental skills required to use computer programs to simulate random phenomena is to see how to make use of a random number generator to create random observations from a particular distribution. This skill requires an understanding of the concept of distribution: a good starting point is to see how the random number generator itself behaves. In *Excel*, the function RAND() is the most basic random function available. It generates a 'random' decimal value greater than or equal to zero and strictly less than 1, such that the values generated are uniformly distributed in the half-open interval [0,1).

Of course, like any other computer-generated 'random' number, it is really only a pseudo-random number, in that there is an algorithm programmed into the computer to generate the value each time. However, since we (as users) have no knowledge of how this algorithm behaves in any particular instance, and the outcomes generated share the long-run features of randomness, we can treat the successive observations as being random. The following is a useful sequence of exercises in developing understanding of how to use the RAND() function.

First, generate a column of 20 values using the formula =RAND(). Notice how the values displayed in these cells change every time the spreadsheet is altered or if the F9 key is pressed to recalculate the spreadsheet. This instability in the contents of the 'random' cells reinforces for me the dynamic sense of randomness. It is useful to adjust the cell width to display the full precision of the value, so that students see how many figures are calculated. *Excel* usually displays decimal values to 15 places of decimals. However, some cells may only show 14 (or 13) decimal places; this is because the figure in the 15th (and 14th) decimal place is zero and the spreadsheet does not display trailing zeros unless you tell it to – using Format, Cells, Number, Number, Decimal places.

Next, consider how these values could be used to simulate the results of tossing a fair coin. Most students in Year 9, and many in Years 7 or 8, can suggest rules for deciding whether a particular value represents a head or a tail. For example, if the value shown is greater than or equal to 0.5 the outcome is deemed a head, otherwise the outcome is to be a tail. An alternative rule could be, if the first digit after the decimal point was odd, consider the outcome to be a head, otherwise the outcome is declared a tail.

Having seen how to simulate the toss of a coin, some students are subsequently able to see how to simulate a fair six-faced die, but most require some help. The formula =1 + INT(6 * RAND()) produces the desired result. But it is important that students learn to see why this is so. They need to develop the confidence to create equivalent forms of this formula, such as = INT(1 + RAND() * 6), and to modify this formula to select from some other set of consecutive integers such as 4, 5, 6, 7, 8, or to simulate a tetrahedral (or other Platonic solid) die.

Think for yourself why the formula =1 + INT(6 * RAND()) produces the desired result. (The function INT in the above expression has the effect of returning the integer part of the input: thus, INT(2.3) is 2, and INT(3.75) is 3.)

It is now possible to use the FREQUENCY function to display the frequencies of the six possible values in a sample of 20 observations. By repeating these calculations in many columns, you can experience how these frequencies can vary across a large number of samples. Many students are surprised when they find that somewhere in 1,000 samples they have one sample of 20 values that has more than half its values the same. By pressing the F9 key to repeat the calculation, thereby generating a new set of samples, they can get a sense of how often this 'unusual' event occurs when looking at a large number of samples.

Once you are able to simulate the result of rolling one die, many other experiments can be simulated. For example, to explore the distribution of the sum of three dice rolled independently, place the formula to generate the value from rolling each die in three adjacent columns and calculate the sum of the three values in a fourth column. This is shown in Figure 6.18. Each time the F9 key is pressed, the values are recalculated and a new graph is displayed.

Similar experiments can be carried out using dedicated statistical software such as *Fathom*, usually much more easily than with *Excel*. There are also numerous probabilistic simulations available on the internet (see

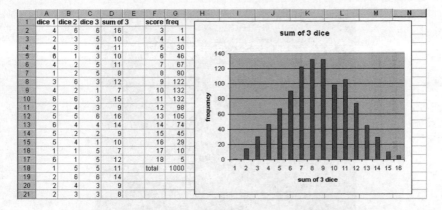

Figure 6.18   The sum of three dice (simulated 1000 times).

Chapter 12), some of which can be useful in the classroom to demonstrate particular concepts or tools, such as the central limit theorem or scatterplots and covariation.

Simulation with NetLogo

A different experience of distribution as an 'emergent phenomenon' (Wilensky, 1999) arises from experimenting with software such as *NetLogo*. Within *NetLogo*, the programming language is essentially the same as *Logo*, enabling the movement of a 'turtle' on the screen to be controlled by instructions such as move forward a distance or turn through an angle. *NetLogo* enables the user to set up a large number of turtles, distributed randomly on the screen and/or each moving initially in a randomly chosen direction. The turtles can be programmed to interact with each other according to some simple rule, which might express what happens when two turtles collide or when turtles are less than some distance apart. When such a system is left to run for a length of time, certain features of the system may display some emergent pattern.

For example, in a simple simulation based on the 'random balls' model taken from the *NetLogo* website (Wilensky, 1998), 100 turtles are scattered randomly in the bottom left-hand quarter of the screen, each moving at the same speed and with a randomly chosen heading (Figure 6.19 over-leaf). The turtles are programmed to bounce off the edges of the screen, as though they were billiard balls bouncing off the cushion of a billiard table, and they are assumed never to collide with each other. The centre of mass of the 100 turtles is marked on the screen and its motion is traced as the simulation is allowed to run. Initially, their centre of mass is in the bottom left-hand quarter of the screen, but it very soon moves towards the centre of the screen. It then moves around, apparently randomly, within a

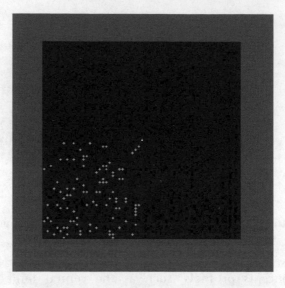

Figure 6.19   Random balls – initial set-up.

confined area in the middle of the screen. Initially, the area within which it moves appears to be approximately circular, but in the longer run it appears to be slightly distorted (Figure 6.20). Here is an emergent pattern involving the set of places to which the centre of mass of this system can move in the long run.

Figure 6.20   Random balls – after several minutes.

A variety of ready-made *NetLogo* simulations are available on the internet. Many of these simulations use pseudo-random numbers to represent a random aspect of the process, and some offer powerful tools for exploring and experiencing distribution as an 'emergent phenomenon'.

Conclusion

Several different kinds of software environment have been discussed in this chapter. They each offer experiences of working with statistical concepts and facilitate statistical thinking in various ways. While spreadsheets such as *Excel* are widely available in schools, and can offer some tools to support the development of statistical thinking, the tools are often relatively inaccessible and sometimes pedagogically unhelpful. Teachers are inevitably looking at how they can make effective use of statistical facilities in *Excel*, in order to take advantage of its existing availability and skillbase among both teachers and students. However, its clear limitations mean that it is important to look at the alternatives that are now on the market.

Fathom is an important package for schools to consider, as it has been written specifically for use within the school curriculum. It takes advantage of the powerful 'drag and drop' metaphor that is widely used in other software in the school curriculum and its design has incorporated some insights from research into students' learning of statistical concepts.

Current developments, such as 'statistical minitools' (Cobb *et al.*, 1997) and the *Tinkerplots* software (Konold and Miller, 2001) both being developed by researchers in the USA, indicate ways in which new software developments are arising out of current research. Bakker (2002) suggests that: 'Students tend to see data as individual values and find it hard to reason with data sets as a whole that have certain characteristics such as an average representing the group, a majority and outliers, or a constant shape'. The developments within new tools such as *Tinkerplots* are seeking to address difficulties like those highlighted by Bakker. However, it is to be hoped that the flexibility and student control built into *Tinkerplots* can eventually be incorporated into a larger, more powerful, and in the end more widely distributed statistics package like *Fathom*.

Tools for random simulation are built into most statistical software. Students can gain insight from experiencing randomness as unpredictability in the short run and seeing pattern and order emerge in the long run. With computer simulation, it is possible to experience the emergence of a distribution over 10, 100, 1,000, 100,000 or even 10,000,000 trials. Such experience is unique in collective human history. Students can practise building simulations of their own in many software environments; even *Excel* is quite accessible in this regard. However, the experience of experimenting with models within a visual environment like *NetLogo* may offer the possibility of extending students' imaginations and hence of encouraging them to consider applying randomness as a model to a wider variety of situations and contexts.

References

Bakker, A. (2002) 'From data via "bump" to distribution'. *Statistics Education Research Journal*, **1**(1), 35.

Batanero, C., Estepa, A. and Godino, J. (1997) 'Evolution of students' understanding of statistical association in a computer-based teaching environment', in G. Burrill (ed.), *Research on the Role of Technology in Teaching and Learning Statistics (Proceedings of the 1996 IASE Round Table Conference)*. Voorburg, The Netherlands: International Statistical Institute, pp. 191–205.

Biehler, R. (1995) 'Towards requirements for more adequate software tools that support both learning and doing statistics'. Occasional paper 157, University of Bielefeld, Germany. (Revised version of a paper first presented at ICOTS-4.)

Cobb, P., Gravemeijer, K., Bowers, J. and McClain, K. (1997) *Statistical Minitools*, Memphis, TN: Vanderbilt University.

Cobb, P., McClain, K. and Gravemeijer, K. (2003) 'Learning about statistical covariation'. *Cognition and Instruction*, **21**(1), 1–78.

Finzer, W., Erickson, E. and Binker, J. (2000) *Fathom: Dynamic Statistics Software*. Emeryville, CA: Key Curriculum Press.

Hatsell, M. (2000) *Autograph v. 2.00*. Oundle, Northants: Eastmond Publishing.

Konold, C. (2002) 'Teaching concepts rather than conventions'. *New England Journal of Mathematics*, **34**(2), 69–81.

Konold, C. and Miller, C. (2001) *Tinkerplots, Version 0.42, Data Analysis Software for the Middle School*. Amherst: University of Massachusetts.

Noss, R., Pozzi, S. and Hoyles, C. (1999) 'Touching epistemologies: meanings of average and variation in nursing practice'. *Educational Studies in Mathematics*, **40**(1), 25–51.

Statistics Education Research Group (2002) *Building Plots*. Amherst, MA: Statistics Education Research Group, SRRI, University of Massachussetts.

SMILE (2003) *Real Data*. London: SMILE (http://www.smilemathematics.co.uk).

Wilensky, U. (1998) 'NetLogo "Random balls" model. Evanston, IL: Center for Connected Learning and Computer-Based Modeling, Northwestern University (http://ccl.northwestern.edu/netlogo/models/RandomBalls).

Wilensky, U. (1999) 'NetLogo'. Evanston, IL, Center for Connected Learning and Computer-Based Modeling, Northwestern University (http://ccl.northwestern.edu/netlogo).

7

THE SCHOOL MATHEMATICS CURRICULUM IN A TECHNOLOGICAL AGE

Douglas Butler

It is a sobering thought that every 16-year-old in the world who attends school learns some mathematics, all in different languages of course, but essentially the same subject. This represents an extraordinarily uniform view of education departments around the world that mathematics is indispensable, even though very few students ever get anywhere near appreciating the scope or the power of the subject. Some countries allow children to give up academic mathematics at age 14, most allow students to stop their mathematical studies at 16, while others require some form of mathematics for all to age 17 or 18.

Despite this enormous effort, most adults recall very little of the mathematics that they learnt at school. If asked what mathematics they use in their adult life, many are at a loss to think of anything beyond simple arithmetic. So why is mathematics taught in schools so extensively? What should the mathematics curriculum look like in a technological age?

At the present time, the subject is being buffeted by several disturbing trends, all of which threaten to answer this question with the most depressing scenario possible. There is a severe shortage of suitably quali-fied teachers joining the profession and an increasing tendency for teachers to leave the classroom for other ways of earning a living. Furthermore, too many able students are losing interest in taking the sub-ject further in their own programme of studies. This is all happening at a time of rapid technological advances most of which could not have come about without a mathematically trained population. These amazing technologies should themselves be the perfect inspiration to the young to improve their own mathematical understanding, but somehow this is not happening.

Previous generations of schoolchildren built models, went fishing and played board games. This required much more of a 'hands-on' approach to problem-solving than many students of today get to employ. So it could be argued that the new technologies are themselves forcing the general public, and school students alike, into thinking that they no longer need to know how anything works. Most people now assume that, in general, things (games, cars, etc.) seem to work with so little effort that they require minimal 'under-the-bonnet' knowledge.

The impact of ICT on other subjects

Before considering what can be left out of and what can come into mathematics teaching, it is worth considering how the impact of ICT on mathematics compares with other subjects. No subject has escaped the ICT revolution and teachers in disciplines as diverse as Latin and music are finding electronic resources for their teaching (http://www.tsm-resources.com/subj.html). For example, music teachers now have software and hardware that effortlessly transposes, arranges, plays back, and even composes music for you (http://www.tsm-resources.com/music.html).

This may be considered a threat to the very subject itself. On the positive side, ICT has lowered the threshold for music as a subject to be enjoyed by very many more students (and music technology itself is a fast-growing subject in its own right and about to overtake straight music). On the other hand, the real worry is that fewer students will want to put the effort in to learning the subject from the bottom up, as previous generations had to.

The impact of ICT on mathematics

The impact of ICT on the subject of mathematics can be profound, but only if adequate and ongoing in-service training is in place.

ICT can help to make the teaching of mathematics more effective

This assertion is discussed in detail in earlier chapters in this book. ICT has the dual benefit of increasing the motivation of students towards the subject and at times making the subject more enjoyable to teach. It therefore has the potential to increase the numbers of students wanting to take the subject seriously and to make the teaching profession more attractive to those considering it as a career. The use of modern computer-generated images can also make the subject seem more 'up to date' and 'relevant' and therefore more appealing to students.

ICT can help to make the teaching of mathematics more efficient

There is plenty of anecdotal evidence that teachers can cover topics in less time (and more effectively) when ICT is used. This is not an easy point to prove with formal research, but it has important implications on the main thrust of this chapter concerning curriculum change. Mathematics as a subject has a phenomenal and rapidly growing suite of electronic resources, both web-based (http://www.tsm-resources.com/mlink.html) and in the form of commercial software (http://www.tsm-resources.com/suppl.html). Looking round other subjects' resources, mathematics would appear to have by far the widest range of software tools, especially if you include the web and spreadsheets.

Most of the major mathematics software environments, whether on hand-held or conventional computers, are gradually aiming for the same

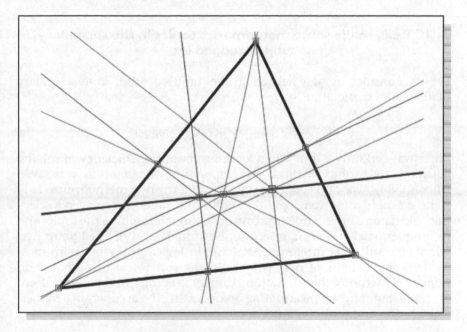

Figure 7.1 The Euler line.
The Euler line is one of the wonders of Euclidean geometry, but presents a formidable challenge in the classroom. The teacher needs to raise expectations of a great discovery without revealing too much; however, if the teacher reveals too little, students can get nowhere and lose interest.

point: to give users an easy-to-use, all-purpose tool for symbolic algebra, dynamic graphing and statistical analysis. This, together with the regular 'office' tools and internet resources, is becoming established as the standard tool-box for the modern mathematics teacher.

In nearly all cases, students will get meaningful results from ICT only if they understand the underlying mathematical principles. A student who cannot factorize will not be able to do much that is meaningful with symbolic algebra, in the same way that a spell-checker is relatively useless to someone who cannot spell. Without giving the matter much thought, many people might pose the question: if a machine can solve, factorize, integrate and plot anything, can we not dispense with most of the curriculum that was designed before these tools were invented?

The real difficulty here is that all the people making decisions about the impact of ICT on mathematics have learnt the subject the 'hard' way. To them, the new ICT approaches open a fabulous window of visual opportunities, which sit beautifully on their rich body of mathematical knowledge. The danger is that teachers will forget that their students do not have this body of knowledge and wonder why their students are not as excited or as insightful as they are about what they are seeing.

ICT can make some mathematics topics in the secondary subject redundant

Let us consider now what could be omitted from the secondary mathematics curriculum.

Numerical methods to solve equations

There was certainly a time when learning about the efficiency of solving equations by various methods was important. Valuable time was saved when solving awkward equations by choosing the best method, especially if the available tools were logarithm tables and slide rules or even a scientific calculator. This is hardly the case now, though teaching the topics and techniques (trial and error, bisection, Newton–Raphson, fixed-point iteration, etc.) still offer interesting exercises in logical thinking. With most modern applications of mathematics in the real world being based on numerical methods, there is a strong case for keeping this on in some form at school, but maybe concentrating on discussing the accuracy of a numerical solution and possible causes of error.

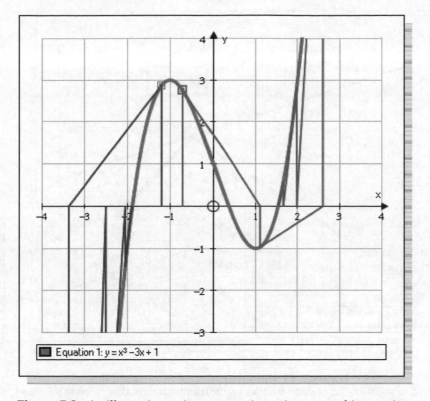

Equation 1: $y = x^3 - 3x + 1$

Figure 7.2 An illustration, using two starting points on a cubic equation, that the Newton–Raphson method is unreliable and inefficient when the starting points are a long way from any root.

When solving for intersections, *Autograph* itself uses a decimal search method to find a starting point near to each root, then uses Newton–Raphson to find the root when it is at its most efficient.

Simultaneous equations

Some students can become really good at solving two linear equations and enjoy the challenge, while others struggle and never understand the idea of eliminating a variable from two implicit linear equations (especially when put like that!). On the other hand, they can see perfectly well that they have two straight lines that cross, and then – click! – there's the answer.

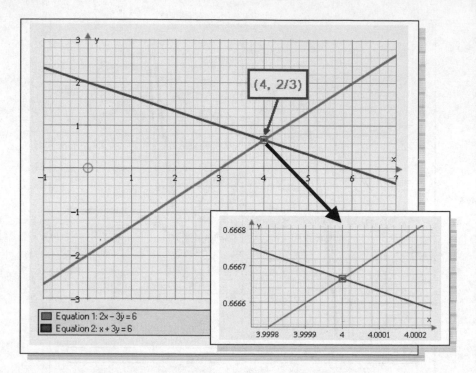

Figure 7.3 The intersection of two straight lines.
The visual link between the algebraic solution for the intersection of two straight lines
and the graphical representation is often one of the first uses of graphing technology.
Zooming in is one of many ways to find the answer. This topic also provides one of
the first uses of the implicit form of the straight line.

Statistics

Many older teachers learned little or no statistics at all at school, so for
them this can still be a new and exciting branch of mathematics, which
gives daily opportunities to bring in 'real' data for analysis. There is one
area that is widely taught in the UK and which is really redundant now:
the Poisson and the normal approximations to the binomial distribution.
These comprise a nice topic to teach specialists, but both came into being
to alleviate the calculation difficulties when the binomial probabilities
involve large combinations or when p was very small. Equally, the various
tricks employed to calculate population mean and variance with working
means have also served out their time.

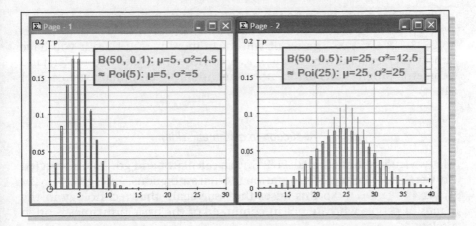

Figure 7.4 An illustration that the Poisson distribution is a good fit to the binomial when *p* is small.

In these diagrams, the thin line sticking out of the top is the binomial. In each case, the two distributions have the same mean, but the variances are very different for larger values of *p*.

Reduction in routine algebra

This is a tempting thought, but algebra is the grammar of mathematics and mathematics cannot progress much beyond simple arithmetic without it. There are no short-cuts to acquiring algebraic competence and fluency – for example, to get to the stage of simplifying $\frac{x^2-1}{x-1}$ without making one or more serious errors! There is certainly a case for reducing the learning of some of the more advanced techniques which the calculator can perform, once the underlying principles are secure. A computer algebra system (either hand-held or computer-based) can produce a chart like the following to help students see a pattern and hence derive a rule:

a	$(x + a)^2$	a	$(x - a)^2$
1	$x^2 + 2x + 1$	1	$x^2 - 2x + 1$
2	$x^2 + 4x + 4$	2	$x^2 - 4x + 4$
3	$x^2 + 6x + 9$	3	$x^2 - 6x + 9$
4	$x^2 + 8x + 16$	4	$x^2 - 8x + 16$

Likewise, it could be argued that long division in algebra could go from post-16 teaching. However, if you have manually divided $(1 - x^4)$ by $(1 - x)$ to get $1 + x + x^2 + x^3$, the result will mean more to you than if you have simply pressed a button. You are, as a consequence, likely to understand geometric progressions better, not to mention the binomial expansion of $(1 - x)^{-1}$.

Reduction in arithmetic skills

Many a student has entered $-1/2^2$ into a calculator and got an unexpected answer, since Mathematics notation is often ambiguous. *Excel* gives $-1 \wedge 2 = 1$, yet $1 - 1 \wedge 2 = 0$. So this raises the issue again that technology in the hands of people who are not in command of the basic principles is often useless.

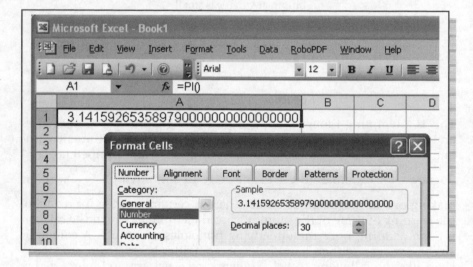

Figure 7.5 π, apparently to 30 decimal places.

Here, *Excel* (which performs all its calculations to 15 significant figures) can display its cells to 30 decimal places. Most users do not know this and could be forgiven for thinking that π is rational!

Hand-sketching of graphs

In a way, the hand-sketching of graphs is more important than ever, as no software is free of error; students must not think they can draw graphs on a machine without the requisite knowledge to detect an error (either in the software or, more likely, in their entry). For example, most graphing tools will 'mess up' the drawing of $y = \tan(x)$ eventually and many cannot cope with $y = x^n$ for values of n that are not positive integers. Other entries can also be ambiguous: for example, what is meant by $y = \sin(x^2)$?

So, the hand-sketching of more advanced graphs could be reduced, but again only if the underlying principles are secure.

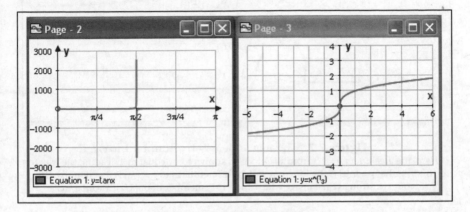

Figure 7.6 Problem graphs for graphing software.
The graph of $y = \tan(x)$ should go to infinity at $x = \pi/2$, but all graphing tools will give up at some stage. Here, *Autograph* seems to fizzle out at about 2500. Fractional indices of x often cause problems because the underlying calculators written in C++ and Java cannot evaluate them for $x < 0$. Most graphing tools therefore need to be 'trained' to include the negative branch.

Analytical calculus

It could be argued that since the world of work uses largely numerical methods to study the relationships of variables, school-level calculus could be far less algebraic. Also, the principles of the calculus, especially the idea of rate of change, could be introduced visually at an earlier stage. More advanced techniques, such as integration by parts and any definite integral, can be removed.

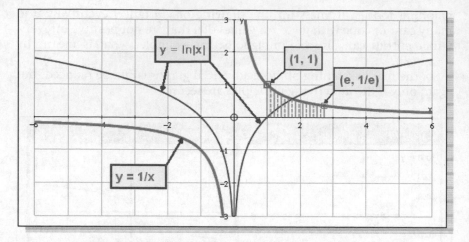

Figure 7.7 The area under $y = 1/x$ from $x = 1$ to e.
Here, the area under $y = 1/x$ from $x = 1$ to 'e' is shown to be equal to 1, leading the way to finding that $y = \ln|x|$ is the function which differentiates to $y = 1/x$. A diagram like this offers a strong visual image with which to remember that $\int(1/x)dx = \ln|x| + c$.

Consideration of ICT in assessment

Another related problem is assessment. If ICT is to have a real impact on the subject, then the method of assessment should embrace it too. Computer-based technology is simply not appropriate for an examination environment (size of footprint, operating system crashes and power supply problems). However, new hand-held products are becoming available (e.g. the Casio ClassPad and the TI Voyage 200) which seriously challenge mathematics educators to rethink the content and its assessment. There will, however, always be two stumbling blocks: there must be funds to equip the students; and both the students and the teachers need training in the use of these products.

Can the mathematics curriculum be extended?

There has been a lot of experimentation in the past few decades, some of which has survived the test of time (for example, statistics), and some of which has faded away (for example, set notation). Having access to modern software should allow the teaching process to be conducted more efficiently, with improved understanding following access to visualization. Improved efficiency and some time saved by shaving some of the more advanced drill and practice outlined above should leave room for a number of extensions and interesting new threads.

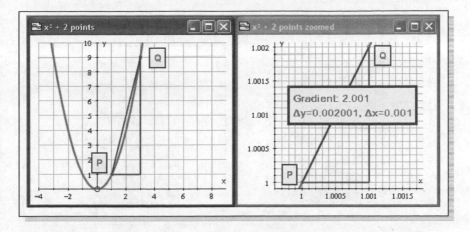

Figure 7.8 A graphing facility that zooms.

A graphing facility that zooms can give new insights into the principles of differentiation and the associated and essential concept of 'local straightness'. Here *Autograph* shows that two lengths can each become very small as Q gets closer to P, yet the ratio remains finite and reaches a limit.

Statistics

The study of statistics could be extended to include large, real data sets and more involved tests. The important central limit theorem is at the moment studied only by the more advanced students. Software methods can make it easier for younger students to understand its basic principles, allowing everyday statistics, such as opinion polls, to be better understood.

There is a good case for improving the statistical understanding of school-aged students so that, in time, the adult population can cope with data more intelligently than it does at present. A glaring example of this can be seen most days in the newspapers: facts and figures are often cruelly misinterpreted by journalists, who display a poor grasp of basis statistical concepts.

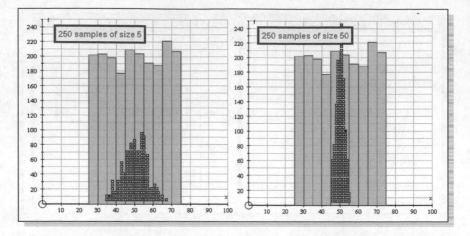

Figure 7.9   Illustrating the central limit theorem.
The central limit theorem forms the basis of much of the sampling used every day, including election opinion polls. Here, *Autograph* has generated 1000 samples of uniform data between 25 and 75 and then taken 250 sample of size 5 and then 50 samples and drawn the distribution of the sample means. The accuracy of the estimate of the population mean can be seen to have increased dramatically with the larger sample size.

Probability

An understanding of this important discipline is central to many occupations, including insurance and the provision of public services. At the moment, only post-16 students have the opportunity to understand what is meant by a probability distribution, but ICT simulations are readily available to demonstrate the concept with ease to younger students.

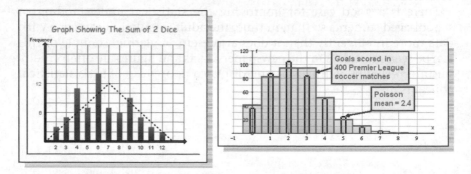

Figure 7.10   Using *Autograph* for simulation.
The idea of a probability distribution could be introduced earlier through commonplace situations. Computers allow large experiments and simulations. Here, the start of a long progression of dice throws can be simulated and the Poisson distribution used to model goals scored (with surprising accuracy).

Coordinate geometry and trigonometry

This whole area comes to life with dynamic software, and is much more approachable to school-level students. The properties of conics can be reintroduced without resorting to heavy algebra. And trigonometric functions are much easier to understand if they are dynamic objects with variable amplitude, period, phase and offset of $y = \sin(x)$ in degrees and radians.

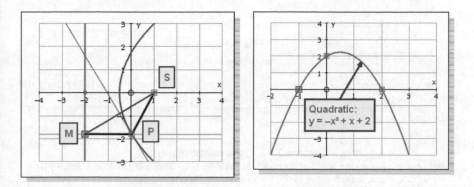

Figure 7.11 Two approaches to the parabola.
In (a) the parabola is constructed using the definition (SP = PM). In (b) it is done by fitting a second-order curve through three points and, in this case, noticing that it factorizes.

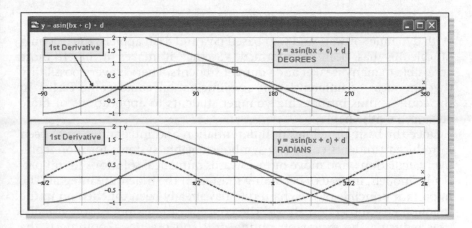

Figure 7.12 The difference between degrees and radians.
The difference between degrees and radians is nicely illustrated here by two diagrams that look very similar, but the first derivative shows the real difference. Varying values of a, b, c and d in either diagram can illustrate the true meaning of these parameters and, with the first derivative drawn as well, the properties of the chain rule can be explored. These are all topics that have the potential of being understood earlier in the curriculum through the use of dynamic coordinate geometry objects.

Other graphic coordinate systems could regain some of their former prominence, e.g. parametric (particularly useful in kinematics) and polar (obvious applications in radar). Both of these are much more approachable with modern dynamic software.

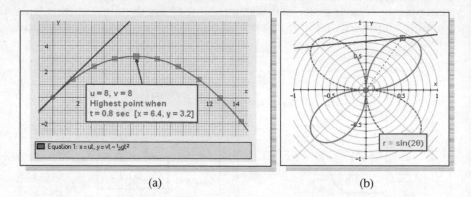

(a)   (b)

Figure 7.13 Parametric graphs.
The idea of a parameter 'driving' a coordinate system is an important concept. Appropriate visualization can make it more easily understood and accessible. (a) The idea of a projectile modelled using constant acceleration formulae: $x = ut$, $y = vt - \frac{1}{2}gt^2$. (b) There is no reason why students should not be introduced to the polar coordinate system visually.

Calculus concepts

With dynamic software and web-based Java and flash applets, the teaching of calculus has been transformed. 'Seeing' it makes it much more accessible to many weaker and younger students. There is every possibility that the ideas of differentiation and integration could come earlier in the courses, thus introducing younger students to applications of more advanced mathematics.

Once the basic principles of differentiation and integration have been introduced, students could use symbolic algebra systems for more complex calculations, and move more towards numerical solutions to suit particular models, instead of becoming masters of the indefinite integral. The important principle of the chain rule has already been touched on in the trigonometry subsection above. The concept can be understood visually, thus reducing the extent of routine drill and practice. Zooming is the perfect tool to help students see 'inside' the process, for example that of integration.

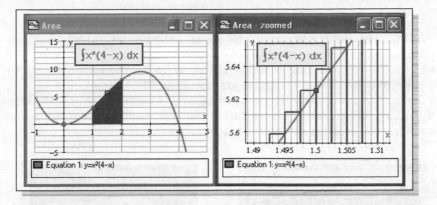

Figure 7.14 Illustrating integration.
Here, the principle of integration by adding up an infinite number of zero-width rectangles can be looked at: the computer can only approximate, of course, but by zooming in with, say, 500 rectangles, it can be shown that there is always an error (an overestimate in this case), so long as there is a finite number of rectangles.

Modelling

The concept of modelling could be freed up to include situations where the equation (or, at a higher level, the differential equation) only has a numerical solution. This should allow much more interesting situations to be included. This particularly provides opportunities to reinvigorate the teaching of mechanics (post-16). If you add some of the science software titles (e.g. *Interactive Physics*) to the dynamic mathematics software, the subject can really come alive.

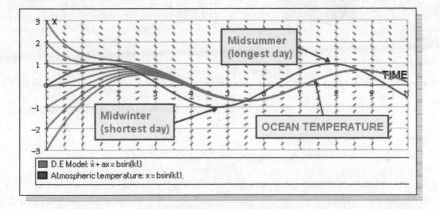

Figure 7.15 The relationship between the atmosphere and the oceans.
Here, the relationship between the atmosphere and the oceans can be explored without the skills needed to solve the resulting differential equation, explaining why people in the Northern Hemisphere tend to take their summer holidays after midsummer.

Visualizing in three dimensions

With the enormous advance in the use of 3-D graphics in films and computer games, in architecture and design, this would be an appealing addition to the curriculum. At more advanced levels, the principles of 3-D perspective and the 2-D representation of a 3-D image could be considered, including parallel perspective and vanishing points. Modern dynamic software now makes this topic very approachable for school students and much easier for the teachers to explain.

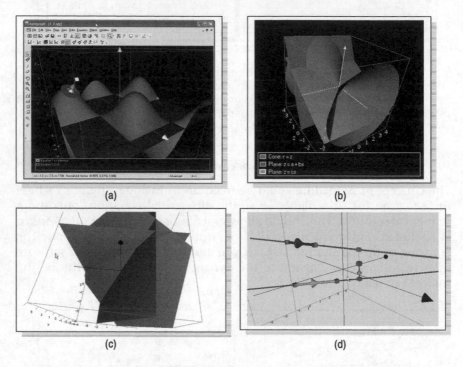

Figure 7.16 3-D topics.
Here are four scenes that could be used to make the teaching of 3-D topics more accessible at school level: (a) the principle of max and min in three dimensions; (b) conic sections; (c) intersection of planes; (d) the shortest distance between two skew lines and the cross product.

Euclidean geometry in 2-D and 3-D

The dynamic software now available should enable a much more discovery-driven approach to Euclidean geometry, in both two and three dimensions. Geometry has been squeezed out of the teaching programme in secondary schools just at a time when new software approaches should have seen it expanding.

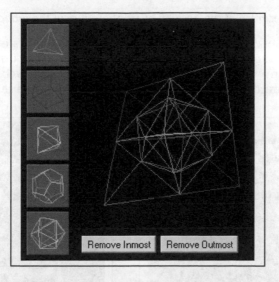

Figure 7.17   Helping students visualize 3-D objects.
This is typical of many websites that can help students visualize 3-D objects. Here, the
five Platonic solids are shown dynamically in a Java applet from Gian Marco Todesco
(http://www.divideo.it/personal/todesco/java/polyhedra/index.html).

An appreciation of the history of mathematics

Mathematics has an incredibly rich history that barely gets a mention at
present. There is scope here, of course, to work with the history department. Resources abound on the web to help and one of the benefits is that
a historical aspect can be inserted transparently into a lesson (e.g. asking
who Pythagoras was, and where and when he lived – many students will
not have much idea that it was as long ago as 550 BC).

Also the recent history is important, and timelines can be a useful tool
here.

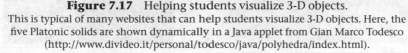

Figure 7.18   The sixteenth Mersenne prime.
The sixteenth Mersenne prime, available from an easy web search, is shown here, together
with an image of Mersenne himself (obtained via the St Andrews history of mathematics site.
Such resources can enrich a lesson an interest in where mathematics has come from.

An appreciation of the position of mathematics in the grand scheme

Few students ever get to realize how central mathematics is to an understanding of structure, from that of quarks to that of the universe. Again, there are plenty of high-quality and totally engaging web resources on hand to illustrate, for example, patterns and chaos in nature.

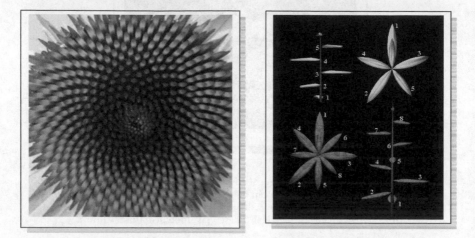

Figure 7.19   Patterns and chaos in nature.
Two images from Ron Knott's celebrated site (http://www.mcs.surrey.ac.uk/Personal/R.Knott/Fibonacci/fibnat.html) illustrating that form in nature is dictated by the rules and symmetries of mathematics. This is not just commonplace, it is central to the structure of all things.

An appreciation of the recreational aspect of mathematics

Mathematical entertainment – two words that few schoolchildren would put together in the same sentence! Yet puzzles, fun and relevant problems to solve are all superbly resourced on the web and so can be effortlessly slipped into lessons.

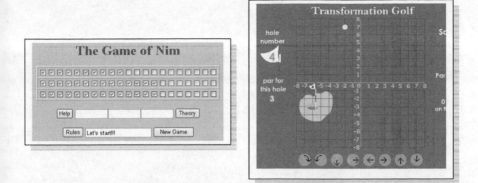

Figure 7.20 Mathematical games.
Two mathematically oriented games that can be accessed through http://www.tsm-resources.com. (a) NIM, a two-player game of strategy that can be played anywhere with three columns, even at the dinner table (knives, forks and spoons!). (b) Transformation Golf – getting the ball in the hole can reinforce lessons learnt about rotation and reflection.

Conclusion

The subject of mathematics is fighting for survival. Arguments have to be won at the highest governmental levels and this often means persuading people of the immediate and obvious dangers of allowing a population to be under-educated in mathematics. ICT in experienced hands can empower and enlighten and thus help to rescue this situation.

In inexperienced hands, images can flash by too quickly and the opportunity for learning is wasted. Students are used to being presented with moving images much of the time. When they meet them in the classroom, they must be challenged by them – preferably *before* they see them. That way they are curious and the learning process can be triggered. (This is discussed further in Chapter 13.)

So, with more efficient and effective teaching of mathematics, there is room for the secondary courses to include a range of new and exciting topics. If all this, including the appropriate training, is put in place, there is a good prospect of mathematics staging a recovery in schools, for the benefit of the whole nation.

Part B

ICT and the mathematics classroom

8

GRAPHICAL CALCULATORS: TOOLS FOR MATHEMATICAL THINKING

David Wright

Graphical calculators (GCs) are an example, perhaps unique, of a maturing information technology that has developed in the educational context. In this chapter, I outline some of the ways in which this technology supports the teaching and learning of mathematics and science. I also discuss how the portability and power of these devices for mathematical and other applications could provide us with an indication of ways in which teaching and learning may develop in a ubiquitous computing environment in the classroom, a mode of pedagogy that is becoming known as 'm-learning'.

Terminology and some history

These devices have been referred to as 'graphing', 'graphic' or 'graphical' calculators as well as 'personal ICT', 'hand-held computers' or just 'GCs'. Apart from problems with perception caused by the 'calculator' label, the term 'graphing' also fails to describe the scope of these devices, and 'graphic' focuses on the passive content, so 'graphical' is my preference as the most appropriate adjective of the three. However, for simplicity, I shall refer to the technology as 'GCs' in this chapter. Manufacturers are trying to change this terminology: Texas Instruments refers to its latest model as a 'personal learning tool' and Casio has introduced what it calls a 'ClassPad'.

The models available in 2003 offered computation, graphing, solving equations, statistical analysis, simultaneous equations, sequences and series, differentiation and integration, evaluation of functions and complex arithmetic. Some models have computer algebra systems (CASs) and interactive geometry software built in. Certain GCs even have 'flash ROM' technology, which acts like the hard disk on a PC and provides an extensive, non-volatile memory (in other words, data or programs will not be lost when the RAM is cleared or batteries are removed). This allows the device to store a range of software such as an upgradable operating system, quite sophisticated applications like spreadsheets, and small, specialized software applications like the SMILE programs. (For details, see http://www.smilemathematics.co.uk/ and for free, downloadable GC versions, see http://education.ti.com/.) Thus, the functionality of the GC can be extended into the same area as the PC.

GCs also have input/output ports and connectors, which allow them to communicate with each other, with computers (and hence with printers and the internet) and with compatible devices such as data-loggers and controllers. Built-in or detachable keyboards are available for some models which allow text to be input directly. There are teachers' versions of most models connecting to a pad of about A4 size with a transparent liquid crystal display which can be placed on an overhead projector and used for whole-class work. Some models have pen-driven interfaces. GCs are manufactured by Casio and Sharp in Japan and Hewlett-Packard and Texas Instruments in the USA.

Educational applications

In the classroom, the graphing and programming facilities of these devices were adopted by schools and colleges for use in advanced mathematics education. In England, schemes such as SMP 16–19 and Nuffield Advanced Mathematics assumed their use. However, adoption has not been universal or uniform. In England, assessment policy for their use in A-level examinations has been inconsistent and led to a reduced level of usage by students and teachers (see Monaghan and Rodd, 2002, for a survey of teachers in Leeds). There have been developments in higher education too, but here again, reactions have varied widely. At official levels, as well as in educational settings in other countries, there has been a range of response to the technology, from ignoring or banning to wholehearted adoption.

Some teachers of primary school mathematics have attempted to use this technology in their classrooms. See Cox (2001) and Hyde (2001) for some useful ideas on the use of GCs in a junior school.

The availability of low-tech, large-scale displays, which can work with overhead projectors, means that the GC is an important asset in whole-class teaching. Teachers are using the technology as a useful addition to interactive, whole-class teaching, which does not need the large investment and complicated arrangements of interactive whiteboard technology. (See Chapter 9, as well as the mathematics section on the Virtual Teacher Centre at http://vtc.ngfl.gov.uk/docserver.php?temid=292 for many useful ideas on this topic.)

The following sections outline the wide range of ways in which the GC can support particular aspects of mathematics. Each of these areas demands far more space to discuss fully; all I can do here is draw the reader's attention to its potential.

Graphing

The most obvious use of this technology is to support graphical understanding. Hennessy (1998), in a comprehensive account of the way in which portable technology supports students' understanding of graphs, explored the following claim by Leinhardt *et al.* (1990, p. 7): 'More than perhaps any other early mathematics topic, technology dramatically affects the teaching and learning of functions and graphs'. An understanding of graphs is generally recognized as being one of the more useful and desirable outcomes of mathematical education. However, research shows that school leavers and college students still experience considerable difficulties with some aspects of using graphs (Hennessy, 1998, p. 29). In particular, although most students seem to be proficient at drawing graphs, their interpretation causes many problems. Among these, Hennessy lists: erroneous concepts of variable and of what constitutes the graph of a function; a tendency towards linearity; a pointwise focus; translation between graphical/algebraic representations; interval/point confusion; slope/height confusion; iconic interpretations; difficulties in choosing, constructing and scaling axes.

The ease with which it is possible to generate and manipulate graphs using GCs allows teachers and students to focus on the interpretive aspects of graphing which cause difficulties without being distracted by the problems of generating the graphs. GCs also embody facilities which allow an approach to mathematical concepts such as gradient through 'zooming in'. 'This approach is more cognitively direct than the elaborate, and often misunderstood, traditional approach to the idea of gradient through the construction of a secant line tending to the tangent' (Ruthven, 1994, p. 161)

Statistics

GCs have a range of facilities for the analysis of data. Data is stored in 'lists', which allow manipulation and analysis such as summary statistics for one- or two-variable data to be produced. Graphs such as bar charts, box-and-whisker diagrams, histograms and scatter plots can be produced from the data.

GCs also have facilities that enable statistical tests or regression analysis to be carried out. For more advanced applications, many GCs also allow the creation and analysis of distribution functions. More sophisticated analysis, such as non-parametric tests, can be carried out through development of small programs for data analysis.

Data can be entered in several ways: manually, by collection from data-logging sensors or by connection to a PC and hence to collections of data available in spreadsheets or on the internet. Data can also be shared with other users in the same way.

Allowing teachers and students to capture, manipulate and analyse large quantities of data with a hand-held device offers a powerful aid to statistical understanding. The speed at which data can be shared, processed and graphed or summary statistics produced means that students and teachers can focus on important aspects of modelling and interpretation which often get squeezed out by concentration on the mechanics of calculation or graphing (see also Chapter 6). The ready availability of the technology means that students and teachers can have the processing power available to use as and when needed, rather than planning teaching around the availability of the technology. The *Census at School* website (also discussed in Chapter 6) gives some ideas for starting to use GCs for statistics (see http://www.censusatschool.ntu.ac.uk/curriculum5.asp).

Geometry

The development of interactive geometry software (for a comprehensive list, see MathsNet: http://www.mathsnet.net) has begun to open up new ways of exploring geometrical understanding. (Jones, 2002, has a comprehensive research bibliography.) This software has also become available for GCs. There are difficulties associated with using this software on GCs such as the size of screen and manipulation of the images via a keyboard. However, the development of large-scale displays or pen-driven interfaces can overcome these problems: for example, the Casio ClassPad has a pen-driven interface and interactive geometry software.

Teachers have also explored how GCs can support understanding of coordinate geometry using the plotting facility of the GC to draw pictures and produce animations.

Data-logging

The powerful data-logging applications available with GCs allow data to be collected from motion sensors or other probes and stored in the list registers of the GC for analysis or graphing. These activities are also valuable in cross-curricular applications, particularly in science, but also in other areas such as geography and PE. The portability of the technology means that data can be collected *in situ* outside the classroom and retained for analysis upon the students' return. A comprehensive account of the potential of this way of using GCs can be found in Oldknow and Taylor (1998).

At least one GC will allow data from a motion sensor to be displayed graphically. This facility can allow even very young children to gain some understanding of notoriously difficult concepts, such as time and distance graphs. (For a description of Year 1 aged children learning with this technology, see Burkholder, 2001.)

Computer algebra systems

Several models of GCs are supplied with CASs. These are applications which can carry out sophisticated algebraic manipulations, including calculus, up to at least first-year university level. They were developed to support scientists and engineers in solving problems which involved the manipulation of algebraic models.

CASs were not developed as pedagogical tools and considerable mathematical expertise is needed to interpret their output, because it is not always in the form used conventionally in the classroom. However, there are teachers who are successfully using the power of these systems to support their mathematics teaching. (For an interesting application to an optimization problem, see Forbes, 2001.)

What might be of more interest for secondary teachers is the development of applications which take the power of CAS and apply it to support students' algebraic understanding by providing a context-dependent environment in which they can explore. In other words, the system provides students with a starting point and a goal (or they choose their own) and offers them legitimate choices at each stage in the manipulation, then showing them the consequences of their choice. Several of these systems are available for the PC and at least one has been developed for the GC. (For a description of using the Symbolic Math Guide for the TI-89, see Child, 2001; the Symbolic Math Guide is available to download from http://education.ti.com.)

Seeing connections

The ability of a GC to display mathematical information both dynamically and simultaneously in tabular, graphical and algebraic form is one which provides a power greater than the sum of its parts. This feature of technology enabling students to see connections between different representations was highlighted by the National Council for Educational Technology in 1992 as one of the six 'entitlements' for students using ICT in mathematics (see Chapter 1). Figure 8.1 (Teacher Training Agency, 1999,

---

Specific teaching points
Now that the pupils were familiar with the problem the teacher reminded them how to enter a function such as "Y1 = X√(5²-X²)" on the graphic calculators and show the class how to use them to produce automatically a table of values of the areas Y1 for the values as before for the heights X, as in Fig. 4a. (She would expect pupils to explain why the word "ERROR" appeared against the value X=6.)

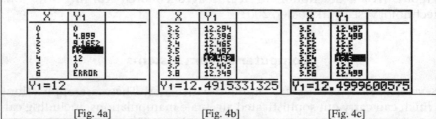

[Fig. 4a]   [Fig. 4b]   [Fig. 4c]

Step 5 - drawing graphs of functions
The teacher now discussed with the class how the data might be represented differently and more accurately using a graph. She then checked whether the pupils remembered how to use the graphic calculators to draw the graph of the function stored in Y1.

The teacher worked through a complete example with the class using the values in Fig. 4a as co-ordinates for the graph.

Commentary on teacher's decisions about whether or not to use ICT in meeting the teaching and learning objectives and justifying and explaining any use of ICT
The teacher judged that graphical calculators were the best resource for this as pupils could produce graphs quickly using the data. The split screen facility which allowed pupils to view the graph with the table of results alongside it, gave the teacher the opportunity to draw out in discussion with pupils the connections between the two representations.

Specific teaching points
The teacher checked that pupils knew how to decide upon suitable values for the scales on the X- and Y-axes based on the data in their tables: *"What's the smallest value X can be? What's the largest...."* She checked that pupils remembered how to trace along the graph. She also reminded them how to "zoom in" on places of interest on the graph, and also how to arrange the scale on the x-axis so that each sideways movement of the cursor corresponded to a "round number" for X (as in Figs 5 a, b, c).

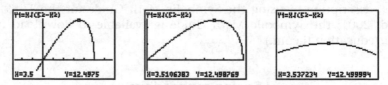

[Fig. 5 a, b, c Tracing the graph of the area function on a graphic calculator]

Finally she showed pupils how to arrange the screens of the graphic calculators so that the table and the graph were displayed alongside each other. Now when the graph was traced the pupils could see (a) the point on the graph, (b) the algebraic expression for the function which generates it, (c) the co-ordinates of the point, and (d) the corresponding entry in the table (Fig. 6).

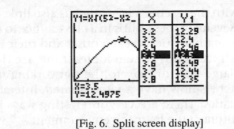

[Fig. 6. Split screen display]

Figure 8.1   Teaching with multiple representations.

pp. 34–47) illustrates how this facility can be used to support teaching in mathematics.

Programs and applications

The availability of larger memories for GCs has meant that developers are now able to write significant applications for them. The programming can be done in either the higher-level pseudo-*BASIC* language or in low-level assembly code. Applications written in low-level code can be sophisticated: for example, it has allowed the development of a spreadsheet application for GCs. Further applications, which could be used across the curriculum, such as text processing or revision aids, have also been produced. Some manufacturers have released their software developers kit to allow third parties to do this. (For the Texas Instruments download, see http://education.ti.com.)

One of the most effective ways of using ICT to support mathematical understanding has been through small software programs that focus on particular concepts – these are now being produced in versions for the GC. (See the BECTa report edited by Oldknow and Taylor, 1998, on the use of small software in the classroom.) The advantages for the teacher of having these applications available on request in the classroom are obvious, but there are more subtle cultural changes emerging in classrooms that have ICT on demand. I will discuss these in more detail later.

Networking

The development of networking facilities for GCs adds another dimension to the way in which this technology can be used in the classroom. Texas Instruments has recently developed a system (TI Navigator: http://education.ti.com) which links four GCs to a 'hub' allowing them to communicate wirelessly with the teacher's PC, which is also linked to a GC and a large-scale display. Several of these hubs in a class suffice to allow a whole class to communicate mathematics to each other and their teacher. (For a description of a teacher using this system for teaching, see Hopley, 2002.)

The addition of a large-scale display to the networking facility means that students and teachers now have a large, shared, interactive space in which to do mathematics. There are very interesting ways in which this facility adds to the culture of the learning environment.

Here is a simple example. The teacher asks all the students to choose a square number and input this on their GC. The results are all displayed simultaneously (and anonymously) on the large-scale display (although the teacher can identify which student has contributed each number). The teacher and students then discuss the range of numbers chosen and whether they all have the desired property.

Here is another example: students each control a cursor on the large-scale display on which the axes of a graph are displayed. The students are asked by the teacher to move their cursor to a point with the property that the x coordinate is double the y coordinate. The teacher and students then discuss the pattern formed by the cursors. In a lesson that I observed, a girl had moved her cursor to an incorrect position. Since no individual cursor was identifiable (to the students), there was no fear of anyone being identified as having made the error. In the course of the discussion, however, the girl was able to identify which cursor was in the wrong place and why, without having to admit to any mistake publicly.

This is a very important facility. Notice that all students are required to participate, but they do so anonymously. This both encourages participation but removes the fear of being publicly embarrassed by being in error. Good teachers always aim to promote an environment that reduces fear, and this system supports such an approach, leaving students and teacher space to make guesses and discuss their outcomes.

Portability

Many of these activities are possible using a PC. However, the portability and accessibility of GCs, particularly when students can own one, brings another dimension to their use in educational settings. Hennessey (1998) reports the following findings from the studies on portable technology she surveyed.

> *Student empowerment* ... It gives students an experience of personal computing which is under their own control and accessible whenever they choose. Students rarely get the opportunity to appropriate sophisticated equipment of any kind for themselves and the very fact of being entrusted with a valuable machine increases their self-esteem. (p. 22)

Active participation and investigative learning . . . A fundamental distinction from more typical curriculum activities is that students with access to portables – whether individually or in groups – become actively and productively involved in their own learning activities from beginning to end. . . . As well as offering students opportunities for involvement in setting up, running and reporting on the whole investigation, the speed of operation also means that students often have more time for exploration and hypothesis testing. (p. 23)

Independence . . . and differentiation The privacy afforded by a personal machine encourages experimentation, self-help and individually paced work, playing a critical role in enhancing learning. . . . Taking the machines home seems to allow students to complete work more quickly, to develop and build on the mathematical ideas and procedures they have already grasped. (p. 15)

Collaboration

The addition of portability to the availability of small software can have some interesting and unexpected results. In one class I was observing, students were using a 'drill and practice' program which, ironically, was designed to test their 'non-calculator' calculation skills. (For a version for the TI-83+, see http://vtc.ngfl.gov.uk/docserver.php?docid=4445.) The program generated numerous examples of the same type of calculation, but with random data. Thus, the students were unable to give each other the correct answer without carrying out the calculation themselves.

Since discussion was allowed in the class, they began to discuss the method to solve the problem rather than simply give each other the answer. This was a spontaneous development, prompted by the fact that stimulating technology was available on the students' desks, in their normal working environment. However, the teacher was able to take advantage of this development to talk about appropriate ways of tutoring peers and to plan for further interventions when using the resource again.

ICT capability

I have shown ways in which the graphical calculator has evolved into a powerful tool to support mathematical education. However, a tool is not simply a given, inanimate object, which has a passive relationship with the user. The use of the tool shapes the user's experience of the way they interact with the world. It is a dialectical relationship in which the tool and the user are changed by their interaction.

An example is given in Oldknow and Taylor (2000, p. 167). Students were using a GC to explore a variety of trigonometric identities such as

$\sin(2x) = 2\sin(x)\cos(x)$ by looking at the zeros of these functions graphed by the GC. Using a range of [–360, 360] one girl claimed that she had demonstrated that $\sin 4(x) = -2\sin(x)\cos(x)$. This certainly appeared to be the case (see Figure 8.2). However, when the range was changed to [–90, 90], it was seen that the apparent coincidence of zeros was an artefact of the way the GC plotted graphs.

Such artefacts appear in other situations with GCs. An asymptote, a discontinuity or a rapid change in the graph being plotted may not be visible to the user because of the way the GC draws the graph. The student using the GC needs to have some understanding of the nature of the function being plotted, in order to use the tool effectively. Indeed, this can motivate the necessity for learning graph-sketching skills, when it might appear that the introduction of technology has removed it! This is very similar to the procedure encouraged when students use a simple four-function calculator.

If the GC or computer is being used in mathematical modelling or running simulations it is also necessary for the student to consider the underlying model used by the programmer as part of their work in using the tool (for a detailed discussion of this issue, see Noss, 1998).

Thus the introduction of technology into mathematics also introduces a new skill. The choice of when and how to use the technology appropriately becomes part of the problem-solving strategies needed by students as part of their studies. Teachers need to be aware of this aspect of technology when planning their teaching and be prepared to introduce examples that demonstrate how the technology can affect the mathematics. Students should also be encouraged to justify their choice and application of a particular tool as part of their reporting of their work and expect to be assessed on this aspect of their work.

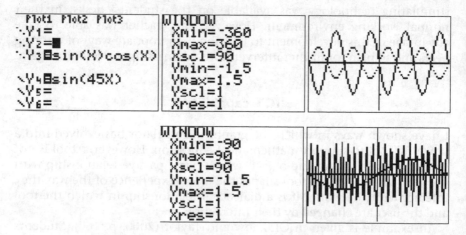

Figure 8.2   An artefact of the way GCs plot graphs.

Conviviality

The introduction of ICT introduces new learning skills. The user has to become aware that the 'window' on mathematical meanings which ICT can give learners is not transparent, but can influence the meanings themselves. The extent to which this relationship is supportive of the user can be described by the term 'convivial'.

> The extent to which a tool may be seen as convivial is the extent to which the use of the tool creates meanings for its user, catalyses intellectual experience and growth.
>
> (Noss and Hoyles, 1996, p. 56)

The same tool may or may not be convivial to a user depending on their relationship with it. Noss and Hoyles continue:

> The essential difference is the way in which the tool enters the personal and cultural space of the user. [. . .] For most people involved in computer use, the computer is far from convivial.
>
> (p. 58)

Finally, the tool must offer the user opportunities for expressing thoughts. They observe:

> Expressive power opens windows for the learner, it affords a way to construct meanings.
>
> (p. 59)

An interesting example of how GC technology enables new approaches to learning and new areas of knowledge, where the modellers' rules are accessible, is 'participatory simulations' (for a full description, see http://ccl.northwestern.edu/ps/). In these activities a model of some situation, such as a population or a traffic system, has been developed using a version of *Logo* called *StarLogo*, which allows students to control individual 'turtles' on a whole-class display through a wireless GC network. This permits an exploration of complex dynamic systems in a participatory and accessible way, allowing even young children to gain some understanding about how the interactions of individuals can result in large-scale effects. (For more projects and access to *Starlogo*, see http://education.mit.edu/starlogo/.)

GCs could also be said to be an instance of an 'intermediate' technology in the sense of Schumacher (1993): that is, one which enables people to satisfy their needs, while making the most of their time, capabilities, environment and resources. For many teachers and students the GC, as a more portable, accessible form of computer specifically developed to give access to mathematics, is a 'convivial' tool. Conversely, there is also potential for users to change the tool. Some calculator manufacturers have developed extensive programmes for professional development, which also serve to give feedback about the ways in which teachers and learners would like the technology to be developed. (Texas Instruments sponsors T^3 – Teachers Teaching with Technology – training programme. For more details, see http://education.ti.com/uk/teacher/training/training.html. Casio education programmes are available too – see http://www.casio.co.uk/dt&i/education/.)

Conclusion

Teachers' and students' ownership of small, hand-held, powerful computing devices described in this chapter allows ICT to act as a bridge across which data, information and learning can flow. It can bridge the gap between classroom and ICT suite, between school and home, between student and teacher, between student and student, and between teaching and learning. The sorts of powerful aids to mathematical understanding that I have illustrated are not confined to graphical calculators: it is the combination of these aids with the feature of portability that makes the difference.

The GC is still evolving and other technologies are converging on its niche. There are already emulators of GCs available, which run on personal digital assistants (PDAs). Some believe that the GC is old technology, a 'monster in monster's clothing' as a student said to me, with its array of multi-function keys, dazzling access to powerful mathematical functions and tiny screen. 'M-learning' is the generic term for the use of mobile devices, including mobile phones, PDAs and GCs, to support learning. There is a growing realization that this form of technology may be the most appropriate for educational applications. (For more examples, see http://www.m-learning.org/background.html.)

However, as Ruthven (1994, p. 165) predicted:

> a new mathematical tool, even one so readily available as the conventional calculator, may have little influence on the curriculum. Not only may the tool fail to penetrate the classroom . . . but even where the machine is accepted, its use may be largely assimilated to traditional mathematical practices.

Research into the extent of classroom adoption or how the technology is actually used in the classroom by teachers and students is limited, although recently TI has commissioned a survey of research into classroom practices using GCs (see Burrill *et al.*, 2002). Leeds University also carried out a small-scale, but indicative survey of secondary schools in

Leeds (Monaghan and Rodd, 2002). The findings from these surveys confirm Ruthven's prediction that where the GC is used, it is largely deployed to support traditional modes of learning in the classroom. This may be a stage through which teachers pass as they gain confidence, but they may also require a vision of possibilities in order to move forward.

The current availability of GCs as a specialist, portable, ICT tool for mathematics could allow us to explore and develop a pedagogy for a ubiquitous ICT environment in the classroom. The availability of such systems provides a powerful challenge to the traditional mathematical curriculum similar to the way in which the availability of the four-function calculator challenged the basic numeracy curriculum. Some countries are beginning to take on the challenge of providing a mathematics curriculum which uses the opportunity given by this technology. Scotland, for example, embarked on a discussion about a constructive approach to using advanced calculators in mathematics education (http://www.svtc.org.uk/sccc/acme/).

The history of the adoption of ICT by the mainstream mathematical education community in England shows that mathematics teachers will probably not be ready for students who have access to powerful, hand-held devices with the full range of GC facilities, in addition to the other functionalites available on PDAs, including access to the internet through wireless connections. However, there are already primary and secondary classrooms in the UK where this is commonplace and we need to be ready for the raised expectations generated by the availability of portable technology (Perry, 2003). More powerful hand-held computers are just around the corner.

References

Burkholder, M. (2001) 'Kindergarten data logging'. *Micromath*, **17**(2), 21.

Burrill, G., Allison, J., Breaux, G. *et al.* (2002) *Handheld Graphing Technology at the Secondary Level*, publication CL2872.
(http://education.ti.com/us/resources/research/graphingsecondary.html).

Child, D. (2001) 'The symbolic math guide and laws of exponents'. *Micromath*, **17**(2), 32–5.

Cox, S. (2001) 'Using the TI-73 at Ringwood school'. *Micromath*, **17**(2), 17–20.

Forbes, I. (2001) 'The circle of understanding'. *Micromath*, **17**(3), 15–18.

Hennessy, S. (1998) 'The potential of portable technologies for supporting graphing investigations'. Available at http://www.education.leeds.ac.uk/research/mathseducation/gcalc_hennessy.pdf. Summary version (1999) in *British Journal of Educational Technology*, **30**(1), 57–60.

Hopley, N. (2002) 'Calculator network'. *Micromath*, **18**(1), 14–15.

Hyde, R. (2001) 'Ideas for using graphics calculators with middle school pupils'. *Micromath*, **17**(2), 14–16.

Jones, K. (2002) 'Implications for the classroom'. *Micromath*, **18**(3), 18–20, 44–5.

Leinhardt, G., Zaslavsky, O. and Stein, M. (1990) 'Functions, graphs and graphing: tasks, learning and teaching'. *Review of Educational Research*, **60**(1), 1–64.

Monaghan, J. and Rodd, M. (2002) 'Graphic calculator use in Leeds schools: fragments of practice'. *Journal of Information Technology for Teacher Education*, **11**(1), 93–108.

Noss, R. (1998) 'New numeracies for a technological culture'. *For the Learning of Mathematics*, **18**(2), 2–12.

Noss, R. and Hoyles, C. (1996) *Windows on Mathematical Meanings: Learning Cultures and Computers*. Dordrecht: Kluwer Academic.

Oldknow, A. and Taylor, R. (eds) (1998) *Data-Capture and Modelling in Mathematics and Science*, Coventry, Warwks, British Educational Communications and Technology Agency. (http://vtc.ngfl.gov.uk/uploads/application/datacapture16796.pdf).

Oldknow, A. and Taylor, R. (2000) *Teaching Mathematics with ICT*. London: Continuum.

Perry, D. (2003) *Handheld Computers (PDAs) in Schools*, Coventry, Warwks, British Educational Communications and Technology Agency (http://www.becta.org.uk/research/reports/portableict.cfm).

Ruthven, K. (1994) 'Supercalculators and the secondary mathematics curriculum', in M. Selinger (ed.), *Teaching Mathematics*. London: Routledge, pp. 154–68.

Schumacher, E. (1993) *Small is Beautiful*. London: Vintage.

Teacher Training Agency (1999) *Identification of Training Needs: Secondary Mathematics*. London: TTA.

9

INTERACTIVE WHITEBOARDS: DEVELOPING A PEDAGOGY FOR MATHEMATICS CLASSROOMS

Alison Clark-Jeavons

The introduction of the interactive whiteboard to the secondary mathematics classroom encourages a review of the interactions among the teacher, students, technology and mathematics. It is my intention in this chapter to describe the main features of the interactive whiteboard and to exemplify how its use can promote successful teaching and learning of mathematics within an ICT-rich classroom environment (see Wood, 2001). Although many of the features and modes of use that I describe are appropriate for all levels of mathematics teaching, the examples are taken from mathematics at the secondary level.

A brief history

The first interactive whiteboards were designed for the business sector in the early 1990s and began to appear in schools a few years later. Initially, their use was limited by the availability of suitable software, specifically for mathematics education. Research (e.g. Greiffenhagen, 1999, 2000a, 2000b; Greiffenhagen and Stevens, 1999) focused on how the interactive whiteboard could be developed to support teaching and learning mathematics in the secondary classroom. Greiffenhagen used his observations of how the conventional classroom board supported whole-class teaching, with the intent to inform interactive whiteboard designers about desirable features and modes of use.

A government report on the use of ICT in schools (Ofsted, 2001) refers to PCs for whole-class displays:

> Many schools have invested in interactive whiteboards and computer projection equipment. Generally these have led to more effective whole-class teaching, with all pupils able to see a large, clear display. Pupils too have made good use of this new equipment, for example in illustrating a prepared talk with the aid of presentational software.
>
> (p. 17)

It is worth noting that this comment makes no direct reference to the features of the interactive whiteboard itself and the example of good practice that has been described here could have been achieved using a data projector connected to a computer.

A recent project (funded by the Department for Education and Employment (DfEE)), which developed a technologically rich course for Year 7 mathematics, used an interactive whiteboard central to the lesson and has been extensively evaluated (Passey, 2001). Chapter 10 describes this project in some detail.

How the interactive whiteboard works

An interactive whiteboard, when connected to a computer and a data projector, acts as an interface between the user and the computer. Figure 9.1 shows this diagrammatically. The data projector can be free-standing or ceiling-mounted. In effect, an interactive whiteboard allows you to 'drive' the computer from the whiteboard rather than by using the keyboard and mouse. The 'driving' is done either with an electronic pen or by using a finger, which relays to the computer its relative position on the board. Consequently, all interactive whiteboards have to undergo a calibration process to ensure their subsequent accuracy. If the data projector and/or interactive whiteboard are mobile, this calibration would need to be carried out each time the board is used. If the equipment is fixed in the classroom, a weekly calibration is normally sufficient.

The pointing device (pen or finger) can be used in two ways: as an electronic pen for use with supporting software for annotation purposes; or as a pointer enabling the selection of options and the highlighting or dragging of objects within a software package.

The software that supports the interactive whiteboard allows the user to annotate screens from any software package and then take 'snapshots' to form a series of lesson notes, which can be saved and printed. An initial

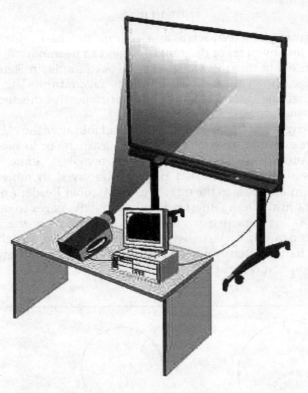

Figure 9.1   Set-up for an interactive whiteboard.

attraction for many teachers would be the facility to offer students the opportunity to revisit a lesson by reviewing a series of saved files.

Some interactive whiteboards have additional features, such as a remote tablet or electronic slate, which can be passed around the class to offer students the chance to interact with the board without leaving their seats. This facility can also be achieved by using a remote mouse connected to the computer.

It is possible to buy a kit that 'converts' a conventional whiteboard into an interactive whiteboard: however, these systems can be less sensitive to pen location, especially when working in an interactive geometry software environment.

Modes of use

I will consider four modes of interactive whiteboard use in this chapter: the flipchart, the pointer, the annotator and the recorder.

Flipchart mode

Used in this way, the screen acts as an electronic flipchart, with the facility to save or print any notes or diagrams. Images can be imported, which can be snapshots of another software package. For example, in Figure 9.2, the flipchart page shows a series of snapshots taken from *The Geometer's Sketchpad*, enabling three diagrams and their respective measurements to be captured and compared.

Flipchart pages can be saved and made available after the class to other students (for example, absentees or distance learners) or to support note-taking and enable previous learning to be reviewed. Some interactive whiteboards allow such flipchart pages to be saved in more generally accessible formats, such as the ones used by Acrobat Reader (.pdf files) or the internet (.html files). Others will only allow the pages to be viewed if the appropriate interactive whiteboard software is on the computer. Character recognition facilities within some interactive whiteboard software allow handwritten notes to be converted to text to give a more presentable outcome.

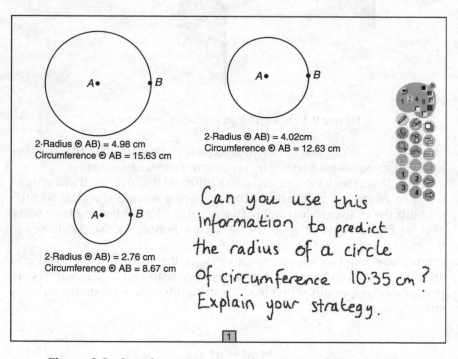

Figure 9.2   Snapshots on an interactive whiteboard flipchart page.

Pointer mode

In this mode, the software is being driven at the interactive whiteboard without the need to use the computer keyboard and mouse.

PowerPoint presentations can be made in this mode, with slides being advanced by touching the interactive whiteboard. However, this use should carry a government health warning – more interesting uses of interactive whiteboards occur when the interactivity of the board is used in conjunction with an interactive software package. Some interactive whiteboards have accompanying features that allow *PowerPoint* slides to be annotated during the presentation and converted to text to be saved within the *PowerPoint* file itself. These features help promote a more inter-active presentation style, as does using hyperlinks within slides that connect to other software.

The use of interactive geometry, integrated mathematics or concept-mapping software involves a higher level of interactivity and, as such software is of a visual nature, requires little keyboard use. If the software is being driven at the whiteboard, a floating (on-board) keyboard is used to enter alpha-numeric characters. This is sufficient for entering small amounts of text, but is laborious and slow for larger amounts. Having a remote keyboard in the classroom, which can be passed around the class, overcomes this drawback. Concept-mapping software offers an ICT environment in which explicit visual connections can be made between mathematical concepts. On paper, these strategies are known as 'mind' or 'model' maps.

Caviglioli and Harris (2000, p. 11) demonstrate how model mapping can:

- teach thinking skills as part of subject delivery;
- support each stage of the accelerated learning process;
- demonstrate and develop intelligence;
- develop four essential learning skills that all learners need – irrespective of their preferred learning style;
- transform the teaching and learning systems in operation in classrooms. (p. 11)

Prestage and Perks (2001) discuss how the use of concept maps (they call them 'splurge diagrams') can support the development of mathematical understanding. Some interactive whiteboards have accompanying concept-mapping software.

The advantage of using such software in an interactive whiteboard environment is in the way the user can connect kinaesthetically with the process of mapping the idea or concept. The use of hyperlinks enables such maps to be expanded to reveal diagrams, text, video images and sound clips within or outside the concept map. Figure 9.3 overleaf exemplifies this for the central theme of 'linear functions'. Both the table and the graph are hyperlinked to integrated mathematics software, which

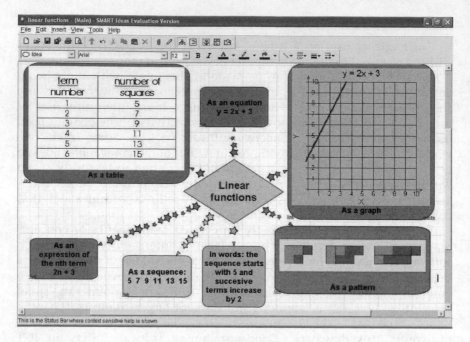

Figure 9.3   An interactive concept map.

means that both can be changed, enabling learners to observe the effect. The sketch is a hyperlink to a graphics package, which allows the squares to be manipulated to form other configurations. The ICT supports the teacher making changes to any aspect of the representation and questioning learners as to how the other features will change. An immediate advantage of reviewing mathematical topics in this way is the support that it provides for individual learners.

Since Howard Gardner (1983) introduced his list of 'intelligences', teachers have been encouraged to consider providing support for different types of learners. With an initial focus on supporting predominantly visual, audio and kinaesthetic learners, the concept map has the advantage (assuming that practical resources are also being used) of providing a stimulus for each. However, the more powerful advantage is that, in doing so, students are making connections between topics within the mathematics itself.

Annotator mode

This mode of use enables written notes to be made over the top of another piece of software that is running: for example, if a dynamic geometry package is being used, annotations can be added using the pen.

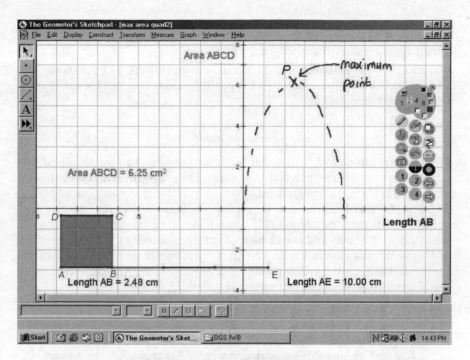

Figure 9.4 Annotating with the pen.

In the example in Figure 9.4, the dynamic construction allows the investigation of the maximum area of a rectangle ABCD with fixed perimeter equal to AE. The point P graphically represents the area of the rectangle ABCD (the ordinate) plotted against the length AD (the abscissa). The interactive whiteboard annotation tool has been used to draw a prediction of the path of point P. Within the geometry package, the locus of this point has been constructed and clicking on the Show Locus action button will reveal the correct path. This particular package makes it possible to drag the variable itself (the point A) and connect the path of the locus both visually and kinaesthetically. Colour is explicitly used to highlight the visual connections between the length AB and the area ABCD in the geometric construction, as well as to the plotted point P. Although this feature is (at the time of writing) not yet available, the addition of a sound effect, whose pitch varies with the area of rectangle ABCD, would complete a visual–aural–kinaesthetic learning experience.

I strongly encourage the reader to explore this example with an interactive whiteboard, as there is a powerful phenomenon emerging here. The learner is physically able to alter a variable and then observe the effect on the plotted point, locus and depicted function in a completely new way. Although the same mathematical exploration can be explored using ICT in a spreadsheet, graphical calculator or interactive geometry setting, it has not previously been possible to connect the whole system together in this way, with the learner physically 'driving' the model.

The screen shown in Figure 9.4 can then be saved as a 'snapshot', as reverting to the software will cause any annotations to be erased. The annotation facility is useful when preparing guidance notes for using tools within a software package.

Recorder mode

With some interactive whiteboards, it is possible to record all of the actions that have taken place at the board. For example, if a perpendicular bisector has been constructed using an interactive geometry package, the steps in the construction can be replayed like a video clip (see the perpendicular bisector gsp.avi on this book's website). The viewer will see the selection of the tools and the choice of actions, as well as the construction of the geometric object itself. This particular mode of use is particularly useful in mathematics when teaching geometric construction techniques. A still from this video can be seen in Figure 9.5.

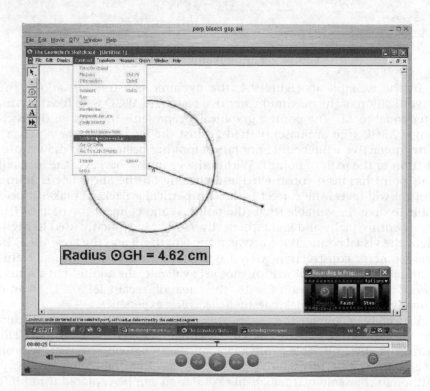

Figure 9.5 A still from a recording of a geometric construction.

Developing a pedagogy for mathematics

Before a teacher can even begin to think about *how* to integrate the use of an interactive whiteboard into classroom pedagogy, there are a few very practical points to make. First, the height and position within the classroom at which the board is mounted are crucial to its future accessibility. In a fully inclusive classroom, all students and staff should be able to reach the top of the board comfortably. This is most apparent because the majority of computer software is currently designed with the menu and tool bars across the top of the screen. In time, I would expect software designers to respond by including an option to switch the menu and toolbars to the bottom or sides of the screen page. The sides are a preferable location, in order to reduce the likelihood of standing in front of the projected image as well as to accommodate both left-handed and right-handed users.

Second, depending on the amount of natural light in the classroom, the usual background colour of white in most software packages does not provide sufficient contrast for a good display.

Third, default font sizes need to be at least 36 point and font colours should also be chosen to provide a good contrast with each other, as well as with the background colour.

Observations of teachers using interactive whiteboards in the classroom have revealed several levels of use, as reported in the Teacher Training Agency (2002, p. 22):

- low interactivity – for example, you move from one slide to the next in a *PowerPoint* presentation by clicking on an on-screen icon;
- medium interactivity – for example, where teachers and students are able to control relevant software from the front of the class for whole-class teaching and discussion;
- high interactivity – for example, where students are able to interact with geometrical constructions produced using dynamic geometry software by dragging diagrams into different configurations. The evaluation of the Year 7 project referred to this as 'Pupils touching the mathematics'.

The teacher's physical position in the classroom also changes with the development of more confidence both with the technology and with an interactive, whole-class teaching style. Initially, teachers tend to stand close to the board and limit the amount of use by learners. Often, teachers adopt a very closed stance, with their back to the class, and can be quite tentative in their actions. A certain hand position is necessary to avoid obscuring the image from the data projector. With experience, the choice of software evolves, students become the focus of the interactivity and teachers are more likely to stand back from the board.

Initiatives such as the National Numeracy Strategy (DfEE, 1999) and the Key Stage 3 strategy for mathematics (DfEE, 2001) have promoted interactive, whole-class teaching as a strategy for raising achievement in mathematics. The word 'interactivity' conjures a range of mental images and, specific to the context of the teaching and learning mathematics, offers exciting prospects.

Perks (2002) places importance on teachers displaying images that are 'large enough to see' (p. 57), whether through a large display monitor or data projector. Indeed, an overhead projector could be interpreted as exemplifying the 'C' for communication in ICT and achieves just this aim. However, many schools are bypassing overhead projectors in favour of expensive interactive whiteboards, without first having exploited their use in the development of a more interactive teaching style. Perks takes this view further, by considering how using large images then demands large, exaggerated (theatrical) body movements and actions when discussing or explaining them, thus creating a 'public mathematics moment' (p. 60).

What is in it for the learner?

No change in the classroom can be effected without considering the impact it will have on the critical features of the classroom. Hiebert *et al.* (1997, p. 12) summarize these features as the 'five dimensions of the effective mathematics classroom'. The core features they identify are given in Table 9.1.

Table 9.1 Five dimensions of the effective mathematics classroom

Dimension	Core features
Nature of classroom tasks	Make mathematics problematic
	Connect with where students are
	Leave behind something of mathematical value
Role of the teacher	Select tasks with goals in mind
	Share essential information
	Establish classroom culture
Social culture of the classroom	Ideas and methods are valued
	Students choose and share their methods
	Mistakes are learning sites for everyone
	Correctness resides in mathematical argument
Mathematical tools as learning supports	Meaning for tools must be constructed by each user
	Used with purpose – to solve problems
	Used for recording, communicating and thinking
Equality and accessibility	Tasks are accessible to *all* students
	Every student is heard
	Every student contributes

There is a distinct difference between the nature of traditional mathematical tools (Cuisenaire rods, Dienes apparatus, cubes, etc.) and ICT tools for mathematics. With traditional tools, the meaning has to be constructed by the learner. However, a feature of the most effective ICT tools for mathematics is that they have inherent mathematical features. For example, in an interactive geometry environment, the software 'microworld' places constraints on its use based on a set of mathematical axioms. This creates a completely new mathematical environment.

The choices behind the selection of the mathematical tool, which is likely to be the mathematical software, for which the interactive whiteboard is the user interface, directly affect how the tool is used. For example, given the task to construct a square using dynamic geometry software and an interactive whiteboard, with the range of Euclidean and transformation geometry construction tools at the learners' fingertips, a variety of approaches can be used. Contrast this with tapping the board to advance *PowerPoint* slides!

From the perspective of equality and accessibility, the interactive whiteboard clearly offers support. However, is the classroom culture such that all students are regularly heard? Do students have the opportunity to touch the board? Has the board been mounted high on the wall so that 'children don't fiddle with it'? My 10-year-old niece recently commented that her primary school had now got an interactive whiteboard, but, at the moment, only the Year 6 students were allowed to touch it.

The Ofsted (2001) report also makes the following comment about the use of interactive whiteboards in this context: 'the use of interactive whiteboards is bringing benefits to pupils with [special educational needs], for example by making teachers' presentations clearer and more interesting, and by providing instant notes via printouts of the text and examples used in presentations' (pp. 17–18). Any initiative which improves the experience of lower-attaining students is also going to have a positive effect on the learning of *all* students. While the addition of an interactive whiteboard in the classroom has been welcomed by some teachers and is dreaded by others, it will undoubtedly lead to a review of practice, a very steep learning curve and, with appropriate mathematical software, a completely new engagement with mathematics.

Pimm (1995) has written on the process of manipulation within mathematics and comments that 'Actions guide understanding and understanding in turn guides action. Eventually, many things can be carried out virtually, in the mind, with no action in actuality at all' (p. 25). Learners can experience this physical connection with mathematical systems and processes by the use of slider bars and 'turn handles' while in 'touch and drag' mode.

The nature of the function $y = mx + c$ can be explored using an integrated mathematics package (see Figure 9.6 overleaf), by means of dragging slider bars to change the values of m and c. The connection between the

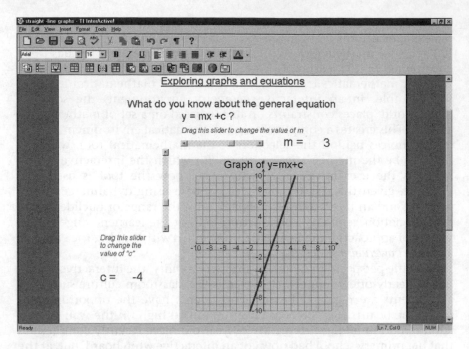

Figure 9.6 Exploring $y = mx + c$ with slider bars.

movement of the vertical slider bar controlling the value of c and the position of the intercept on the graph supports the students in making this visual link. An improvement to this software would be to allow circular sliders, in order to relate the concept of angle to the value of the gradient and the resulting position of the line.

An example of such a 'turn handle' is shown in Figure 9.7, within the context of transformation geometry. The object is rotated through the angle ABC which can be varied by dragging the point C: dragging the point P can alter the position and size of the object.

There is clearly an advantage in exploring rotation within an interactive geometry environment over a static text page. However, connecting the learner to the physical act of rotating an image exemplifies the process suggested by Pimm. Initially, the learner could observe the effect of altering the angle of rotation on the object. At a later stage the student, questioned on the expected result of, say, a rotation of 25°, could draw on a mental image to suggest an answer. Drawing on a student's comment, Passey (2001) describes separation from the mouse in an interactive whiteboard environment as having the effect of letting the user touch the mathematics.

The use of a graphing calculator emulator suitable for the interactive whiteboard (currently under development) provides a 'floating' calculator

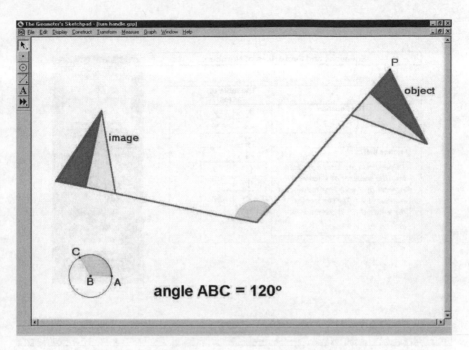

Figure 9.7 Exploring rotation with a turn handle.

with full functionality. The role that this tool could have within, for example, a lesson plenary allows explicit connections to be made. Figure 9.8 shows the calculator emulator floating above a text page on which students record their responses.

The power of hyperlinks within visually creative software tools, rather than text-rich web pages, enable students to dig deeper and make connections within and across mathematical topics in a way that a textbook could not facilitate. And 'making connections' has been widely cited as a fundamental aspect of teaching mathematics for understanding (Hiebert *et al.*, 1997; Perkins *et al.*, 1995).

The ultimate goal is to enable 'learning for understanding' within an ICT-rich environment, defined by Perkins *et al.* (1995) as: 'the possession of a rich, extensible, revisable network of relationships that explain relevant aspects of the topic' (p. 74). The interactive whiteboard offers learners opportunities to get closer to mathematical systems and processes in an exploratory way, over and above the use of a computer and data projector.

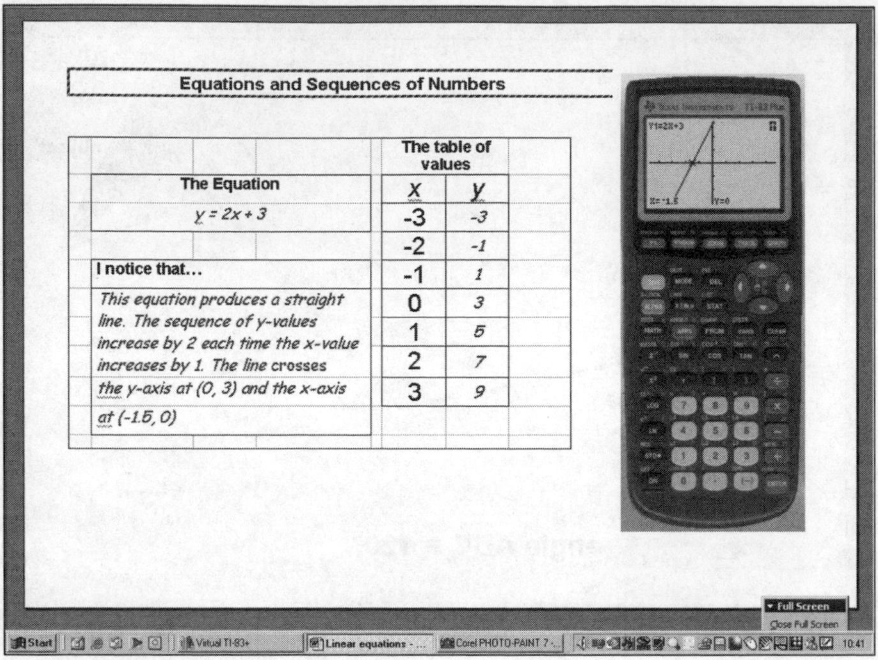

Figure 9.8 Calculator emulator with space for student responses.

References

Caviglioli, O. and Harris, I. (2000) *Mapwise: Accelerated Learning through Visible Thinking*. Stafford: Network Educational Press.

Department for Education and Employment (1999) *Framework for Teaching Mathematics: From Reception to Year 6*. London: DfEE.

Department for Education and Employment (2001) *Framework for Teaching Mathematics: Years 7, 8 and 9*. London: DfEE.

Gardner, H. (1983) *Frames of Mind: The Theory of Multiple Intelligences*. New York: Basic Books.

Greiffenhagen, C. (1999) The use of the board in the mathematics classroom: a pilot study to inform technology design. Unpublished master's thesis, Department of Educational Studies, Oxford University.

Greiffenhagen, C. (2000a) 'From traditional blackboards to interactive whiteboards: a pilot study to inform technology design', in T. Nakahara and M. Koyama (eds), *Proceedings of the 24th International Conference of the Psychology of Mathematics Education Group*. Hiroshima: Hiroshima University, Vol. 2, pp. 305–12.

Greiffenhagen, C. (2000b) 'Interactive whiteboards in mathematics education: possibilities and dangers'. Paper presented at WG11 The Use of Technology in Mathematics Education, 9th International Congress on Mathematical Education, Tokyo/Makuhari, Japan.

Greiffenhagen, C. and Stevens, A. (1999) *Mathematics Teaching Project: SMART Technologies Interim Report.* Technical Report, Oxford University Computing Laboratory.

Hiebert, J., Carpenter, T., Fennema, E. *et al.* (1997) *Making Sense: Teaching and Learning Mathematics with Understanding.* Portsmouth, NH: Heinemann.

Ofsted (2001) *ICT in Schools: the Impact of Government Initiatives – an Interim Report.* London: Office for Standards in Education.

Passey, D. (2001) *MathsALIVE! Final Evaluation Report of the RM/DfEE Project to Develop Year 7 Mathematics On-line Course Materials.* Oxford: RMplc.

Perkins, D., Schwartz, J., West, M.M. and Wiske, M.S. (1995) *Software Goes to School: Teaching for Understanding with New Technologies.* New York: Oxford University Press.

Perks, P. (2002) 'The interactive whiteboard: implications for software design and use', in S. Goodchild (ed.), *Proceedings of the British Society for Research into Learning Mathematics,* **22**(2), pp. 55–60.

Pimm, D. (1995) *Symbols and Meanings in School Mathematics.* London: Routledge.

Prestage, S. and Perks, P. (2001) *Adapting and Extending Secondary Mathematics Activities.* London: David Fulton.

Teacher Training Agency (2002) *ICT and Mathematics: a Guide to Teaching and Learning Mathematics 11–19,* London, Teacher Training Agency/Mathematical Association.
(http://www.m-a.org.uk/education/teachers_teaching_with_technology).

Wood, C. (ed.) (2001) 'Interactive whiteboards – a luxury too far?'. *Teaching ICT,* **1**(2), pp. 52–62.

10

'MATHSALIVE': LESSONS FROM TWENTY YEAR 7 CLASSROOMS

Adrian Oldknow

Through an unexpected stroke of good fortune, a government initiative led to an innovative project in the application of ICT in the mathematics classroom in 2000–01. This chapter considers:

- the UK government's educational initiatives which led up to that project;
- the decisions the project took about ICT in the mathematics classroom;
- the impact the project had on the students and teachers participating in it;
- the extent to which subsequent government initiatives have taken heed of it.

Background to the MathsAlive initiative

In order to put this project into context, I first review other relevant government educational initiatives in ICT and subject-matter teaching. These were outlined in Oldknow (2000).

Schools in the UK participated in a very ambitious continuing professional development scheme funded through the New Opportunities Fund (NOF) to the tune of £230 million. It was to provide some 30 hours of subject-specific ICT training for virtually every primary and secondary school teacher. Originally intended as a three-year exercise, the scheme was extended to a fourth year and was completed in 2003. It is fair to say that this programme did not have the impact on classroom teaching in secondary school subjects, such as mathematics, that was hoped for. References to its evaluation by Ofsted appear later.

In preparation for this NOF training, the Teacher Training Agency produced booklets and CD-ROMs in order to help teachers identify their ICT training needs (TTA, 1999). These were carefully designed in order to avoid 'leading edge' subject approaches which might deter teachers, to be as neutral as possible about promoting ICT use and to emphasize that the use of ICT needed to be justified in subject-specific terms.

Video excerpts from the case study (on the secondary mathematics CD) show the use of:

- dynamic geometry software with a Year 7 class in an ICT suite for geometry;
- spreadsheets with a Year 8 class using networked PCs in a mathematics classroom for data handling;
- small software (a place-value game) with a Year 9 class using PCs in a mathematics classroom for number;
- graphical calculators with a Year 10 class in a mathematics classroom for algebra.

In each case, the video excerpt also shows ICT used for whole-class teaching with:

- a teacher's PC projected onto a wall with a data projector;
- a teacher's lap-top connected to a large-screen TV with a VGA/video interface;
- a teacher's lap-top projected onto a screen with an overhead projector (OHP) tablet;
- a teacher's graphical calculator projected onto a whiteboard with an OHP tablet.

These materials were produced before the introduction of the Key Stage 3 strategy (Department for Education and Employment (DfEE), 2001), but remain one of the few resources to offer insight into how teachers manage different forms of organization and activity using ICT to support the teaching of mathematics. The National Numeracy Strategy had published its Year 7 mathematics framework in March of that year. This document contained very little mention of ICT at all – see Oldknow (2000) for a criticism of its lack of vision.

Against that background, we can plot the development of the DfEE-funded Year 7 curriculum project announced (at BETT 2000) by Michael Wills, the then minister responsible for educational ICT. With hindsight, it is possible to see that the project fitted into the government's plans for the broadband connection of schools and the provision of on-line curriculum resources (now referred to as 'e-learning'). The rationale for choosing the three subjects Japanese, Latin and mathematics for the project remains a mystery – but a plausible reason from the government's perspective may well have been the need to promote the development and trialling of subject 'content' for electronic distribution by the commercial sector.

The development of the project

The contract for the mathematics project was eventually won by Research Machines (RM), but was only confirmed several months after the date originally planned. So instead of 'going live' at the start of the autumn term 2000, the 'MathsAlive' project had to wait until January 2001 to start in earnest. By that time 20 pilot sites, each with one identified teacher and a Year 7 class, had been selected – drawing on middle, secondary and home-hospital schools. The sites were provided with hardware and software and the teachers were given a very small amount of preparatory training. RM developed a web-based management system for lesson planning and teacher support.

The lesson plans and associated resource materials were written for the project by a team of authors based at the Mathematics Centre of University College Chichester, led by Professor Afzal Ahmed. The project specified that these materials had to conform to the objectives of the Year 7 mathematics framework. RM employed a team of teachers with both primary and secondary teaching experience to help support and train the pilot teachers. Further support for the training was provided through the Mathematical Association's 'Teachers Teaching with Technology' (T³) programme.

An educational advisory group was set up, drawn from RM, the National Numeracy Strategy, the Mathematical Association and the external evaluator. This group advised on both the hardware and software base and also on the in-house development of tools such as games, simulations and videos.

The ICT infrastructure for the project

The hardware provision followed a 'mixed-economy' approach – with the underlying assumption that as much of the teaching as possible would take place within the normal mathematics classroom, without a need to move to an ICT suite. With the Framework's emphasis on interactive whole-class teaching, it was imperative that ICT was available to support such use. The main tool was a classroom PC, with printer, displayed through a ceiling-mounted data projector on a Smartboard interactive whiteboard.

Because of the height of Year 7 students (and some of the teachers), it was necessary either to mount the board slightly lower than would normally be the case in a secondary school or to provide a raised step. At that time, interactive whiteboards were just beginning to become more common in secondary schools, as their prices had begun to fall. However, their use in mathematics classrooms was not at all common.

As an alternative, each teacher also had use of a TI graphical calculator to project onto the board, screen or wall using an LCD tablet in conjunction with an OHP. The teachers also received lap-tops, printers and internet connections for use at home to download materials and prepare lessons. Each classroom was equipped with two further PCs – this decision being made more from reasons of space than economics. Again, an alternative means of student access to ICT was provided in the form of a half-class set of TI student graphical calculators. The final element in the hardware collection was a TI Calculator-Based Ranger (CBR) data-logger. The illustration in Figure 10.1 shows one typical classroom configuration, where one wall is set up for interactive whole-class teaching with ICT, while the opposite wall (not shown) is set up for conventional teaching using an ordinary whiteboard.

The software provision was also a 'mixed economy' of generic software, display software, small programs, simulations and videos, together with

Figure 10.1   Classroom with interactive whiteboard.

mathematical tools for dynamic geometry and more general computation including symbolic algebra. While all the PCs and lap-tops had the *MS Office* suite, the main programs used were *MS Word* and *MS Internet Explorer* for accessing the project's materials.

The display software was developed from RM's own *Easiteach Maths* which had been produced for primary schools using interactive whiteboards. Here, teachers could load pre-prepared screens containing text, numbers, symbols, diagrams, etc. for display and manipulation on the interactive whiteboard. Students could come up and enter their own suggestions, drag objects about with their fingers or uncover hidden text. Teachers could bring up number lines, number grids, coordinate axes or 'function machines'. While visually very attractive and motivational, the software was not at all intelligent – you could write 2 + 3 = 6 and the system would not detect that there was anything amiss.

RM's production company, 3T, wrote a large number of games and other software for students to practise mathematical skills. Sample programs, such as *Codebreaker*, can be accessed from http://www.becta.org.uk/ks3online/maths/index.html. A particularly popular game, called *Sub-Patrol*, was available to students to use outside lessons via the project's website.

The main mathematical software tools chosen were *The Geometer's Sketchpad* (*GSP*) and *TI InterActive!* (*TII!*), together with the freely available *MSW Logo*. Such software was new to both the teachers and students in the pilot classes. It proved ideal for use with the interactive whiteboard, where students could come and drag a vertex of triangle using their finger to see whether any properties seemed to remain invariant. The materials provided for teachers included a large number of pre-prepared *Sketchpad* files ready for use in interactive teaching (Figure 10.2). The aim was to encourage teachers to edit and adapt these materials and to develop the confidence to produce their own resources.

Because of some of the mathematically undesirable limitations imposed by standard spreadsheets, such as *MS Excel*, it was decided to look for software to support work in number, algebra and data handling. Desirable features included allowing values to be easily changed and dependent ones to be recomputed, but also included more mathematically familiar styles for writing functions, drawing graphs, etc. There were just two candidates at the time.

Mathsoft's *Studyworks* is a low-cost, educational version of the professional *MathCAD* software, with many powerful tools for presenting and solving mathematical problems. Unlike a conventional spreadsheet, *Studyworks* is not a rectangular array of cells. It allows the user to design the page in any way desired, with a mixture of text areas, formula areas and graphing areas. It was originally designed for engineers to produce reports in the form of 'live' documents, where parameters could easily be altered and where every area depending on those values would then be

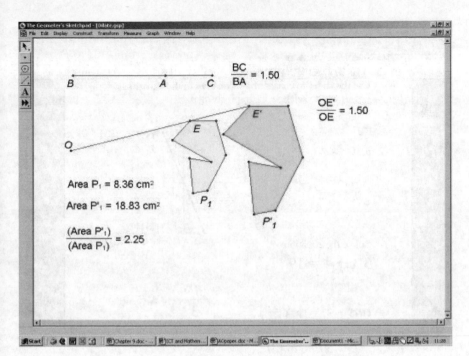

Figure 10.2   An example of a pre-prepared *Geometer's Sketchpad* file.

recomputed and displayed. Its user interface requires a number of key-board 'short-cuts' and the MathsAlive team decided that it was probably rather too complex for use in Year 7.

Fortunately, Texas Instruments had recently brought out a completely new, and also low-cost, piece of software, *TI InterActive!*, which has most, if not all, of the desirable features of *Studyworks* (Figure 10.3 overleaf). It is contained within a more familiar interface which blends the familiar features of *MS Office* with those of a graphical calculator. It combines the features of *MS Word*, *MS Excel*, *MS Internet Explorer* and *MS Outlook Express* with the computational and graphical features of the TI-83+ graphical calculator – and also includes features for symbolic manipulation from *Derive*.

As with *Sketchpad*, this type of software was quite new to the pilot teachers and their students – though many had some experience in using spreadsheets. Again the authors developed files of materials for *TII!*, which teachers could use for whole-class, interactive teaching, but they too were developed with the intention that teachers could modify the files and create their own. The ability to use large fonts, thick lines, strong colours, etc. easily made it another mathematical tool well adapted to interactive, whole-class teaching via the interactive whiteboard. Teachers were very

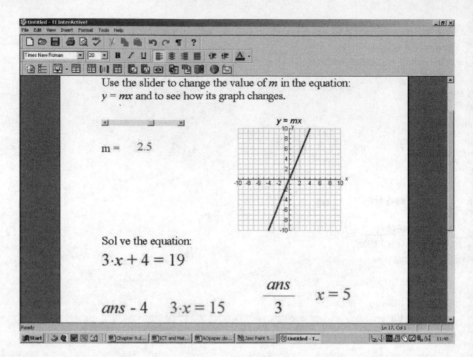

Figure 10.3   An example of a pre-prepared *TI InterActive!* file.

impressed with the features for symbolic manipulation to help with algebraic manipulation.

The PCs also had links to the graphical calculators and data-logger, so that data, programs, screens, etc. could easily be transferred. The advantage of the newer models of graphical calculators (GCs), like the TI-83+, is that with their large amounts of 'flash-ROM' new application software, large data sets and suites of programs can be downloaded from the internet, or CD-ROM, and transferred to the GCs. The *TII!* software also provided an easy interface between GCs, CBR (Figure 10.4) and other software, with its ability to import and export files in *Excel*, *Word*, rich text (.rtf) and internet (.html) formats – see Oldknow and Taylor (2000) for many examples of applications of *TII!* in mathematics teaching.

For a number of good reasons, the potential of this wide base of ICT support was not by any means fully realized during the pilot. Yet many aspects of the project gave cause for encouragement.

The effects of the project on the pilot teachers and students

Just as the project was preparing to start in schools, the Key Stage 3 mathematics strategy was announced as a national programme and the first

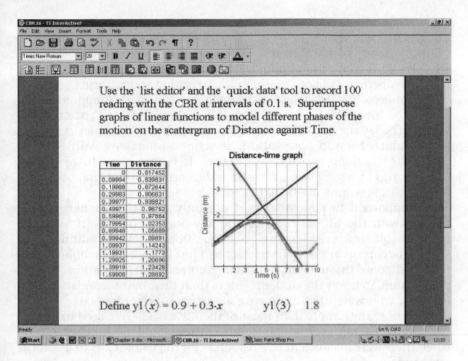

Figure 10.4 *TI InterActive!* with the results from a Calculator-Based Ranger.

drafts of *Framework for Teaching Mathematics: Years 7, 8 and 9* (DfEE, 2001) were put into circulation. The impact of the framework is commented on further below, but it immediately made the authors' task much easier, since its exemplar material showed many more imaginative uses of ICT, including graphical calculators, data-loggers and interactive geometry.

The MathsAlive project's materials contained teacher notes, lesson plans, student task sheets, assessment and homework sheets in the form of *Word* documents which teachers could adapt as desired. Together with the *Easiteach, GSP* and *TII!* files, the materials were organized in blocks of work to conform to the medium-term planning document produced by the Key Stage 3 mathematics strategy. Given their authors' previous involvement with innovative government mathematics projects such as LAMP (Low Attainers in Mathematics Project) and RAMP (Raising Achievement in Mathematics Project), it was not surprising that these materials were also quite ambitious in their scope. Far from just creating a package of electronic resources, the project had grown into an ambitious test-bed for developing new teaching approaches for a new framework using state-of-the-art ICT.

So how did the teachers, and their students, cope with the demands of all this material, together with the new hardware, software and the Key

Stage 3 framework? The answer is remarkably well under the circumstances. The teachers were not selected by the project as being either expert mathematics teachers or for their ICT expertise. They were nominated by the schools which applied to be pilot sites – and these schools included a wide range of experience of both mathematics teaching and ICT use.

The project was evaluated externally by consultants appointed by BECTa and internally by an expert in ICT evaluation from Lancaster University. The latter evaluator visited each of the 20 sites on three occasions and conducted lesson observation, structured interviews with teachers and students, along with questionnaires. It is important to remember that this was by a long way the most ambitious classroom trial of ICT for teaching and learning mathematics for a decade in England.

It is important to remember that not only were the teachers having to cope with the introduction of the Key Stage 3 framework, with its emphasis on structured lessons, pace, questioning, etc. In addition, the Year 7 students involved in the project had just left primary schools where they had come through the National Numeracy Strategy's Key Stage 2 programme. So it was the students, more than their new secondary school teachers, who were used to playing an active role in interactive, whole-class lessons. They, more than most of their teachers, were used to lessons organized on a 'carousel' principle, where they would move between tasks when there were insufficient ICT resources for the whole class to use at the same time.

The following extracts are taken from the evaluator's final report, September 2001.

The initiation of the pilot project and its challenge

This project has been a large undertaking, involving a great deal of ingenuity on the part of the development teams in RM, and a great deal of trust and forward thinking on the part of the DfEE (latterly the Department for Education and Skills (DfES)) who had the foresight to instigate such a project. All those involved, in both its instigation and implementation, should feel proud of their achievements.

Overall indicators of success of the pilot project

At this stage, the project and its outcomes have undoubtedly been a success. The evidence from the evaluation indicates that success has been achieved in a wide range of ways:

- teachers have been extremely positive about the value and usefulness of the resources throughout the project, and have wanted to continue with the project beyond the period of the pilot;
- teachers have felt that the resources and the training offered have enabled them to implement the objectives and needs of the National Numeracy Strategy, using technology to support their teaching;

- teachers have felt that the technology has added to their teaching strategies and approaches;
- students have reported positively throughout the period of the project on the value of the resources and the impact it has had on their learning and on their positive attitudes towards mathematics;
- the resources have been shown in practice to support both teaching and learning.

It will be seen from the evidence which is presented in this report that it is difficult to identify any major weaknesses in the resources. Where any weaknesses have emerged, these were reported to the RM development team and these were dealt with and addressed as a part of ongoing development informed through regular teacher and evaluator feedback and response.

Most teachers (14 or more out of 16) have indicated that their interest in teaching mathematics this year is more than last year. They understand how to use the technology in most lessons, their skill in using computers and technology has increased, they enjoy using the interactive whiteboard and the technology, they think topics are easier to teach when carried out on the interactive whiteboard and that MathsAlive has given them ideas of how to teach mathematics.

This resource was used with classes of Year 7 students, i.e. at a time in school when student attitudes towards mathematics are known to decrease. Hence, the identification of positive attitudinal shifts towards mathematics for this group of students involved would undoubtedly be a major outcome of the resource. This has been the case.

Students report that:

- they had more interest in mathematics in the pilot year than in the previous year (in 69% of 425 cases);
- MathsAlive made mathematics easier (in 73% of cases);
- they discussed mathematics more in the pilot year (in 60% of cases);
- they used technology more in the pilot year (in 85% of cases);
- they believed mathematical games helped them to remember (in 75% of cases);
- they believed they learned from the video (in 61% of cases);
- they enjoyed school more in the pilot year (in 64% of cases);
- they enjoyed using a computer at school (in 92% of cases) or at home (in 87% of cases), but they did not enjoy doing homework in any subject (48%).

In terms of differences between responses of girls and boys, few differences existed. However, far fewer girls did not enjoy doing homework in any subject and fewer girls understood most things in mathematics lessons and could answer questions more easily.

How would the project have been more successful?

Here we come to the main weakness of the project – too many new things for the teachers to take in, without enough time for training, discussion, revision and maturation. With hindsight, it would have been much better if the sites had been chosen in regional clusters, so that groups of teachers could have met more frequently (at least fortnightly) outside the five dedicated days (one per half-term) of training. Also basing the project on just one pilot teacher and class per school meant that many of the teachers were quite isolated and opportunities were not there to spread the initiative load in the way a whole-department project would have enabled.

The priority in the training had to be for teachers to be able to use the RM management system to gain access to, trial and assemble the resources when planning lessons. They were also effectively receiving their Key Stage 3 mathematics training in advance of the national programme of training which was to follow after March 2001. All the teachers rapidly became accustomed to the use of the interactive whiteboard and saw its advantages for interactive, whole-class teaching – but some found it more difficult to share control with the students. All were enthusiastic users of the *Easiteach* and *The Geometer's Sketchpad* materials designed to support whole-class work. But in the short time available to the project, relatively few adapted such materials and even fewer designed their own. *TI Inter-Active!* appeared to be 'a tool too far' for most teachers, since it did not appear in the training schedule until almost at the end of the project.

Most teachers found it very difficult to arrange group work with some students using the three classroom PCs, while others either used GCs or worked without ICT. This was not surprising, given the very short time scale for the project, but the classroom model is such that it could allow students to make decisions about which ICT resources to use for a given task. With even three PCs linked to either an intranet or the internet, students could gain access to resources such as encyclopaedias, search engines and databases, as well as using mathematical and presentational software. It would have been interesting, for example, to see how the teachers might have deployed the equipment to support the subsequent Qualifications and Curriculum Authority (QCA) coursework requirement for data handling in GCSE mathematics. Certainly with tools like GCs and *TII!*, they had all the analytic and display power they needed.

Again the real power of tools like *GSP*, *TII!*, *Logo*, GCs and CBRs did not become sufficiently apparent to many of the teachers because of lack of time for training, lack of support within school, the time pressure of the project, and the restriction of materials to use with Year 7 students.

But the great advantage of the chosen mathematical software base is that it is not at all restricted to any year group or aspect of the mathematics curriculum. Between them, these tools are more than sufficient to support the teaching of mathematics from Year 7 to A-level Further Mathematics – see Oldknow and Taylor (2000) and TTA (2002).

What the project's evaluations showed quite convincingly was the manner and extent of the impact of ICT on both teachers' and students' enjoyment and understanding of the mathematics involved. In particular, many students commented positively on the ability to review work done in their own time after lessons – and how often rereading at their own pace made 'the penny drop' in a way that had not been previously possible without access to ICT.

Since the project has finished, RM have gone on to develop a full Key Stage 3 mathematics package known as the 'Mathematics Alive Framework Edition', which is now available as a subscription service. One of the few hardware changes is that they now recommend a video interface (TI Presenter) to connect the teacher's graphical calculator to the video input of the data projector for use with the interactive whiteboard, and so avoid the need for an OHP.

Have things improved since MathsAlive?

In charting the development of the Year 7 project, we have already seen the impact of the Key Stage 3 mathematics strategy's document (DfEE, 2001). In my original Mathematical Association presentation (Oldknow, 2000), I referred to the need for encouragement from the QCA, the examination boards and the National Numeracy Strategy:

> More depressingly, the National Numeracy Strategy has virtually nothing to say about the use of ICT to enhance mathematics teaching at KS1/2. The QCA commissioned them to write a scheme of work for Year 7 which has now been published. Needless to say, there is also virtually no reference to ICT except in the context of data handling and the critical use of calculators for computation. The lack of vision shown here is most regrettable. (p. 12)

Just as the Year 7 framework was 'ICT impoverished', so the Key Stage 3 one is 'ICT rich' and provides ample encouragement, together with exemplification, for the use of a range of ICT approaches to enhance teaching and learning. But, as we know, no printed material, however persuasive, is likely to make an impact unless other resources are available to provide the necessary hardware and software and to provide training and support.

A good example of the breakdown of the government's much-vaunted 'joined-up thinking' was the DfES's Computers for Teachers phase 2 scheme. Only Key Stage 3 mathematics teachers already signed up for the NOF-funded ICT training were eligible. But the scheme only provided for the purchase of the hardware, and had no provision for ensuring teachers had access to appropriate mathematics-specific software or supporting materials. Such a fundamental oversight in ICT provision has been perpetuated both in the recent provision of lap-tops to all Key Stage 3 mathematics consultants and in the current DfES scheme providing lap-tops for teachers – neither of which includes any element of specialist software provision. So the message which such schemes unfortunately perpetuate seems to be that *MS Office* provides all that a mathematics teacher could possibly need.

The most recent Ofsted (2002a) report on mathematics teaching is not encouraging reading as far as ICT practice is concerned.

The use of ICT to support learning in mathematics is good in only one quarter of schools. It is unsatisfactory in three schools in ten. Typically there is some use of ICT with some classes, but it is not consistent across the department. Students' access to a range of mathematics software also varies greatly. Most departments have access to spreadsheets, graph-plotting software, LOGO and specific items of software to support skills learning. In general, however, very little use is currently made of the powerful dynamic geometry or algebra software available.

Many mathematics teachers use ICT confidently outside the classroom in the preparation of teaching materials and in the management and analysis of students' achievement. Despite this, only a small proportion of departments has reached the point where they can evaluate critically their use of ICT and decide where it most benefits learning in mathematics. Too often, teachers' planning and schemes of work lack any reference to specific ICT applications, and students have difficulty recalling when they have used ICT in mathematics. (pp. 8–9)

Ofsted has also been evaluating the impact of the government's initiatives in ICT in schools. In their first interim report (Ofsted, 2001), we find some general comments about ICT provision, such as the following.

69. Many schools have invested in interactive whiteboards and computer projection equipment. Generally these have led to more effective whole-class teaching, with all students able to see a large, clear display. Students too have made good use of this new equipment, for example in illustrating a prepared talk with the aid of presentational software. . . . In an effort to provide more flexible access to ICT resources for students, some schools have increased the availability of lap-top computers. Many teachers have benefited from the DfEE scheme for part-funding computers, although demand has outstripped the available funding. Other teachers have benefited significantly from Government schemes to provide lap-tops for personal use. (pp. 17–18)

The Ofsted (2002b) ICT Secondary Mathematics report also has sections on managing ICT in mathematics and on staff development. Overall, the report appears to paint a rather depressing picture. The following extracts give a taste.

2. The effect of government ICT initiatives on the quality of teaching and learning in mathematics varies considerably among schools. Overall, good practice remains uncommon. . . .
6. However, good, consistent and progressive use of ICT in mathematics is found in only a small minority of schools. In around two-thirds of mathematics departments some use is made of ICT, but not to the extent that it is an established part of the curriculum. . . .
13. . . . although they know the general advantages of ICT use, many mathematics teachers remain unaware of the potential of specific software and tools: for example, the power of the data-handling facilities on graphical calculators or the facility of graph-plotting software to transform general shapes. They are less able to employ ICT to meet the different needs of students and because of weak planning are more liable to be drawn into teaching ICT skills to the detriment of the mathematics which the ICT is intended to support. . . .
16. The management of ICT developments within mathematics departments is generally weak. . . . most mathematics departments do not have ICT as a priority. . . .
29. In the small minority of schools where ICT resources and accommodation are very good, these have a favourable effect on achievement in mathematics. However, even where mathematics departments have their own computer rooms, their use is not always well planned and in several cases they are insufficiently used.

Comments with regard to the NOF-funded training also make rather grim reading.

25. However, the overwhelming view of mathematics teachers is that the NOF-funded training has not met either their personal or pedagogical needs. In about two out of three schools, there is little evidence that the training is yet having an effect on either the quality of mathematics teaching or on students' achievement. Teachers are frustrated by the lack of subject-specific focus in the training. In particular, many teachers feel strongly that the training involves a daunting quantity of material and relies too much on teachers' own time. Some teachers feel that the training has been counter-productive, coming at a time of other key initiatives, especially the Key Stage 3 Strategy.

Also we find in the general ICT report (Ofsted, 2001) another aspect of NOF training:

77. NOF training has been most successful where it has been preceded by thorough preparations. However, no consistent national assessment of teachers' professional ICT requirements was undertaken in relation to the expected outcomes for NOF training. Generally, teachers' needs with regard to the pedagogical use of ICT in their subject or phase were not ascertained effectively in advance by schools or [accredited training providers]. The needs analysis materials provided by the TTA were used infrequently. (p. 20)

While one might have expected the momentum from the ICT exemplars in the Mathematics Framework at Key Stage 3 to be continued by the strategy, this has yet to prove the case. Again, Ofsted (2003) had a tough message in its most recent evaluation of the second year of the Key Stage 3: 'The potential of ICT to enhance teaching and learning of mathematics was under-exploited, as were opportunities for investigative work' (p. 9). So the inspection evidence gives a pretty unequivocal 'no' to the question 'Have things improved since MathsAlive?'.

Can we expect any improvements in the near future?

There have been major changes since Charles Clarke became Secretary for State for Education in 2002. In an early speech, he signalled his intention to involve professional subject associations more centrally in future. He also took personal charge of subject developments in both ICT and mathematics. The National Grid for Learning section of his department has been renamed the 'ICT in Schools Division' and has undertaken a major strategy review. Opening the National Association for Advisers in Computer Education conference in Torquay in February 2003, Clarke offered the challenge for ICT to become embedded in subject teaching. He also announced increased expenditure on continued professional development (CPD) in the use of ICT by teachers. Opening the Advisory Committee on Mathematics Education conference on CPD in London in March 2003, Clarke announced the creation of a national centre of excellence in mathematics teaching.

Schools have been allocated funds to use to help purchase ICT-based materials, including software, through 'e-learning credits'. The strategy will focus on ICT across the curriculum in 2004. The Key Stage 3 mathematics consultants' training in March 2003 included specific ICT content (interactive geometry and graphical calculators) for the first time.

The QCA is extending its five school-based projects in algebra and geometry for another year. This includes one directed by Kenneth Ruthven of Cambridge University looking at the potential for the newer version of dynamic geometry software with facilities for graph plotting in bridging across work in both algebra and geometry. In GCSE mathematics, there is now compulsory data-handling coursework which specifies the use of ICT. The revised A/AS mathematics criteria state that graphical calculators should be available, and used, for examination papers in all but one module.

The TTA has been working with subject professional associations to produce guidance on the use of ICT in subject teaching. The mathematics guide (TTA, 2002) was produced by a team drawn from the Association of Teachers of Mathematics (ATM), Mathematical Association (MA) and other groups. It can be accessed from the MA's website (http://www.m-a.org.uk). The Key Stage 3 mathematics strategy has also produced its own guide to integrating ICT, which should shortly be available on its website.

It has also commissioned a group drawn from the ATM and MA to produce sample lesson plans showing cross-curricular use of ICT in mathematics. The lessons are all from the mathematics framework, but also cover objectives from the ICT framework. These lesson plans and supporting materials are also to be made available on the Key Stage 3 website. The BECTa website includes many useful items of ICT advice for mathematics, such as on GCs. It also has downloadable versions of useful documents such as those produced by the DfES's former Mathematics Curriculum IT Support (CITS) group. More recently, it has posted a number of useful tools for departmental review under the name 'Timesavers'.

Summary

A rather unlikely government project aimed to stimulate the generation of content for the 'on-line curriculum' provided a testing ground for an ambitious project aimed to embed ICT in teaching and learning mathematics. Important lessons were learned about the ways this can have an impact on teachers' and learners' attitudes and enthusiasm for the subject.

The impact was limited by the small amount of time the pilot teachers had to adjust to a wide range of innovations and by the restrictions imposed in the way the project was organized – one teacher in one class in each school. Opportunities to disseminate the results and to encourage further such developments have not been forthcoming. The observed state of ICT use in mathematics teaching and learning leaves much room for improvement. Recent changes of direction in government strategies look to be heading in the right direction, but only time will tell.

References

DfEE (2001) *Framework for Teaching Mathematics: Year 7*. London: Department for Education and Employment.

Ofsted (2001) *ICT in Schools: the Impact of Government Initiatives – an Interim Report*. London: Ofsted (http://www.ofsted.gov.uk/publications/docs/1043.pdf).

Ofsted (2002a) *Mathematics in Secondary Schools* (HMI 818). London: Ofsted.

Ofsted (2002b) *ICT in Schools: Effect of Government Initiatives – Secondary Mathematics* (HMI 705). London: Ofsted. (http://www.ofsted.gov.uk/public/docs02/ictsubject/maths_ictsec.pdf)

Ofsted (2003) *The Key Stage 3 Strategy: Evaluation of the Second Year* (HMI 518). London: Ofsted.

Oldknow, A. (2000) 'The government's strategy for ICT in education – what's in it for mathematics?'. *Micromath*, **16**(2), 9–13. (http://www.m-a.org.uk/tc/ac000416.doc)

Oldknow, A. and Taylor, R. (2000) *Teaching Mathematics with ICT*. London: Continuum. London.

Teacher Training Agency (1999) *Identification of Training Needs* (booklet and CD-ROMs). London: TTA (http://www.canteach.gov.uk/info/ict/nof/paper.htm).

Teacher Training Agency (2002) *ICT and Mathematics: a Guide to Learning and Teaching Mathematics 11–19*. London: TTA/Mathematical Association. (http://www.m-a.org.uk/)

11

VIDEO-CONFERENCING: CASE STUDIES IN MATHEMATICS CLASSROOMS

Jenny Gage

When I first started working with video-conferencing, former teacher colleagues asked me why I would want to do it. My response, based on experience, was that video-conferencing can have a very positive impact on raising the status of mathematics, making it seem both up to date and exciting for school students. Having a live audience can be very motivating and also helps them to value their own work more. It can be very easy for mathematics lessons to run in much the same way week in, week out, with no special events to break the routine. Video-conferencing can provide a 'special event'. There are many ways in which it can be used to enhance students' participation in mathematics lessons and develop greater skills in mathematical communication (some ideas are given later), as well as bringing them in contact with people they would otherwise be unlikely to encounter.

Often when schools acquire video-conferencing equipment, teachers look for opportunities to use it. However, as in so many other circumstances, this can lead to the technology driving the curriculum. There needs to be a purpose for a video-conference, other than just to demonstrate that it can be done. This purpose could include objectives directly related to the curriculum: for example, post-16 students accessing Further Mathematics A-level lessons, which would not be available to them in their own school or college. It could include objectives to do with increasing mathematical communication: for example, students could video-conference once a week for half a term with a similar class at another school (which might be anywhere in the world), taking turns to lead each other in solving mathematical problems.

A video-conference is not a single entity: rather, it is a medium which allows access to a wide variety of people and resources not normally available in the classroom. Successful use of video-conferencing occurs when the act of video-conferencing is not in itself the primary focus, but merely the means of achieving a justifiable educational objective.

As with every other form of ICT, introducing video-conferencing can lead to successful practice, but may not do so. Just including a video-conference in a lesson is not a strong practice in itself: above all, video-conferencing is about interaction. A lecture may not be a good use of video-conferencing. The same objectives might be more easily achieved with a videotape, which could be stopped and started, allowing discussion to take place, as necessary. On the other hand, if the students can ask questions and receive direct answers from the lecturer, then the interactivity of the video-conference is drawn upon, providing a valid reason for its use.

Using video-conferencing in the mathematics classroom

There are many different ways to use video-conferencing in the mathematics classroom. Whatever is happening, the teachers may well find that – at the outset at least – they are very necessary facilitators, orchestrating student contributions and responses. Students who would normally show no hesitation in taking part in an in-class discussion may initially be overawed by the occasion and may need prompting to ask questions or to respond. The teachers of the respective classes may need to repeat anything which is not very clear in their own class or the one at the remote end. In the normal classroom environment, students often interrupt or talk across each other. This just comes across as jumbled noise at the remote end and the teacher may well need to intervene. Students do not usually take long to learn the protocol of a video-conference.

Once everyone has become comfortable with the medium, video-conferencing can give students opportunities to hear other voices and views. It gives them the opportunity to engage in mathematical discovery, to meet potential role models, to consider a wider future for themselves and to enlarge their experience of the world. A teacher, talking about a girl who, before taking part in video-conferences, had never participated in class discussion, commented:

> One of the girls afterwards, she's been contributing in class, she's been putting her hand up . . . you know . . . it's just made her world a little bit bigger.

It is well known to teachers that it is often only when you have to teach a mathematical topic that you really come to understand it for yourself; having to teach peers is a very good way for students to learn a new topic. Video-conferencing can be used to facilitate peer teaching, providing distance and significance to their task. One way this might work is for one class to be taught a topic and, in addition to the normal exercises on that topic, plan teaching approaches and materials which they then use with the remote class. Then, in a subsequent video-conference, the classes can reverse their roles.

In a case study (Bell *et al.*, 1993), the teacher organized her students to teach those from another class in the same school and also to teach each other within their own class: 'The two-class approach was much more of an "occasion". It was perceived by students as an exciting event. The latter approach [students teaching others within their own class], in contrast, was much more mundane' (p. 92). One of the girls involved commented: 'It probably didn't help the classes, but it helped us understand'. (It may well be necessary for the teacher of the remote class to follow this up, to make sure that her/his students have fully grasped the topic, of course.)

Here are some other specific ideas to get started. As with any form of unfamiliar ICT, it is usually best to start with something simple and build up gradually so that everyone has time to develop the necessary skill. One possibility is to connect with another school you already have links with and plan a few straightforward tasks. For example, two classes could set short problems for each other in advance, which could be worked on before the video-conference, and subsequently discussed live. Other possibilities include:

- small schools linking up to collaborate on projects;
- students making a presentation to another group of students;
- a class working with another class on some aspect of the curriculum;
- sharing visitors;
- cross-phase links (primary/secondary – see Walsh, 2002 – or secondary/ sixth-form/tertiary);
- specialist teachers/lecturers giving occasional lessons to a primary or secondary school, using specialist equipment not available at the school;
- joint delivery of lessons to one or more classes by an outside expert or by one or more teachers involved;
- post-16 courses, such as Further Mathematics, using an external provider, or sharing teaching expertise, and backed up with in-house support and good written materials – this increases the viability of small groups, and provides students with valuable opportunities to manage their own learning in preparation for higher education;
- continuing professional development, such as joint INSET courses or meetings with staff of linked schools, including feeder schools;

- opportunities for inexperienced or poorly qualified staff to watch strong practice, either elsewhere in their own school or in other schools.

Whatever you decide to do, identify your objectives on several levels for the session. What are your objectives in terms of communication, interaction, educational gain, professional development? How will face-to-face contact with the remote site make a difference? If it is not going to provide something not otherwise available, is a video-conference really necessary?

A case study: Motivate

The Motivate project (http://www.motivate.maths.org) provides an example of a video-conferencing project set up to exploit the ability of video-conferencing to bring outside experts to school students. It also offers them an outside audience for whom they can describe their own mathematical project work. This project originated in 1996 because a school had video-conferencing equipment that was not being used and teachers wanted to find ways of using it that would enrich the students' mathematical experience. The main objective was and continues to be to use video-conferencing to bring people for whom mathematics is a significant part of their working lives together with school students of all ages (Gage *et al.*, 2002).

Since the first conference in 1996–7, well over 100 schools from all parts of the UK have been involved (in both the primary and secondary sectors), together with schools in South Africa, India and Singapore. The project particularly tries to involve schools where there is some degree of disadvantage, which could be the number of students whose first language is not English, some social or educational disadvantage or geographical isolation.

Students have the opportunity to interact with mathematical experts talking about their own lives and discussing some area of mathematics (which they may never have realized existed previously) and then to ask questions. They carry out their own work away from the camera (either the same day or over the following weeks), so that they can follow up problems posed by the speaker and can engage in mathematical inquiry for themselves. Finally, the students present an account of what they have discovered to all of the other video-conference participants.

The Motivate project aims to enrich the students' mathematical experience, broaden their mathematical horizons and generally raise their aspirations for their own futures. It also aspires to offer them a chance to develop greater fluency in communicating about mathematics and to experience collaborative working on a mathematical task. Finally, students have a chance to present their own work to an audience of their peers and discuss it with their peers and an expert. For some students, this causes them to consider how mathematics might play a role in their futures. (Sixty per cent of participants claim to be more likely to take mathematics at a higher level as a result of taking part in a Motivate video-conference.) They can also gain a greater confidence in themselves.

A teacher commented at the end of one such event:

Video-conferencing was definitely a positive experience for the children. It [the ICT element] definitely inspired participation in the mathematics 'side' of the project.

A further comment from a 12-year-old secondary student was:

This project was very enjoyable and interesting. ... I think about mathematics a bit more differently than usual.

How to run a successful video-conference

A successful video-conference requires the technology not to be foremost in everyone's minds, but to be purely a transmission medium for the content. It is a good idea to start small and informal. A small, relaxed conference gives everyone the chance to get to know the equipment (and to get an idea of what happens) in a less threatening situation.

There are several books and websites which discuss equipment (see the resources list on this book's website). Basically, video-conferencing needs a camera, microphone, speakers and TV/monitor/screen/whiteboard at each end, plus a way of sending sound and images between them. This can be done via either ISDN telephone lines, which are dedicated phone lines providing a greater capacity than normal voice-only lines, or via the internet. ISDN phone lines incur costs each time a video-conference takes place and there are also installation and rental costs.

The quality of the video-conference depends on how many lines you use. A minimum of two lines is necessary for video-conferencing. Alternatively, you can use IP, which is an internet-based method of transmission. This requires a fast computer and sufficient bandwidth to carry the video-conference. Using IP is free, but most schools will have 'firewall' issues to contend with. Schools are usually within the firewall of their local grid for learning or internet provider, which protects them from unwanted internet access. Video-conferencing outside the local area requires the manager of the firewall to allow the video-conference signals through, so this is an issue which needs consideration in advance.

A simple video-conference involves two users on a point-to-point conference. If more participants are involved, or if you are mixing ISDN and IP calls, you will need to use a bridge, which connects all the users together, giving a multi-point conference. The users can be in the next classroom or spread throughout the world. The difference from normal video or TV broadcasts is that it is interactive in real time.

If you are just involving a few students around a camera, you can use desktop video-conferencing, which uses a small camera attached to a PC. However, this is not suitable for more than four or five students. For whole-class work, a proper video-conferencing camera is necessary. You also need to consider the size of the screen the remote image will be displayed on – it needs to be big enough for students at the back of the group to see comfortably, so that they can remain focused on the video-conference.

Sound is also an important consideration. Poor sound kills more video-conferences than almost anything else – if the students are unable to hear each other easily, interaction between them will not happen. Testing sound quality in advance is a good idea, as is getting the students to prac-tise using the microphone, so they know how loudly to speak, where to hold it and where to stand. Hand-held microphones are ideal – you can be heard easily and it is obvious when someone is speaking. There may be a slight time delay on the sound, and this has to be allowed for. It means waiting for the person at the other end to answer you or to finish what they are saying and not jumping in too quickly.

Images on the screens are updated when there is movement, so the less movement there is, the quicker the image settles down. Everyone there-fore needs to be careful not to move about unnecessarily. If students are holding up items to show people at the remote end, they need to hold them steady for long enough for the image to settle. The quality of the image will depend on the precise method of communication you are using. If you are using ISDN2, the quality will not be as good as TV, but once you have become used to it, it should not be an issue. ISDN6 and IP both give an excellent image.

On the technical side, it is a good idea for students to know how to operate the equipment as well as the teacher or technician. They will then be able to take turns in overseeing the technical operation of the video-conferencing. This frees up the teacher for other activities, as well as offering students a sense of ownership of the video-conference.

A telephone in the room (whether a landline or a mobile) enables com-munication between sites if connection via the video link is delayed or drops for any reason. There is nothing worse than sitting waiting for a link which does not become established and having no way to find out what is happening. If it does take a little while to establish the connection, it is a good idea to have a task for your students to get started on.

Students need to be aware of the aims of the video-conference, as well as what they will be expected to do while it is in session. They also need to know the skills and behaviour required for an effective video-conference – hence the need for informal initial activity to allow awareness to build up. Those in the home site need to see who is at the remote site and find out a bit about them. This gives everyone a chance to take part at an early stage, thus reducing shyness later on. Allowing students to chair the sessions helps them to feel in control and also further develops a sense of ownership.

Preparation is crucial: both teachers and students have to be fully prepared for the event. Students should be involved in this, perhaps by brainstorming questions to ask or by preparing short sections of the conference. Having everything written down is a good idea in case of attacks of nerves when it comes to delivering the material over the video-conference! You may also need to prepare materials to send to the other site beforehand.

Visual props help to provide variety: to be effective, these will need to be very simple, with text large enough to be seen on a small screen. Lights sometimes can cause glare on white posters so that they cannot be seen at all. Colours need to contrast well. You could use other software, such as a dynamic geometry package, a spreadsheet, interactive whiteboard or a *PowerPoint* presentation. You should aim for frequent changes of activity, and never more than 20 minutes or so without some kind of off-screen activity. Initially, 30 minutes for the whole video-conference, with groups of students taking turns to present, is probably quite long enough.

Finally, you will have to think about how you follow up the video-conference. It is a good idea for students to have the opportunity to reflect on what happened, what worked, what did not and to consider how they might improve things for another time, in addition to specific follow-up on the tasks involved.

What are some of the problems?

In this section I discuss five commonly perceived problems with video-conferences.

It is not as good as a first-hand experience

This assertion can be challenged on several levels. To begin with, a first-hand experience may simply not be available in the classroom. A video-conference may be the only way to bring an expert to your students or to enable them to interact with other students elsewhere in the world. Second, there are aspects of video-conferencing that are better than a first-hand experience. Students (and teachers) may be overawed by the presence of a world authority in their own school (even assuming this could be arranged), finding it difficult to work out what to say.

A video-conference, perhaps where several schools are taking part, allows the burden of talk to be shared, and gives a certain sense of distance. Students can stay in their own familiar environment, which can also add to their confidence in a strange situation. Third, using video-conferencing successfully requires its own skill, which can be of benefit – particularly skill at communicating – and can contribute to student confidence.

It is not the same as meeting face-to-face

It is much easier to interact directly with someone face-to-face, and inter-activity via video-conferencing has to be worked at. This means that the session has to be planned very carefully, with at least some questions worked out in advance and materials prepared which are easy to see on screen. However, these are aspects of all good teaching. With greater familiarity with the medium, video-conferencing becomes easier and interactivity becomes much more natural.

Sometimes there are technical failures

Indeed there are! A connection failure can mean the end of all the careful plans that have been made. It is always necessary to have an alternative plan, so that if connection cannot be made, is delayed or fails part-way through, everyone is not just hanging around. The likelihood of technical failure will be lessened, however, if the person operating the video-conference has had the chance to practise and the connection is tested shortly beforehand. Familiarity with the technology helps connection failures to be kept to a minimum. The main technical difficulties likely to cause problems during a video-conference concern the size of the screen the students are watching and sound. If these are carefully considered in advance, the session should go well.

What about training, confidence and workload of teachers?

Teachers need training and experience in order to have confidence in the medium, including the chance to practise using the technology and to talk to others on a video-conference for themselves before trying to use it with a class. This could be achieved by you talking to other teachers via a video-conference during the planning stage, so that when you involve your class, initial problems have been overcome and con-fidence gained. Inevitably this means a temporary increase in workload, as does the additional planning needed, but the familiarization stage probably will not last very long, with most teachers rapidly adjusting their teaching style.

Finding the time for people to get to know each other

A successful video-conference requires time for the students and teachers involved to get to know those they are meeting in this way. If students are going to work with another class over a period of time, it is worth building in time for them to find out about each other before starting work on the mathematical tasks planned. This may mean allowing time for e-mailing each other or for talking about themselves at the beginning of the first video-conference. It is no different from the situation at the beginning of a new school year really, when teachers expect everyone to need time to find out a bit about each other. Thereafter, at the beginning of each video-conference, students need to find out who is at the other end, to be able to greet each other and to re-establish a relationship with the remote class. Time spent in this way will mean that the students feel comfortable interacting with the remote class. If this aspect is cut short, interactivity will be much harder to achieve and the video-conference is likely to consist of students talking to the camera, rather than to each other.

The context for video-conferencing in mathematics education

Video-conferencing is necessarily a social medium, with communication issues paramount. It can therefore be situated in the context of social theories of learning and theories of the function of communication in mathematics learning.

Social theories of learning

The socio-culturists have provided a theoretical background which emphasizes the social nature of learning and the importance of inter-actions in the classroom (Nickson, 2000, p. 176). Students learn both from the teacher and from each other, and discussion is seen as the means by which the students construct meaning for themselves, with the teacher's interventions being vital to the process (Lerman, 1998).

The socio-constructivists form part of the neo-Vygotskian theoretical background to mathematics education. Vygotsky claimed that all higher mental processes in the individual have their origin in social processes, with the role of parents and teachers in creating (and being part of) a learning environment being fundamental.

Every function in the child's cultural development appears twice: first, on the social level, and later, on the individual level; first, *between* people (*interpsychological*), and then *inside* the child (*intrapsychological*). This applies equally to voluntary attention, to logical memory, and to the formation of concepts. All the higher functions originate as actual relations between human individuals.

(Vygotsky, 1978, p. 57; emphasis in original)

Vygotsky described the 'zone of proximal development': this is the difference between what a child can perform unaided and what s/he can
perform with the assistance of a teacher, parent or more experienced peer.
'What the child can do in co-operation today he can do alone tomorrow'
(Vygotsky, 1986, p. 188). Performance can be assisted by the more experienced person acting as a model, by giving feedback, by specific instruction, by questioning or by structuring a task (Tharp, 1993): in short, by all
the strategies an experienced teacher uses with her/his students. Video-
conferencing increases the number of experienced people available to
students and increases opportunities for students to collaborate with their
peers.

The role of communication in the mathematics classroom

There has been a perception of mathematics as a quiet, largely written
activity, rather than a subject for lively discussion and oral negotiation of
meaning. However, much recent research based on Vygotsky's theories of
learning has emphasized the need for talk in the mathematics classroom,
and this is recognized in the National Numeracy Strategy in the UK. The
Key Stage 3 National Strategy (Department for Education and Employment,
2001) states that:

> better standards of mathematics occur when:
> • there is whole-class discussion in which teachers question students
>   effectively, give them time to think, expect them to demonstrate and
>   explain their reasoning, and explore reasons for any wrong answers;
> • students are expected to use correct mathematical terms and notation
>   and to talk about their insights rather than give single-word answers.
>
> (p. 6)

Two decades earlier, the Cockcroft Report (Department of Education and
Science, 1982) claimed that:

> mathematics provides a means of communication which is powerful,
> concise and unambiguous. Even though many of those who consider
> mathematics to be useful would probably not express the reason in
> these terms, we believe that it is the fact that mathematics can be used as
> a powerful means of communication which provides the principal
> reason for teaching mathematics to all children.
>
> (para. 3)

According to Pimm (1987, p. xvii) mathematics is a 'social activity,
deeply concerned with communication'. Trying to articulate their
thoughts helps students to understand better, and trying to organize the

language they use helps them to organize their thoughts. However, much informal talk in the classroom contains half-finished and vague utterances with many immediately modified phrases. Students' difficulties in expressing themselves mathematically are well documented: 'School introduces children to aspects of the mathematical and scientific register (e.g. vocabulary items) but provides them with relatively few opportunities to practise these registers' (Forman and McPhail, 1993, p. 226).

One of the intentions of the Motivate project is to offer just such opportunities to the participating students. Video-conferencing provides a forum for purposeful mathematical talk. This adds an extra dimension to normal classroom discussion, by providing students with an audience outside their own classroom. The external audience does not have the same shared experience and so better communication is needed if the external audience is to understand what is being said. When students are asked to explain something to their peers in the same classroom, they can often get away with 'You know what I mean', or other vague utterances. This will not do if the audience does not have a shared experience.

I have carried out research (supported by a BECTa bursary) to see whether regular video-conferencing could lead to better mathematical communication skills in students (Gage, 2003). Two schools held fortnightly video-conferences during one term between two classes of 12–13-year-olds to see if this had an effect on both their oral and written fluency in mathematical investigations. The classes doing the video-conferences showed greater improvement in both, compared to similar classes not taking part in video-conferences. The students and teachers involved also commented that the students had both gained significantly in confidence as a result and had enjoyed the extra opportunities for collaborative learning which had occurred.

Conclusion

It is my view that video-conferencing has enormous potential benefits to offer the education world and mathematical education in particular. Mathematics in UK schools is going through a difficult time at the moment, with fewer students choosing to take mathematics through to the end of secondary school and even fewer following through to university level. There are many reasons for this, of course, but it is well known that mathematics is perceived as difficult. My experience as a teacher would indicate that many also perceive it as boring.

Video-conferencing can offer real gains in students' mathematical fluency, plus the potential benefits that come from raising the status of mathematics, and making it more exciting. It can also offer students the opportunity to participate in events that challenge their thinking and enable them to raise their mathematical standards.

More generally, video-conferencing has a significant role to play in students' social and cultural education through the prospect of meeting and exchanging ideas with others worldwide. It broadens students' horizons, offering them the opportunity to look outside their own classrooms and communities. It also provides students with the chance to develop themselves through making presentations to their peers and through collaborative working. Having a real audience gives a purpose to planning their contributions to the video-conference and offers students of all ages the opportunity to take responsibility for their own learning, leaving a lasting sense of achievement.

References

Bell, A., Crust, R., Shannon, A. and Swan, M. (1993) *Awareness of Learning, Reflection and Transfer in School Mathematics*. ESRC Research Project, Nottingham, Shell Centre, University of Nottingham.

Department for Education and Employment (2001) *Key Stage 3 National Strategy*. London: Department for Education and Employment.

Department of Education and Science (1982) *Mathematics Counts* (Cockcroft Report). London: HMSO.

Forman, E. and McPhail, J. (1993) 'Vygotskian perspective on children's collaborative problem solving activities', in E. Forman, N. Minick and C. Stone (eds), *Contexts for Learning: Sociocultural Dynamics in Children's Development*. Oxford: Oxford University Press, pp. 213–29.

Gage, J. (2003) *Video-conferencing in the Mathematics Lesson*. BERA Conference. (http://www.leeds.ac.uk/educol/documents/00003288.htm).

Gage, J., Nickson, M. and Beardon, T. (2002) 'Can video-conferencing contribute to teaching and learning? The experience of the Motivate Project'. *BERA Conference* (http://www.leeds.ac.uk/educol/documents/00002264.htm).

Lerman, S. (1998) 'A moment in the zoom of a lens: towards a discursive psychology of mathematics teaching and learning', in A. Olivier and K. Newstead (eds), *Proceedings of the 22nd Conference of the International Group for the Psychology of Mathematics Education*. Stellenbosch, South Africa: Faculty of Education, University of Stellenbosch, Vol. 1, pp. 66–84.

Nickson, M. (2000) *Teaching and Learning Mathematics: A Teacher's Guide to Recent Research and Its Applications*. London: Cassell.

Pimm, D. (1987) *Speaking Mathematically: Communication in Mathematics Classrooms*. London: Routledge & Kegan Paul.

Tharp, R. (1993) 'Institutional and social context of educational practice and reform', in E. Forman, N. Minick and C. Stone (eds), *Contexts for Learning: Sociocultural Dynamics in Children's Development*. Oxford, Oxford University Press, pp. 269–82.

Vygotsky, L. (1978) *Mind in Society: The Development of Higher Psychological Processes*. Cambridge, MA: Harvard University Press.

Vygotsky, L. (1986) *Thought and Language*. Cambridge, MA: MIT Press.

Walsh, G. (2002) 'Mathematics – long distance'. *Primary Mathematics*, December.

12
MATHEMATICS ON
THE INTERNET

Nathalie Sinclair

Like the Swiss army knife, the internet is a multi-purpose tool with several functions. Some people use the internet as a library, others as a platform for running interactive programs (such as Java applets), while others still see it as a virtual post office, a professional development centre, a collaborative network, a shop, a bank or a newspaper.

In this chapter, I highlight some of the most relevant features of the internet to the teaching and learning of mathematics – whether they are currently being fully exploited or not – and indicate ways in which these features productively serve the interests and needs of teachers and students. I also draw attention to a few of the complicating social and economic issues that may eventually compromise some of its currently promising features.

The web: library or conference centre?

Picture a typical upper secondary mathematics classroom. A teacher stands at the front of the class and the students are writing in their notebooks; the lesson is about parabolas. The teacher introduces the general equation for a parabola and describes the parameters involved, providing a small set of examples drawn by hand on the blackboard. What role could the internet play in this scenario?

Perhaps the teacher found her lesson plan or some of the homework questions she will subsequently hand out on one of the thousands of websites that catalogue secondary mathematics lesson plans. Maybe, as she was searching for a lesson plan, she located a research-oriented site that had some good advice about the particular examples that would help her students better understand the parabola. She might even belong to a discussion group of secondary mathematics teachers whom she met at university.

The teacher could enhance her lesson with a little historical anecdote on Diocles' use of the parabola for burning mirrors – something she could easily print off from the MacTutor History of Mathematics site at the University of St Andrews (http://www-groups.dcs.st-and.ac.uk/~history/) – or even assign it for homework reading. Her students could then appreciate the long, rich history of their classroom mathematics. With a little net-searching, she could show her students pictures of parabolas used in architecture or videos of paths traced out by water fountains – thus using the internet as a 'wired' blackboard. The students could then see how parabolas are used and are related to phenomena in the physical world.

This teacher could ask her students to go on-line and carry out some of their own research on parabolas, after which they could even create a web page that illustrates what they now know about parabolas. And in the course of searching for information on the web, the students might come across third- and fourth-degree equations. This might be the perfect take-off point for independent, student-motivated investigations. Or perhaps she could ask her students to e-mail a mathematician to ask a few questions she herself might not know the answer to: for instance, what does a parabola 'look like' in four dimensions?

Using the web to share and find mathematics

The possibilities described above reveal two features of the web that have been central to its growing success both inside and outside the classroom. First, it functions as an open repository, similar to a library or an encyclopaedia, one with an ever-increasing and ever-changing amount of information. On the web, however, teachers and students can contribute information instead of only 'borrowing' it or looking something up. Second, the web allows for communication in both real-time and elapsed-time modes through on-line discussions, e-mail and 'chats'.

These two features of the internet – serving as both reference and communication tool – offer several possibilities to the mathematics teaching community. Klotz (1997) outlines some salient ones (and I have added exemplary instances of each), suggesting that the web can:

- provide a repository and conveyer of instructional resources and course materials for face-to-face and distance mathematics education (e.g. NRICH: http://nrich.maths.org);
- allow mathematicians, teachers and students to discuss mathematical ideas and publish them, formally or informally, in text and hypermedia (e.g. Plus Magazine: http://plus.maths.org);
- foster the formation of new mathematical communities (e.g. the Math Forum: http://www.mathforum.com);
- house numerical data that can be located, collected and shared (e.g. the Data and Store Library: http://lib.stat.cmu.edu/DASL/DataArchive. html);
- feature mathematical software that can be published, purchased and demonstrated (e.g. MathsNet: http://www.mathsnet.net);
- virtually host professional organizations and programmes for curricular reform (for example, as discussed in Chapter 11, Motivate: http://www.motivate.maths.org).

Although the web offers an enormous amount of educational resources, data and software – more than any library and available at any time of the day or night – relevant ones are buried amid the vast, unorganized range of sites available. How is someone to find them? Many search engines allow internet-savvy surfers to locate resources using keyword searches. By typing "high school mathematics" into Google's search engine (http://www.google.com), approximately 65,000 'hits' show up, but adding "linear functions" narrows it down to less than 10,000, while adding "domain and range" as well further reduces it to a far more manageable number – around 1,000 (at the time of writing).

This type of searching may work well when one is looking for specific information about, say, the colours of the Canadian flag, but many teachers and students need access to the type of information that is customized for pedagogical use. Fortunately, several reference sites now exist that are devoted to gathering, categorizing, reviewing and indexing mathematics education materials, thus offering teachers and students increased accessibility and reliability. Many such sites have succumbed to the pressure of constant updating (adding new and removing extinct sites): a notable exception is the US-based Math Forum (http://www.mathforum.org). In fact, a closer look at the services offered by the Math Forum will illustrate the varied ways in which web-based technologies can address aspects of both the professional needs of teachers and the learning needs of students.

More than a library: the Math Forum

Since its inception in 1994, the Math Forum (see Figure 12.1) has been establishing itself as the premier site for the mathematics education

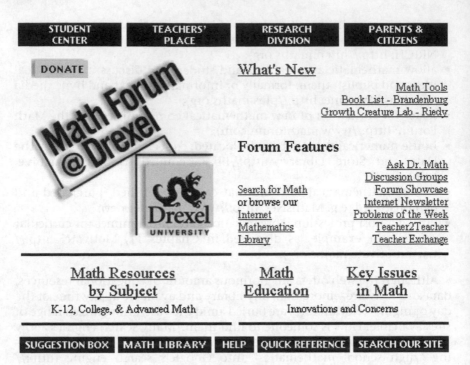

Figure 12.1   The Math Forum website.

community in North America (effectively combining the services of the UK-based NRICH (http://nrich.maths.org) and Motivate (http://www.motivate.maths.org) sites). It provides both an up-to-date, comprehensive reference service through its *Internet Library* and several communication tools such as discussion groups (including mathematical topics such as geometry, as well as educational topics such as the use of technology itself).

Early on, the Math Forum recognized that most teachers did not have the knowledge or support available to take advantage of these services. Consequently, it tried to support professional development initiatives which would allow teachers to participate in an interactive mathematical community. In 1998, it launched the Teacher2Teacher program (T2T), with the goal of generating more focused conversations on the internet by providing a peer-mentored, question-and-answer service, answering questions from teachers and parents about mathematics teaching and learning. T2T also features discussion areas that range from ideas on using software for teaching algebra to strategies for teaching how to factor trinomials, from how to help gifted students to factors that affect girls' success in mathematics.

As teachers increase their familiarity with the web and thus their ability to find sites and answers on their own, sites such as T2T might no longer be needed. However, researchers interested in using the web for systematic professional development argue that, in order for teachers to learn new skills and adopt new approaches, they need to engage in more collaborative, real-time activities (Schlager and Schank, 1997). Projects such as Tapped In (http://www.tappedin.org) have used emerging internet technologies to provide teachers with conference-centre-style facilities where they can create and share documents, 'attend' lectures and communicate in real time.

Even though Tapped In is seeded by means of face-to-face workshops or summer institutes, it still has trouble reaching the critical mass of participating users needed to sustain a virtual community. This is a recurrent theme in web-based professional development projects. Although the opportunities are exciting, successful, scalable and sustainable, on-line teacher professional development will require changes on other social and political fronts: in particular, the time and effort teachers spend will have to be valued, supported and rewarded by colleagues and administrators.

The services mentioned above mostly serve teachers: however, the Math Forum also offers model interactive projects geared specifically to students. Ask Dr. Math is one such project; this archived, 'ask-the-expert' service for students answers over 2000 questions per month. Students can submit questions through web forms and answers are e-mailed to the submitter, as well as posted to the website. Student questions are answered in an in-depth, pedagogically sound way, and the most popular questions are given more extensive and coherent treatment through the medium of frequently asked questions (FAQs).

In this case, the web not only is useful in facilitating the communication, both in terms of access and speed, between student and expert, but also allows the interaction to be made available to other students, in a keyword-searchable way. As with NRICH's Ask a Mathematician service (see http://nrich.maths.org/discus/messages/board-topics.html), Ask Dr. Math is essentially building a reference library tailored to the needs of students, thus providing the kind of guidance and level of explanation that few textbooks can match. It also provides enrichment opportunities, as curious students ready to move beyond classroom material can, and do, ask questions about areas of mathematics not often taught in school, such as fractals and topology.

The Math Forum also offers problems of the week (PoWs), which are moderated by an extensive network of volunteer teachers. A similar service is provided by NRICH, which offers monthly problems that span the primary and secondary levels – as well as the ones directed to an open-ended continuum – and is maintained by the School of Education at the University of Cambridge. The Math Forum's PoWs are designed to provide opportunities for teachers and students to engage in working on the type of problem-solving tasks that are currently emphasized in many curricula and examinations. Six categories of problems are customized for a variety of ages, as well as subject areas, including calculus, geometry and algebra.

Students around the world can submit answers to any problem (all of which receive an individual response from the Math Forum team and an invitation to resubmit if errors are made or confusions are apparent), the best of which are posted to the website each week. This service is one of the Math Forum's most active, widely used by the 'home-schooling' community, but also by teachers who seek to foster student skill at solving non-routine problems and developing fluent mathematical communication. The communication component is significant, since students must explain their answers, using words, to strangers; success at this involves both becoming adept at reasoning and deploying a certain fluency with mathematical terms. The PoWs may also provide a greater incentive for students to explain themselves clearly to a stranger, something they often find tedious and 'unreal' to do for their own teacher.

As is the case with Ask Dr. Math, mathematical communication in response to the PoWs can be hindered by the difficulty involved in writing and displaying mathematical notation on the web. For example, text symbols for exponentiation $(2 \wedge 5)$ must be used instead of the customary mathematical display 2^5. This restriction begins to cause more problems in the upper secondary years, when students need to write more complicated, fractional expressions, as well as work with integrals or geometrical objects such as rays and circles. Although the technology exists to support the web-based display of mathematics (e.g. WebEQ/MathML: http://www.w3.org/Math/), it has yet to become directly incorporated into web browsers.

With the exception of the PoWs, the services of the Math Forum are not explicitly geared toward helping students develop mathematical competence. So, while the Math Forum services are successful in fostering educational interactions, both for teachers and for students, they do not provide environments in which students can *do* mathematics directly – namely solve problems, explore ideas and manipulate representations.

The web: a network?

When mathematical problem solving requires the coordinated efforts of many users, the web can act as a network, facilitating collaborative work. For example, the Great Internet Mersenne Prime Search (GIMPS) co-ordinates the unused number-crunching power of personal computers around the world to search for Mersenne primes (GIMPS has found seven new ones at the time of writing, and there are only 41 such primes known – see http://www.mersenne.org/prime.htm). This use of the web, as a kind of networking tool which allows multiple, geographically dispersed individuals to contribute data needed to achieve a goal that no single person (or computer) could achieve in a timely way, takes advantage of one of its most unique features.

A typical classroom task that may benefit from web-based collaboration involves gathering data. For example, English and Cudmore (2000) describe a project in which students from several different countries engaged in collaborative statistical inquiry. These students, now part of an enlarged classroom, used web pages that automatically accepted, processed and distributed data using interactive forms. Using the forms, students could pose, share and criticize questions and 'publish' their contributions on a web page.

Instead of using classroom-generated data, the students were able to gather an international data set that revealed many cultural differences, provoking more interest, questioning and analysis than their own classroom data would have done. By working with large amounts of messy, 'real' data – data which are difficult to gather within the confines of a single, frequently homogeneous classroom – the students became familiar with some of the basic problems and tools of data analysis. The researchers also report a high level of engagement and interest among the students who took part.

While the web seems well suited to facilitating communication and exchange in data analysis, it is reasonable to wonder whether subjects such as geometry and algebra could benefit from the same kind of classroom enlargement. At first glance, it might seem improbable. However, the Noon Observation Project exemplifies another project that productively exploits the web's networking facility in the context of geometry. This annual event invites students from around the world to estimate the circumference of the earth using Eratosthenes' geometric method, which requires measurements from different geographic locations (see http://www.ed.uiuc.edu/noon-project/). Students at each location measure the length of a shadow cast at precisely high noon local time by a metre rule and submit their measurements via interactive, web-based forms to other participants in the project.

Nevertheless, while this kind of project reaches beyond statistics to include applications of geometry, algebra and trigonometry, it remains quite unique and relatively obscure. For the time being, few tasks in school mathematics require such collaborative work; in fact, few would be improved by using the web. In order to take advantage of the web's networking facility, teachers will either have to create new applications of school mathematics or place more emphasis on collaborative problem-solving.

The web: a laboratory?

In addition to being a reference system, a communication tool and a network, the web also acts as a platform for running interactive programs where students can observe mathematical simulations, explore relationships and manipulate objects. Most of the web-based programs of interest to mathematics education are called *applets*, written in the Java programming language. In theory, applets can do many of the things that desk-top software can and they are as free and accessible as most other internet resources. In addition, applets can be seamlessly combined with other resources: for example, a web page with a Pythagorean theorem applet (Figure 12.2) could be linked to a site with historical information about Pythagoras. Finally, since applets are usually small, restricted computer programs, they are easy to learn how to use, particularly when compared with more multi-purpose desk-top software.

Since anyone can create and 'publish' applets, there is a wide variety in

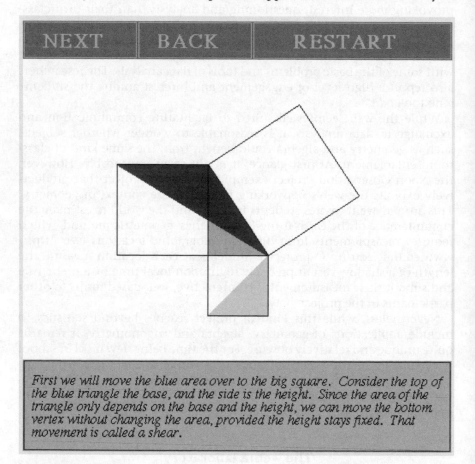

NEXT   BACK   RESTART

First we will move the blue area over to the big square. Consider the top of the blue triangle the base, and the side is the height. Since the area of the triangle only depends on the base and the height, we can move the bottom vertex without changing the area, provided the height stays fixed. That movement is called a shear.

Figure 12.2 Mid-way through an animated proof of the Pythagorean theorem (see http://www.sunsite.ubc.ca/LivingMathematics/V001N01/UBCExamples/ Pythagoras/pythagoras.html).

terms of pedagogical purposes and quality. Teachers new to the internet are frequently excited to discover 'drill-and-practice' applets, which can test student understanding through multiple-choice questions and instant feedback, and 'demonstration' applets, which can visually illustrate the logic of a theorem. (See Mawata's suite of applets at http://www.utc.edu/~cpmawata/instructor/tsukuba1.htm.) However, these kinds of applets are not as popular, nor as pedagogically promising, as the growing number of 'interactive' applets, which frequently involve geometry or probability.

A subset of such applets are what I call *weakly* interactive, in that users are limited to 'click and drag' actions (for extensive collections, see http://www.mste.uiuc.edu/java/ and http://www.ies.co.jp/math/java/). A typical, probability-oriented applet allows students to vary the number of trials in a Monty Hall simulation.[1] This requires the student to select or input a number and then click a button (http://www.mste.uiuc.edu/reese/monty/MontyGame5.html), thus helping students understand the law of large numbers. A typical statistics-oriented applet allows students to vary parameters of a distribution: for example, the Histogram applet (http://www.stat.sc.edu/~west/javahtml/Histogram.html) allows students to vary the bin width of a histogram, showing the effect of bin-width size on the shape of the histogram. Even weakly interactive applets can offer representations that help students grapple with difficult concepts such as slope (http://www.jamesbrennan.org/algebra/graph_applet.html) and the behaviour of three-dimensional geometrical objects (http://www.mathsnet.net/geometry/solid/icosahedron.html), as shown in Figure 12.3.

Roschelle and Pea (1999) have criticized those applets such as *weakly* interactive ones as being mathematical representations that can only be passively watched. They prefer instead ones that can be 'actively utilized by learners (and teachers) in formulating, expressing, and critiquing ideas' (p. 24). These might be called *strongly* interactive applets, as they offer more possibilities for student mathematical expression, allowing students to create, manipulate and change mathematical objects on the screen.

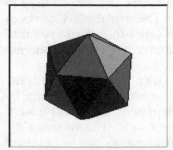

How many faces, vertices and edges has an icosahedron got?

faces:
vertices:
edges:
Check

Figure 12.3 *JavaView* allows this icosahedron to be 'turned' around.

Such applets could exploit many of the cognitive benefits attributed to other well-designed mathematics education software, since they would allow students to act directly on mathematical objects and relations (see Balacheff and Kaput, 1996). Few of these types of applets currently exist, in part because of the technical limitations of Java. Though Java is cross-platform in theory, in practice it is very difficult to create applets that run effectively and consistently on the matrix of different browsers and platforms. In addition, even the small applets available today are too long for classroom downloading, while stronger interactivity requires bulkier applets and continuous connection.

In addition to only being *weakly* interactive, many applets suffer from a problem of lack of context. Such applets can suffer the same fate as many other web-based learning resources, because they are not coupled to the curricula and textbooks used by most teachers (see Chapter 14 for more on this). There are, however, some notable exceptions to this. The Shodor Educational Foundation's Project Interactivate (http://www.shodor.org/interactivate/) embeds applets in lessons that are directly linked with the US National Council of Teachers of Mathematics' *Principles and Standards for School Mathematics* (NCTM, 2000; http://standards.nctm.org). Many of these applets are *strongly* interactive; see, for example, the transformation applet at http://www.shodor.org/interactivate/activities/transform2/index.html, which allows students to create polygons and then translate, reflect or rotate them. The site provides teacher support in the form of curriculum connections and strategies for classroom use. Extensive instructions are also available, as well as explanations of the 'big ideas' drawn on in the applet. More than any other initiative, Project Inter-activate has made a strong, exemplary commitment to attractive and easy-to-use applet design.

The NCTM has also launched the *Illuminations* website (http://illuminations.nctm.org), which offers 'math-lets' that are supported by ready-to-use lessons also linked to the US national standards and which are strongly interactive. For example, the Spreadsheet and Graphing Tool (http://illuminations.nctm.org/mathlets/grapher/index.html) provides spreadsheet functionality with graphing capabilities and can be used to investigate rational and exponential functions. These 'math-lets' can even be downloaded onto a computer network, in order to increase speed of access and to decrease reliance on schools' frequently tenuous internet connections.

As with well-designed desk-top mathematics education software, *strongly* interactive applets can contribute to mathematics learning by providing students with linked, interactive representations and instant feedback. They can also offer teachers windows onto student meaning-making, since students' decision and thought processes can be observed through their interactions with the computer.

Finally, I would like to mention two other aspects of currently available web-based applets that are relevant to student learning. The first relates to visualization and the second concerns the structure of student activity.

The Colour Calculator applet (http://hydra.educ.queensu.ca/maths/) illustrates the way in which visualization can support student inquiry as well as concept development. It is a regular, web-based calculator that provides numerical results, but one that also offers the decimal digits of its results in a colour-coded table. Each digit of the result corresponds to one of ten distinctly coloured squares in the table. The calculator operates at a maximum precision of 100 decimal digits and, thus, each result is simultaneously represented by a decimal string as well as a table of coloured squares, as shown in Figure 12.4. It is possible to manipulate the way these coloured squares are displayed, by changing the width of the table from, say, ten digits to six. A table width of six would nicely highlight the repeating pattern of digits found in the decimal expansion of 1/7.

Thus, of particular interest in the Colour Calculator are the pattern-rich rational numbers because they can be seen and understood as patterns of *colour*. This visual representation of number calls attention to and facilitates the perception of important classes of real numbers – terminating, periodic, eventually periodic and non-periodic decimals – and some of their properties. Moreover, the calculator operations (addition, subtraction, multiplication, division and square root), as well as the changeable width of the table, enable direct exploratory action on the colour patterns

Width of table: 10 ⇕

Legend (for numbers after the decimal point):

Equation: 1/7

Results: .142857142857142857142857142857142857142857142857142857142857142857142857142857142857142857142857142857857

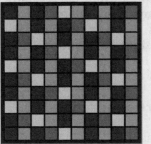

Figure 12.4 The output of 1/7 from the Colour Calculator.

themselves. (For example, how can you create a checkerboard pattern? How can you create an entirely red colour table?) Therefore, through a generative visualization, the Colour Calculator provides students with an alternate means of understanding rational numbers, as well as an *expressive* problem-posing and problem-solving context (Sinclair, 2001).

Much student activity is structured through the use of worksheets, black-line masters or other types of teacher-provided tasks. Just as the reader turns each page of the book to get to continue reading, students regularly follow instructions step by step. This kind of structure makes it more difficult for students to experience some personal agency in the process of inquiry. The stages of exploration and problem-posing are frequently predetermined, at least in the eyes of the student. Could the hyperlink feature of the web provide some alternatives to this linear trajectory?

The eight pages of *Meeting Lulu* (a Javascript module focused on coordinate geometry and algebra: http://hydra.educ.queensu.ca/maths/) can be navigated by clicking on hyperlinks at the bottom of each page. There is a choice of two or three links and each link is in the form of a 'What if?' question which leads the student to a page with appropriate tools for exploring that question. The student is thus, to some extent, structuring her own activity by following the questions that interest her. The hyperlinks are designed so that there are a finite set of paths that can be followed, with each providing enough scaffolding to prepare the student for the final page. Choice is a major motivating factor of mathematical inquiry (Sinclair, 2004); perhaps, then, such hyperlinked task structures may increase student motivation. Moreover, students may learn to adopt the 'What if?' strategy in their own mathematical explorations.

Even in the most strongly interactive applets, assessment and evaluation remain awkward, often non-integrated components of student activity. Few applets allow students to take notes and record their work, activities that help both students and the teacher to keep track of their classroom experiences. Sometimes, the typically cramped quarters of the computer laboratory even make it difficult for students to write things down on a piece of paper. And while most desk-top software at least allows students to save and print what they have created for future reference or for assessment purposes, no web-based applets currently do. Of course, students can take notes, or describe their work using a word-processor, but this often does not capture their rich, on-screen interaction.

Final comments and some future directions

Mathematics educators and teachers should perhaps devote their efforts to capitalizing on the more distinct or even unique features of the web, as mathematicians have done, for example, with Sloane's site (http://

www.research.att.com/~njas/sequences/). This site stores almost 85,000 integer sequences, which are contributed and annotated by mathematicians around the world. While working on a particular problem, a mathematician might encounter an unfamiliar sequence of integers, which, by using a simple on-line search, may be matched to a sequence already identified and described in the constantly updated data base.

As with the data analysis and the Noon Observation projects described above, Sloane's data base takes advantage of the web's capacity to store and give access to large amounts of data for geographically dispersed individuals in a dynamic way: that is, in a constantly evolving and growing way. Are there similar opportunities for mathematics teachers? Perhaps teachers could design problems for students that would lead to unfamiliar sequences and thus to using the web as research mathematicians do. (For example, how many complete squares appear in successive iterations of the dragon fractal? See http://ejad.best.vwh.net/java/fractals/jurasic. shtml. On how to create a dragon fractal, see also http://www.logosurvey. co.uk/interact/dragoncurve.php.)

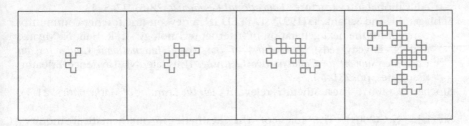

Figure 12.5   The fourth, fifth, sixth and seventh iterations of the dragon fractal.

Despite the disadvantages and challenges outlined above, the web offers unparalleled opportunities to the mathematics teacher. Resources of all kind – from lesson plans to problems of the week, from teaching strategies to mathematics mentors – can help teachers continuously improve mathematics learning in their classrooms. Indeed, the networking and reference features of the web in particular will provide long-term, affordable services both to teachers and to students, who will become increasingly efficient at navigating and using the web.

Note

1. Monty Hall was the (Canadian) host of an NBC television show *Let's Make a Deal* that first aired on 30 December 1963 (for more on the show, see http:// www.letsmakeadeal.com). Contestants were faced with three doors, only one of which had a great prize behind it. After having chosen a door, Monty Hall would open a non-prize door and ask the contestant if he/she wanted to 'switch'. Most

people assume that whether one switches or not does not matter. But, actually, it is better to switch: if you do, you win two-thirds of the time.

References

Balacheff, N. and Kaput, J. (1996) 'Computer-based learning environments in mathematics', in A. Bishop, M. A. Clements, C. Keitel, J. Kilpatrick and C. Laborde (eds), *International Handbook of Mathematics Education*. Dordrecht, Kluwer Academic Publishers, **1**, pp. 469–501.

English, L. D. and Cudmore, D. H. (2000) 'Using extranets in fostering international communities of mathematical inquiry', in F. R. Curcio and M. Burke (eds), *Learning Mathematics for a New Century: NCTM Yearbook*. Reston, VA: National Council of Teachers of Mathematics.

Klotz, G. (1997) 'Mathematics and the world-wide web'. (http://forum.swarthmore.edu/articles/epadel.)

National Council of Teachers of Mathematics (2000) *Principles and Standards for School Mathematics*. Reston, VA: NCTM.

Roschelle, J. and Pea, R. (1999) 'Trajectories from today's www to a powerful educational infrastructure'. *Educational Researcher*, **28**(5), 22–5, 43.

Schlager, M. and Schank, P. (1997) 'TAPPED IN: a new on-line teacher community concept for the next generation of internet technology', in R. Hall, N. Miyake and N. Enyedy (eds), *Proceedings of the Second International Conference on Computer Support for Collaborative Learning*. Hillsdale, NJ: Lawrence Erlbaum Associates, pp. 231–40.

Sinclair, N. (2001) 'The aesthetic *is* relevant'. *For the Learning of Mathematics*, **21**(1), 25–3.

Sinclair, N. (2004) 'The roles of the aesthetic in mathematical inquiry'. *Mathematical Thinking and Learning*, **6**(3), 261–84.

Summary and vision

13

MEDIATING MATHEMATICAL THINKING WITH E-SCREENS

John Mason

In what ways is mathematical thinking altered, enhanced or impeded by the availability of electronic calculators and computers? What opportunities and constraints are offered by ICT and what might learners need to become attuned to, in order to exploit those opportunities effectively?

As with the introduction of other media (such as film or television) into education in the past, there are forces urging everything towards a mechanical rather than creative response. They also point us towards simplicity rather than complexity and towards trying to make things easy for learners rather than stimulating them to use their own powers to overcome challenges. I am concerned that such forces are likely to ensure that the enormous pedagogic potential of ICT for enhancing the teaching and learning of school mathematics is far from actualized.

Isaac Asimov is widely quoted as commenting about prediction that 'The important thing to forecast is not the automobile, but the parking problem; not the television, but the soap opera; not the arms race, but the bomb'. In the case of electronic screens (e-screens), the important forecast is not the pedagogic potential of e-screens but the mental pollution of increasingly fragmentary images being thrust upon us. It is not the enhancement of our mental capabilities so much as the effect on our powers of concentration of being exposed to rapidly changing images, knowing that at the click of a button a new screen can be activated.

In this chapter, I try to demonstrate ways in which e-screens can be used powerfully, while at the same time recognizing their inherent limitations. In passing, however, let me note it is somewhat ironic that my 'demonstration' has to be confined to the static constraints of text.

Thinking screens

Television screens, calculator screens, computer screens, overhead projector screens and touch-sensitive screens are just a few of the ways in which electronics has enabled us to augment the most powerful 'screen' of all – our mental imagery. With cave paintings and sand drawings, with slate, papyrus, paper and now e-screens, various media have been employed to store and present images throughout human history. All can be used to establish a partial image, one which helps stabilize mental imagery, providing a background upon which mental images can be imposed.

As with writing, diagrams and pictures afford an opportunity to go back to review and analyse what was said. Just as writing enhances the possibilities of complex manipulations of strings of symbols by providing a record of previous and current thinking, diagrams and pictures provide similar possibilities. Furthermore, whereas text and symbols are processed linearly, diagrams and pictures exploit human powers to process simultaneously in several dimensions, to detect change and to discern the nature and structure of both necessary and contingent relationships.

Before considering in more detail how e-screens can assist and detract from the teaching and learning of mathematics, it is worth reminding yourself about the powers of your mental screen.

Mental imagery

Imagine a circle. Let it grow and shrink in size, let it slide around on a mental plane. Become aware of the power you have in altering it. Does it seem to you like a single object moving around? Can you change this to experience different circles at different times, as if the plane were alive with them, with different ones being lit up either in some regular sequence or simply randomly?

One changing individual and a family of distinct objects are dual aspects of images which parallel the dual aspect of symbolic expressions as both calculation instructions (take your number, double it and add three: $2x + 3$) and as the answer to that calculation (but stated in general). Geometric objects seen as moving give rise to different kinds of mathematical structures from collections of those objects with different specific individuals seen in turn: one leads to *transformations* of an object, the other to *families* of objects.

Now bring a straight-line segment into your circle picture, fix its position and bring your circle so that it just touches the line segment at a single point (so, unless it is at either end, it is tangential to the line segment). Allow the circle to move in any way as before, but now always just touching the line segment somewhere on that segment and somewhere on the circle. For example, the circle can rotate about its centre.

The circle started with complete freedom, but now its freedom has been limited slightly. You can try to describe the freedom that remains by asking where the centre of the circle can get to in the plane. You will discover that it can get anywhere in the plane as long as you permit circles of zero radius.

Now bring in a second line segment, and bring your circle into tangency (or end-touching) with the second segment as well.

Is that always possible? Asking whether it is always possible (what is allowed to change, what has to remain invariant?) invites a switch of attention from moving the circle to moving one of the segments, trying to eliminate the possibility of a circle touching both. The additional constraint leads to a problem of characterizing where the centre of the circle can now get to in the plane. However, any general description will probably depend upon the relative positions of the two line segments.

On an interactive screen, you may be able to determine how various parameters are to change (e.g. through dragging), but still the choices unfold in time, leading to a sequence of frames which can be replayed as a film. On your mental screen, you can imagine in a linear, cinematic mode, but you can do more. Mentally, you can develop the power to experience a multitude of virtual films all at once, as if two or more parameters varied simultaneously. You can superimpose and adjust several factors at once because you do not have to particularize them to actual numbers and relationships the way you do on e-screens. You can (perhaps after some initial work) imagine the plot of a function with a parameter (e.g. a quadratic of the form $f(x) = ax^2 + 2x - a^2$, *without* having to calculate specific values for a); an e-screen cannot do this.

Mental imagery provides a world in which objects can be more complex than can be presented physically (e.g. non-Euclidean configurations) and in which actions are not confined by time or by physical limitations (e.g. objects can move through each other).

External screens as mediators

Images thrown up on external screens immediately affect what is on your mental screen. It is possible to have multiple images, as well as to think about other things while watching a screen, but the more dynamic and colourful the external images, the harder it can become to handle everything at once. External images can be constructed to try to be the centre and focus of viewer attention, but they can also be used to mediate between the viewer and the mathematics.

Diagrams as posters

When a new picture is put up, it catches the eye and attracts attention. As seeing it becomes part of habit, it almost disappears, until some slight change sets up a disturbance with the habituated 'wallpaper', whereby attention is attracted again.

Diagrams in texts and on posters are apparently static objects and are often treated as wallpaper by learners. Even when they do look at them, it is *only* looking 'at' and not looking 'through'. By pausing, by 'saying what you see' as precisely yet succinctly, as briefly but vividly, as you can, you can facilitate negotiating both what is being stressed by different observers and also the use of language by which to direct the attention of others to what you are stressing. Through this type of task, you can come to learn to control your own attention, to make choices and to detect pattern and structure in diagrams. But to do this you have to slow the pace of exposure to fresh stimuli.

The development of dynamic geometry packages for e-screens (as discussed in Chapter 5) has brought attention to the fact that even an ordinary diagram has implicit structure. In order to get the most out of any diagram, you need to know what is permitted to change and what must remain invariant. You need to work *on* the diagram and not just look *at* it. For example, in Figure 13.1 certain lengths are marked as being equal and some are shown as being parallel. Do you start with a parallelogram and generate a quadrilateral or start with a quadrilateral and generate the parallelogram? What is allowed to change (and in what way) and yet still have the length equalities and parallelisms remain? In fact, the central quadrilateral will always be a parallelogram, as long as its vertices are the mid-points of the edges of a quadrilateral. But can that quadrilateral be non-convex? Can it cross itself? Could mid-points be changed to some other ratio?

Furthermore, in order to draw a diagram yourself (and ones you draw yourself are often much more meaningful than ones drawn by others for

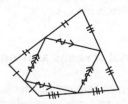

Figure 13.1 Equal or parallel lines.

precisely the reasons being elaborated here), you need to know what to choose 'freely' and what has to be constrained. For example, having drawn 'any' triangle, the centre of the inscribed circle can be found by bisecting the internal angles of the triangle (two will do, because all three meet at the centre) and then 'dropping' a perpendicular to one edge to find the radius (see Figure 13.2).

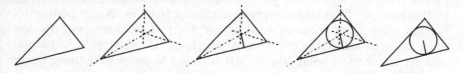

Figure 13.2   Finding the inscribed circle.

All of this is implicit in the fourth diagram of the sequence in Figure 13.2, essential to appreciating the final diagram. Yet much of this is undeclared in the final diagram. You have to know *how* to read it, how to sequence the construction lines. Furthermore, the theorem that asserts the angle bisectors always meet at the centre of the inscribed circle is a justification for the 'sense' that you can alter the triangle in any way you like and still the construction must work. This, in turn, is based on the sense that allowing a circle to be tangent to just two of the edges of the triangle (while tracking its centre) leads to the angle bisectors and their co-incidence at the centre of the inscribed circle. But the fourth diagram can also be seen as starting from a circle and drawing tangents to it, providing an example of converting a 'doing' into an 'undoing'. A constructed sequence of images can be reversed – the film can be run backwards in time.

Working on 'posters' (diagrams) by inviting students to 'say what you see', to ask themselves 'what is the same and what different?', 'how could you build up a construction of such a diagram?' or 'what can change and still preserve specified relationships?' can develop skill, develop a way of working on a diagram and enhance the propensity of students to use these mental resources in the face of more seductive, animated and computationally powerful e-screens.

Animation

Before dynamic geometry software was available, mathematical films were used to animate diagrams (see, for example, Tahta, 1981; Jaworski, 1989). Events happen on an external screen: there is motion, there is change. This change might occur at an apparently alarming rate, just as music videos flash past now. But by reviewing the film mentally, first individually and then collectively, it is often possible to slow the encounter down to a pedagogically effective pace, by reconstructing all or most of a film.

Once a verbal description has been negotiated, it is then (and only then) possible to try to explain *why* certain things happen, why certain things *must* happen as a consequence of the configurations and motions and so reach a geometric theorem or theorems (Love, 1988). It is the desire to make sense of what has been seen on the screen that drives this process. During work on the film, both aspects of objects that I discussed earlier play a part: a single object seen as moving and varied objects seen as instantaneously highlighted representatives of families. Watching mathematical animations without working on them to reconstruct and make sense of them is about as effective as 'watching' TV advertisements while making tea: at most what you are left with is a sense of something being possible, but it usually soon slips from memory.

Dave Hewitt (1991) has proposed reversing the movement from diagram to film, starting with not one but two diagrams. The task involves trying to think of all the different diagrams one could put in between them, so as to make a sequence of frames from a coherent film.

For example, look at Figure 13.3. Seen as two frames from a film, the two triangles could have a variety of different intermediate frames, including the two examples shown in Figure 13.4, as well as the one shown in Figure 13.5, where two intermediate frames have been used in the third interpolation.

Figure 13.3   Two frames from a film.

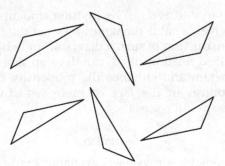

Figure 13.4   Two different examples using one intermediate frame.

Figure 13.5   Two intermediate frames.

Notice the mental imagery work that you need to do in order to make sense of these interpolations: that is, to see them *as* interpolations. Notice, too, how three triangles constrain possibilities more than two. The interpolated triangle in both instances in Figure 13.4 is actually a rotated version of the same triangle, even though it does not immediately seem to be the same size. Other people's interpolated frames have to be worked on much as the original presented frames did, whereas your own interpolation instances a dynamic movement of which you alone, perhaps, are aware.

When watching an animation, it is possible simply to watch images as they have an impact on your eyes. But it is also possible to anticipate, to predict. Clever animations provoke conjecturing in the viewer, whereas many erstwhile 'educational' films and animations try to make the concept development seem unproblematic and inevitable.

Anticipation

Our peripheral vision is particularly good at detecting motion, alerting us to change. And like all of our sensations, attention is attracted by change, by disturbance of routine and the status quo. We discover we have an expectation as a result of noticing and monitoring change.

Paulo Boero (2001) has pointed to the importance of anticipation when carrying out symbol manipulations such as solving equations. Each manipulation is intended to achieve some sort of simplification (or, if working in reverse, some complication). In addition, the choice and execution of some specific action or operation is monitored in relation to meeting that expectation or not. When an expectation is not met, an inner monitor can awaken and ask, 'Why are you doing this?' (Schoenfeld, 1985; Mason *et al.*, 1982). If the pace of encounter is too great for dissonance to come to the surface, and if you know that simply by continuing to watch 'all will be revealed', the TV drama (like film and theatre) and the educational animation both lose their force.

The power to imagine lies at the heart of expectation and planning, for anticipating what is going to happen is part of making sense of something. When surprise is encountered, imagination mobilizes further powers to explain or make sense of what has just happened. So animations need to be worked on, just as diagrams need to be worked on. The power to imagine needs to be mobilized if learners are to gain any pedagogic advantage from watching animations. Descriptions of ways to use both mental imagery and animations to pedagogic advantage in mathematics can be found in Jaworski (1989) and Pimm (1993).

Direct manipulation

Screen manipulation opens up the possibility of going beyond watching things move to being able to grab and move them yourself. The kinaesthetic can thus be experienced directly rather than vicariously through visualization. But as with any medium of expression, there is no guarantee that what a learner does will contribute to, or even provide evidence of, mathematical thinking.

Learners first meeting screen-manipulable objects are quite likely to be taken with what they can do rather than with *mathematical* themes such as 'invariance amidst change' or 'freedom and constraint'. Once they have become aware of freedoms and constraints, they are in a position to reflect on what it is that is constraining the freedom of objects in a way which is quite different from the freedoms and constraints of an arcade game. This is an example of how what learners are attuned to can strongly influence what opportunities can arise.

E-screens go well beyond offering static and dynamic images and user control. They make it possible to carry out manipulation of symbols and images, without you having to go through the details yourself. For example, using the statistical package *Fathom* (which was also discussed in Chapter 6), you can 'grab' a table of values (connecting inputs to outputs) and 'drop' it onto a coordinate grid. The software will then plot the graph. Grab one axis and move it to the other one and the axes interchange. This, together with dynamic geometry, is just the beginning of what will undoubtedly become a much more sophisticated drag-and-drop screen mathematics. Imagine dragging a triangle which has some lengths and angles marked, possibly with letters rather than numbers, and dropping it into a screen box which 'solves' the diagram, perhaps finding all lengths and angles, areas, perimeters, and so on, as required. Forces diagrams could similarly be resolved to produce the equations, which could then be dropped into a 'solve' box.

Conversely, imagine constructing a dynamic geometric image and gaining access to the equations that define the objects. You might then be able to manipulate them algebraically, perhaps in particular, perhaps even at different levels of generality. In other words, users are freed to operate at a far higher conceptual level, reverting to a more technical level if, and when, it seems desirable. There is already software such as *Interactive Physics* (Fable, 2004) which offers a physics environment analogous to dynamic geometry, enabling the user to construct mechanical situations with ropes and rods, with elastics and pulleys, and then to 'run' the system in real time to see what happens.

Care is needed, however. Each increase in software sophistication leads to greater complexity in menus and other choices. Most commonly used applications, including spreadsheets and sophisticated new models of graphical calculator, as well as software for word processing and making presentations, have many features that most people never use – and may not even be aware of. The presence of choices they never use can become an obstruction.

Image 'processing'

Images can be processed *physically*, by developing films: that is, by creating a dynamically changing image which thereby affords access to what is not changing (or not changing rapidly), and what is permitted to change for those attuned to 'reading between the images'.

Images can be processed *mentally*, by acting upon what is summoned onto your mental screen and stabilized by static and dynamic images on a physical screen. It is necessary to be flexible when looking at algebraic symbols to see through them to the generality they signify. It is just as necessary to be flexible with images, looking *at* them as single objects and *through* them to the implied generality (what can change and still preserve the essential relationships and properties).

Images can be processed *mathematically*, by looking for relationships, for properties and by drawing necessary conclusions. But we are some way away from a similar sophistication in image processing enhanced by machines. Symbol manipulation becomes immensely powerful when a collection of objects (often themselves symbols) are denoted by a single letter and then manipulated as such. This activity invokes the dual perception of symbol as condensed operation and as the result of carrying out that operation.

Something similar might be possible for images: we can process images the way we process text, by selecting bits and moving them about, as well as by applying transformations such as reflections, rotations, scaling, etc. This much is available in any drawing package. But we cannot yet sort diagrams, or act upon them according to properties they have, the way we can with text using 'search' and 'replace' features. But then ordinary word-processing packages themselves do not afford access to searching, sorting and replacing on the basis complex 'if . . . then . . .' clauses. Perhaps soon?

What e-screens can and cannot do

E-screens are excellent for presenting phenomena, both dynamic and static, which may stimulate a desire to make sense of and explain them. Those explanations may then lead the explainer to encounter import-ant mathematical objects, topics, links between topics, themes and aspects of mathematical thinking, as well as to highlight personal propensities leading to greater self-knowledge. Thus, e-screens can be used to provide opportunities not just to motivate thinking but to initiate it.

However, e-screens cannot force learning, nor can they teach. They cannot even convey knowledge. But then neither can teachers. All we can do is afford access to phenomena within appropriate constraints and, for those suitably attuned, attract their attention, trigger surprise and, thus, initiate mathematical thinking.

E-screens *can* provide a stable image, so that mental imagination can stress some features in the process of looking through the particular to some generality beyond. Diagrams on non-electronic screens such as paper serve the same purpose. E-screens do more than paper, however, because they support dynamic images and user-manipulable objects. They provide something almost tangible on which to act, to transform. With cleverness, the original and the acted-upon can be juxtaposed, either in time or in space. Through the mouse, and in future through more immediately sensual virtual reality, e-screens add a visceral component to a mathematics classroom, straining to overcome the restriction that any dynamic must occur in time.

More precisely, e-screens, by their simulation of dynamic change, can provide learners with experience of rapid juxtapositions of variation through which a dimension of possible variation can be experienced, labelled and abstracted ready for use in future manipulations. As Marton and Booth (1997) point out, this is the basis for experiencing and making sense of a concept. The central core to be offered is systematic and juxtaposed variation with not too many dimensions being varied at once. This focus is provided in order to draw on the natural power of humans to detect variation and thereby to become aware of dimensions of possible variation.

So what e-screens *can* do is enable generalities to be experienced through visually sequential or juxtaposed variation, stimulating expression of those generalities, perhaps as conjectures. They provide a test-bed for generating examples. Their tremendous computational power means that ideas can be tested in the search for generalizations. But it is up to the learner to articulate those generalities, and to attempt to justify them, perhaps under teacher guidance.

No matter how computationally powerful they become, e-screens cannot do the creative part of algebra in which local patterns are spotted and exploited in order to make sense of large expressions. All they can do is the 'grunt' work of algebraic manipulation: substitution, collection of terms, factoring and the like. They cannot 'partly factor' or collect together similar but not identical terms: this is something the user has to do, making use of the human power of selective attention.

E-screens always and only present particulars, while mathematics is mostly concerned with the general. You can display a sequence of particulars and you can amalgamate a collection of particulars generated by changing a single parameter, by displaying the projection of a surface. For example, you cannot display the graph of $y = ax^n$ without specifying values for the parameters a and n. However, you *can* display a selection of different values chosen for one and a particular value for the other.

This can be done in three ways: simultaneously as a family, sequentially as an animation (drawing on the dual aspects of an image) or as the projection of a surface. But you cannot display the cross-section $y = ax^n$ at a general, unspecified value of the parameters. You *can*, however, learn to do all this in your mind. Making effective use of e-screen images is about 'working on' those images by discerning and looking beyond the particulars on the screen to general relationships which can be turned into properties (Mason, 2003). It is about using computational power to test particular and special cases, while searching for what is invariant amidst some permitted change.

Many mathematical families of objects are best thought of as spatially distributed rather than occurring in time. Seeing a sequence of functions $y = x^n$ for differing n (not just integers) plotted one after the other is not the same as seeing a collection of samples plotted simultaneously, nor the same as seeing a surface $z = x^y$ plotted as a projection in two dimensions. The two-dimensional e-screen projection of a surface rotated in 'space' using mouse control provides a low-dimensional experience through which it may be possible to learn to work in more dimensions. However, having the machine do the work in simple cases may actually make it harder to develop the mental power required to work visually in higher dimensions.

E-screens provide images which can be internalized and then used as eidetic images (things previously seen which can be used as components in further mental constructions). Gavriel Salomon (1979) suggested that such images can supplant, augment and enrich the mental images on which people can call. But care is needed: just because you show me an image, you cannot guarantee that I have seen what you see. Far less can you assume that I have interpreted it in the same way, nor that I have internalized it for future use in the same way that you do. As with any use of screen images, the image itself has to be worked on, in order to integrate it into your functioning.

What e-screens may someday be able to do

The term *visualizing* once meant activating one's own inner mental 'screen', but it has since been usurped by certain ICT enthusiasts: to them, visualizing now means putting pictures on screens. What they fail to recognize is that selection and choice of individual images, the sequencing of such images, as well as the labels used to access them involve socio-political-cultural choices. They follow in the esteemed footsteps of eighteenth-century encyclopaedists like Denis Diderot. Diderot concentrated on collecting and storing knowledge 'once and for all', apparently unaware that each choice, each selection, each organization was the product of editorial bias as well as a reflection of a particular view of knowledge.

In our age, people are developing and promoting CD-ROMs and websites which purport to provide compendia of particular kinds of knowledge. However, they too necessarily reflect a particular perspective, a specific way of thinking and, hence, can be only one among many possibilities. To search such an electronic resource effectively requires becoming familiar with the compiler's way of thinking and classifying.

CD-ROMs are just one source for e-screen images. The tools afforded by each particular software package change what you can do with the virtual objects presented on the screen. Consequently, they alter the supported concept image and hence the sense of the mathematical topic as a whole. Perks *et al.* (2002) have developed this theme by looking, for example, at the notion of area as experienced using dynamic geometry, a spreadsheet and a graph plotter. Each has strengths presented through what it can do and its weaknesses are revealed by what it cannot. As a result, the mathematics itself, as experienced by learners, is partial and restricted (which is natural anyway), but may be misinterpreted by teachers and learners as comprehensive and complete.

The plethora of images from e-screens which bombard us every day could easily have the effect of producing a sort of mental pollution (akin to noise pollution), making us more and more passive with respect to these images. Instead of trying to make sense of them, we may increasingly just 'swim in them'. As the adage has it, if you want to know about water, do not ask a fish. We are swimming in images to the extent that we may find it more and more difficult to be aware of them.

The Italian writer Italo Calvino (1988) expressed a comparable concern in the following extract.

> This leads to another question: What will be the future of the individual imagination in what is usually called the 'civilization of the image'? Will the power of evoking images of things that are *not there* continue to develop in a human race increasingly inundated by a flood of prefabricated images? . . . we run [the danger of] losing a basic human faculty: the power of bringing visions into focus with our eyes shut, of bringing forth forms and colors from the lines of black letters on a white page, and in fact of *thinking* in terms of images.
>
> (pp. 91–2; emphasis in original)

Education will increasingly have to assume the role of educating students' awareness of the presence of images, as well as exploring how they can and need to be worked on. That is, students need to learn how to use them as stable bases for considering what could change and what must stay invariant, as well as identifying what mathematical structures are being instantiated. If we become dependent on having images provided for us, we may also need help discriminating among them in order to identify those which are useful to reconstruct mentally. We will need the impetus and must demand the right to construct our own images.

Mental imagery can be a delicate but powerful ally to mathematical thought: delicate because it makes use of what has been experienced. You probably have the experience of having seen the film of a book you have previously read: the film images dominate, displacing and supplanting the mental images stirred while reading the book. So, too, the myriad of brief images we regularly suffer may weaken our own mental screens. Put another way, we may find that the dynamic images which can be put onto screens become wallpaper for learners who do not discriminate between powerful images and the transitory or idiosyncratic. To avoid this pollution problem getting too serious, it is necessary to derive ways of working on images from e-screens, so that they become available to inform and influence, to provide the basis for further constructive mathematical activity.

Those involved with teaching saluted the classroom educational potential of film, radio, television and videotape as each developed, only to see them become integrated into entertainment. The expectation arising from educational use of a medium associated with entertainment weakens the pedagogic potential of any medium. As Marshall McLuhan (1964) observed, 'the medium is the message' – or is at least a significant part of it.

One challenge for the future is the problem of storing and accessing images imagistically rather than by reference to labels or descriptors. There are huge numbers of screens to be seen and stored, but as yet no effective way to retrieve them the way the brain does, through imagistic association and resonance. Enabling users to search using their own way of classifying is essential if we are not to suffer a tyranny of predigested and preorganized lines of thought. Perhaps this will be Asimov's 'parking problem' as applied to e-screens.

One of the curious features of current computer algebra packages and symbol processors is that they preserve the traditional format of mathematical exposition: line-by-line calculations interspersed with text. The text is usually intended to be helpful, explaining what calculation is to be performed next and commenting on the result of the previous computation. This is in contrast to what happens in a spreadsheet, a screen version of traditional accountant practices. Rather than having to treat each cell as a separate function with computations performed sequentially line by line, in a spreadsheet computations are linked together and a change in one cell value flows or ripples through all the related cells at the same time.

We can expect to see something like spreadsheets become the format behind symbol manipulators and more. We can look for shapes other than a rectangular grid, such as a hexagon, so that cells are linked visually to six surrounding cells rather than just four, and which can also be viewed as a projection onto the plane of three dimensions. Since the principal power of spreadsheets lies in the 'fill down' and 'fill right' features, which enable a calculation format to be iterated, we can expect to see spreadsheets which also 'fill down' other kinds of operations on cells. For example, diagram spreadsheets might iterate geometric constructions in much the same way as arithmetic functions are iterated. But that is yet to come.

Spreadsheets and symbol processors do not do anything until they are instructed: they provide computationally expressive languages (diSessa, 1993). They are of no use unless and until there is something to be expressed and manipulated. They are employed most effectively when their use is delayed until ideas have begun to settle and you know what you want to say and what you want to do.

It is tempting to provide users with pre-prepared sheets, which the user is meant to modify, extend and develop. By seeing how an expert has managed to make something happen, the novice can begin to see how to make the language work for them. But this assumes that novices have something *they* want to explore, to express. Prepared worksheets often serve to limit, restrict and constrain rather than initiate, open up and provoke. Once many different web pages or worksheets are prepared, the desire to click-and-go, to see if there is something better on the next page, can easily dominate. This can make it even harder for an individual to settle down, explore and work on (and at) some experienced disturbance, in order to reach an explanation and generalization of a phenomenon.

Final thoughts

On seeing a newly developed piece of software with new features, it is very hard not to be inspired to ask 'Will it also allow me to . . .?'. Every advance prompts the possibility of further advance. Symbol manipulators once could only manipulate numbers; then you could use letters to stand for values to be stored in locations; after that, letters could be used as parameters: at every stage, further generality is encompassed. Gödel's theorem shows that mathematics is 'recursively unsolvable' (no matter how many axioms you adjoin to arithmetic, there will always be true theorems you cannot prove). So, too, with software. There will always be further levels of generality which machines cannot 'yet' encompass. But the mind is so much richer. These generalities not only occur to our minds, but mathematicians regularly work with them.

However, any tool which extends capabilities also contributes to the atrophy of other human practices, perhaps even of other human powers. The slate, paper and personal organizers reduced our competence at remembering, while logarithm tables and the slide rule perhaps reduced competence at mental and paper-and-pencil arithmetic in the past. The desire to reach for a computer algebra system to do some algebra leads to less algebra being done in the head or on paper. The fear that powers will atrophy without being replaced by something more powerful lies behind the 'ban calculators' movement. Yet, we do not find people demanding that children dig holes with their hands before using shovels, nor before using a digger, nor that they run errands before being allowed to use the post.

Effective educational use of any mediating tool, and especially e-screens, is to go beyond the entertainment value of dynamic images to look at and buttons to click. It is to go beyond setting tasks to do, even where they send the learner away from the machine for a time. The aim is to 'bring forth a world of significance' (Kieren, 1998; Maturana and Varela, 1987), making use of learner's powers (Dewey, 1897), what Kieren calls 'in-person embodiment' (p. 22). The world brought forth, having been mediated at least in part by software that generates screen images, may involve the learner in acting in ways which might not have arisen so readily elsewhere. The effect is to place learners' activity in a context which a wider community recognizes as mathematics, a process Kieren calls 'embodiment in the body of mathematics' (p. 22).

Developing and advancing ICT as a mediator is one thing; squandering our heritage of natural powers which transcend anything a machine will ever be able to do for us is quite another. Exploiting the potential of e-screens means using our powers to work *on* what we see, on what gets thrown up on the screen, on what we can and do express on screen – with the effect of making us more powerful thinkers when the screens are dark. Perhaps the most important thing that someone can learn about an e-screen is when to turn it off.

References

Boero, P. (2001) 'Transformation and anticipation as key processes in algebraic problem solving', in R. Sutherland (ed.), *Algebraic Processes and Structures*. Dordrecht: Kluwer, pp. 99–119.

Calvino, I. (1988) *Six Memos for the Next Millennium* (Creagh, P., trans.). London: Jonathan Cape.

Dewey, J. (1897) 'My pedagogic creed'. *The School Journal*, **54**(3), 77–80.

diSessa, A. (1993) 'The many faces of a computational medium: teaching the mathematics of motion', in L. Burton and B. Jaworski (eds), *Proceedings of the Technology in Mathematics Teaching Conference*. Bromley: Chartwell–Bratt, pp. 23–38.

Fable (2004) *Interactive Physics*. Belfast: Fable Multimedia. (http://www.fable.co.uk/ip.htm)

Hewitt, D. (1991) 'Into our fortieth year: finding our freedom'. *Mathematics Teaching*, **136**, 3–10.

Jaworski, B. (1989) *Using Classroom Videotape to Develop Your Teaching*. Milton Keynes: Centre for Mathematics Education, Open University.

Kieren, T. (1998) 'Towards an embodied view of the mathematics curriculum in a world of technology', in D. Tinsley and D. Johnson (eds), *Information and*

Communication Technologies in School Mathematics. London: Chapman & Hall, pp. 19–28.

Love, E. (1988) *PM647B: Working Mathematically with Sixth Formers on Film.* Milton Keynes: Centre for Mathematics Education, Open University (video).

Marton, F. and Booth, S. (1997) *Learning and Awareness.* Mahwah, NJ: Lawrence Erlbaum.

Mason, J. (2003) 'Structure of attention in the learning of mathematics', in J. Novotná (ed.), *Proceedings of the International Symposium on Elementary Mathematics Teaching.* Prague: Charles University, pp. 9–16.

Mason, J., with Burton, L. and Stacey, K. (1982) *Thinking Mathematically.* London: Addison-Wesley.

Maturana, H. and Varela, F. (1987) *The Tree of Knowledge.* London: Shambala Press.

McLuhan, M. (1964) *Understanding Media: the Extensions of Man.* London: Routledge & Kegan Paul.

Perks, P., Prestage, S. and Hewitt, D. (2002) 'Does the software change the maths? Part 1'. *Micromath*, **18**(1), 28–31.

Pimm, D. (1993) 'From should to could: reflections on possibilities of mathematics teacher education'. *For the Learning of Mathematics*, **13**(2), 27–32.

Salomon, G. (1979) *Interaction of Media, Cognition and Learning.* London: Jossey-Bass.

Schoenfeld, A. (1985) *Mathematical Problem Solving.* New York: Academic Press.

Tahta, D. (1981) 'Some thoughts arising from the new Nicolet films'. *Mathematics Teaching*, **94**, 25–9.

14

UNDERSTANDING AND PROJECTING ICT TRENDS IN MATHEMATICS EDUCATION

Nathalie Sinclair and Nicholas Jackiw

Looking into the crystal ball of educational technology's future, the present inevitably appears as the exact nexus at which the long hard road from the past splits into dozens of the smaller footpaths of possible futures. Thus, before taking stock of the state – and the many possible futures – of ICT in mathematics education, it can first be illuminating to consider the state of ICT within mathematics itself. Just a few decades ago, mathematicians, as a community, mostly expressed fear about the new, encroaching, computer-based technologies. How would computers taint the rigour of their august discipline? Why would any mathematician, dedicated to thinking about abstract ideas rather than crunching numbers, need more than pencil and paper?

This moment and attitude is well captured not only in the professional debate of the time, but in the popular literature – the ominous thriller and admonitory science fiction film – of its day as well. But leap 30 years forward and, nowadays, few mathematicians could function professionally without relying on some form of enabling computer technology, whether to typeset mathematical articles electronically in T_EX or to locate preprint research materials on the internet. And few would deny the importance of fields – fractal geometry, cryptography, dynamical systems – in which the computer has motivated new or renewed interest. Moreover, there are now many mathematicians who bring innovative uses of the computer to the very core of their practice. Experimental mathematicians rely heavily on computer software for doing mathematics: not just for communicating results, but also for building models, gaining insight, verifying hypotheses and identifying solutions.

Will school mathematics ever evolve to this state, where ICT fluency is a baseline state for all teachers and students? Will it ever reach the point where the phrase 'innovation in ICT' reflects not just the *presence* of ICT in a classroom but something positive or exceptional about its *use* in the school, its involvement in the teaching and learning of mathematics? One essential difference between the two communities is the shape of their daily practice. In general, mathematicians spend much of their time working individually, on their own problems, using the tools and resources that suit their specific needs. This individual work is peppered by interactions with colleagues through a variety of means, including journal articles and books, conferences, lunchtime conversations and e-mail.

By contrast, school students spend much of their time working in a classroom full of other students (usually towards a common goal), interacting with their teacher and peers through real-time, verbal communication. In order for ICT to find a comfortable and useful place in the standard – rather than the exceptional – classroom, it has to do more than satisfy the needs of some students some of the time. It should be engaged in the learning of many students most of the time, not only by supporting their individual cognitive goals, but by additionally supporting the full matrix of communication and social interaction that defines the broader classroom environment.

Three waves of ICT development

As this book has shown, there are currently many different computer-based technologies available for mathematics education. Some have been around for decades, while others are more recent in origin; some have already established a wide base of use, while others seem to offer greater potential in the future. It is possible to compare these technologies according to the kinds of mathematics they address, as the chapter structure of Part A of this book has indicated. In this chapter, however, we would like to suggest a different perspective on these and other (possibly future) educational technologies.

We propose to categorize educational ICT less by mathematical content than by the vision offered by specific technologies concerning where learning occurs, by or between whom and how. Our scheme distinguishes the way technologies focus on and support various relationships constituting a pedagogical dynamic, such as the one between mathematics and the learner or that among different learners in a classroom. Consider, for example, some wild future technology that allows the student to read the thoughts of the teacher directly. We would classify such a technology as centred on the relationship between the individual learner and the teacher – the physical classroom, the student's peers and the relevant curriculum contribute little, if anything, to the value (or horror) of such a technology.

Three major waves of ICT emerge when the sea of various technologies is viewed from this organizing perspective. While we chart them separately in this chapter, it is important to remember they are framed here as *waves* – they retain a sense of fluidity and overlap. While consecutive waves can be distinguished by their distinct peaks, judging where one ends and the next begins requires far more subtle discrimination. Although technology itself can seem dry and logical, scientific and mechanical, the human meanings we impose on – or derive from – technology are entirely organic. Thus, we expect to find strange rip currents and eddying backwaters cutting across wavetrains, spreading anomalies and significant exceptions across the overall pattern of our story. We note these where we see them, but you will certainly find others should you look closely.

Many of the technologies discussed in this book seem to fit comfortably into the second of the three waves we describe. By revisiting these technologies from a historical perspective, we intend to highlight some of their relative strengths and limitations. Our wish is that this will help you, likely a teacher faced with many choices and constraints, better understand the potential for each of the technologies described in this volume to inform your own classroom practice. Additionally, we hope the larger framework of 'waves' of ICT provides a useful picture in which you will be able to situate the benefits and drawbacks of the many new technologies you will encounter throughout the entirety of your career.

Wave 1: ICT for learners of mathematics

'First-wave' technologies focus on the direct relationship between the individual learner and mathematics itself, a pedagogical dynamic we represent in Figure 14.1. These technologies attempt to facilitate the individual's learning of mathematical ideas, but speak little to the roles of

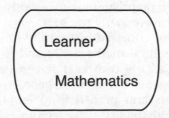

Figure 14.1   The focus of first-wave technologies.

teacher or student, school or home, classroom or classmates. They actually speak little to the entire physical and psychological context of mathematics education as it has been undertaken historically in schools. This is not to say, however, that all first-wave technologies shared a common theory of learning.

First-wave ICT gave rise to wildly different technologies. *Logo* is first-wave, as are the multiple-choice tests of the 1970s computer-assisted instruction (CAI). The theories of learning of the developers of these two technologies could not be more diametrically opposed. But all first-wave ICT, in its exclusive focus on the individual user's direct encounter with mathematical content, at least implicitly agreed on a vision of mathematics learning in which teachers, schoolrooms, curricula and other students had no essential role.

In addition to the differences in their underlying theories of learning, *Logo* and CAI also represent extremes in terms of their *mathematical expressivity*: that is, in the nature of their connection to mathematics. A technology with narrow expressivity relates to a single or small number of mathematical ideas, whereas one with broad expressivity touches on several ideas and perhaps several different ways of approaching those ideas – different representations, examples or forms of reasoning. Some technologies may cover many areas of mathematics, while others may be designed to allow for an in-depth probing of only one.

CAI is very specific in its mathematical content (and always targets a sufficiently small content domain that it can be distilled into multiple-choice logic), frequently limiting users to very procedural ways of mathematical thinking. By contrast, learners, by using *Logo*, can investigate a wide variety of mathematics ideas (see Abelson and diSessa, 1986) and these ideas can be approached using different models, representations and even levels of sophistication, from the primary school to the undergraduate lecture theatre.

From a contemporary point of view, first-wave ICT appears to have achieved individual learning experiences at the cost of neglecting classroom practice, teacher habits and beliefs, as well as the influence of the curriculum, by imposing entirely new and perhaps inappropriate classroom practices. Both CAI and *Logo* illustrate this effect. The behaviourist vision of CAI – learners locked in front of television monitors pressing multiple-choice keys for preprogrammed rewards – imposes classroom practices that are anathema to many teachers.

Likewise, *Logo* has been criticized historically for insufficient transparency of its relation to school mathematics and to school mathematics curricula. To juxtapose a *Logo* computer screen (say, with turtles, procedures and programs) against a traditional geometry textbook (with constructions, measurements and proofs) is to emphasize the difficulties many teachers find in bridging first-wave technologies and their teaching practice. However, as evidenced by its initial inclusion in the UK mathematics national curriculum, *Logo* was able to push classroom practice to evolve, at least in part, towards its singular vision of mathematics learning, although neither as rapidly nor as radically as some had hoped.

Wave 2: developing the context of learning

The second wave of ICT to wash over mathematics education expanded its focus from the learner's relation to the mathematics to include the teacher and the curriculum, as shown in Figure 14.2. Beyond the learning experiences of individuals, technologies evolved to become more transparently related to the school mathematics curriculum and to teacher opportunities for integrating such technology within a familiar classroom practice.

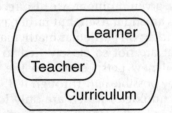

Figure 14.2 The focus of second-wave technologies.

This wave includes many of the technologies you have encountered throughout this book: the graphing calculator, spreadsheets, interactive or dynamic geometry, statistics software such as *Fathom*, and specific microworlds such as Dave Hewitt's *Numbers* (see Chapter 3). For the most part, these tools acknowledge, not only in their design as technological objects but also in the discourse surrounding their development and use, that the learning of mathematics takes place in mathematics classrooms. And this learning is to be led or overseen by teachers pursuing specific mathematical curriculum objectives – or at least the use of mathematical ICT will most often occur in such contexts.

As we have said, first-wave technologies varied in their mathematical expressivity. Second-wave technologies, because of their focus on adapting to the roles of the teacher and the students in a mathematics classroom, also have interesting and substantial variation with respect to their ease of fit to specific sites – locations or moments – within existing mathematics curricula. Technology with a narrow ease of fit can be used directly, without thought as it were, by a teacher using a specific curriculum. Such technologies bear an apparently transparent relation to particular curricula, through the use of explicit correlation, identical language or through similar sequencing of ideas and topics.

Technologies with broader ease of fit, however, have what we might call a family resemblance – but not a genetic identity – to the curriculum. They might involve alternative representations of similar ideas or forms of reasoning that are only implicit in the curriculum. Whereas first-wave technologies had no relation to practice and the curriculum, the mathematical and learning scenarios of the second wave appear as recognizable objects within the classroom. Teachers may still need to build bridges between ICT tools and specific classroom objectives. However, they no longer need to play the more ambitious roles initially of the visionary who imagines the bridge in the first place and subsequently of the architect who plans its every detail before it can be built.

It is important to note that the degree of explicit fit to the curriculum is not a value spectrum. As teachers, we appreciate the convenience and 'sense of fit' of an ICT task that is closely linked to our specific curricular situation. However, at a given moment, we also recognize that the curriculum is not intended as an end it itself, but rather as a means, functioning as a lens with which to focus on particular mathematics. Technologies and technological tasks that are not so closely tied to our specific curricula can also open powerful new perspectives on the same broader ideas – perspectives that may be possible *only* through ICT.

Additionally, ICT technologies which are only loosely coupled to specific curricular contexts or levels remain more flexible and may be usefully brought to bear across curricula and grade levels. If a specific ICT spans multiple topics or even multiple years in students' mathematical experiences, then students can grow and evolve in their use of that particular ICT. In the most sophisticated form of this interplay, the technology may mature into what one might authentically call a tool and the students into craftsmen and craftswomen of mathematics.

In Figure 14.3, we have situated second-wave technologies according to their mathematical expressivity and ease of fit to a specific curriculum (GC refers to graphing calculators, DG to dynamic geometry). These technologies could also be compared and contrasted in different ways (and some of these possibilities will emerge in our discussion). But we find that this two-dimensional scheme provides insight into the reasons why some technologies are currently more widely used or recommended and how other technologies may evolve.

On our grid, a location to avoid would be the lower left-hand corner. We might imagine technologies such as word processors – which have almost no mathematical expressivity and an extremely narrow ease of fit to the mathematics curriculum – occupying this undesirable position. The 'golden' location would be the upper right-hand corner, where both mathematical expressivity and ease of fit to the curriculum are maximal. However, as we have intimated, these two dimensions can be at odds with one another, since the mathematics curriculum tends towards making content knowledge discrete, whereas broad mathematics expressivity implies connections across content knowledge as well as across processes

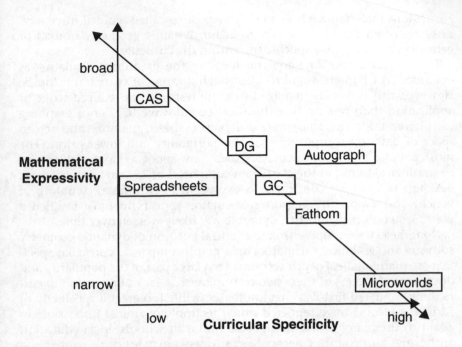

Figure 14.3 Second-wave technologies in mathematics education.

involved in using content knowledge. This trade-off is reflected by the dominant linearity of the plot. We begin by describing the technologies clustered in the middle before turning to the more outlying ones.

Interactive or dynamic geometry ICT, in mature software packages such as *The Geometer's Sketchpad 4.0* or *Cabri-Géomètre* (see Chapter 5), touches a range of mathematical ideas beyond Euclidean geometry, including number operations, probability and calculus at a wide range of sophistication, from elementary school through to undergraduate and even research mathematics. By moving fluidly across mathematics and across representations, it offers in-depth access to these ideas, providing, for example, geometric interpretations of algebraic ideas or visual representations of complex numbers.

It is perhaps because of its mathematical expressivity that its curriculum specificity is only moderate. While it 'speaks the language' of school mathematics more than, say, *Logo* does (a glance at the menus and commands confirms this; 'segments' and 'circles' replace 'turtles' and 'subroutines', for instance), its comprehensive, unifying scope runs counter to the particularized, balkanizing manner in which most school curricula chop up mathematics. However, since it does not explicitly impose any pedagogical models (the same can be said for *Logo*), such geometry software can be configured to suit a wide range of learning modes, from step-by-step student activity to open-ended explorations. In fact, supplemental curriculum materials such as step-by-step or so-called 'guided discovery' tasks are often used by teachers to adapt dynamic geometry's broad or general expressivity to a specific site within the curriculum.

The algebraic and data-analytic tools of the graphing calculator (as described in Chapters 4 and 8) also touch a range of curriculum topics. However, this is usually managed in more restricted or reduced scope or application than one finds with other second-wave ICT, since graphing calculators trade the computational power, speed, memory and screen space of desk-top computing tools for portability and lower price. (The most popular graphing calculators today are about as powerful, in raw technological terms, as the classroom computers of 25 years ago. Whereas desk-top technology continues to evolve with an annual doubling of benefit–cost ratios, the graphing calculator appears to have reached a plateau, so unfortunately this dynamic will likely worsen over time.)

Nonetheless, we propose that the central position of dynamic geometry software and graphing calculators on a graph comparing curricular specificity to mathematical depth accounts for a large part of the popularity and documented success of these two technologies. A lack of attention to curriculum hindered first-wave technologies, while too great a specificity of fit in the second wave rendered much technology almost impossible to adapt to the many different curricula found in schools, local education authorities and counties, across North American states or provinces and even across countries. Dynamic geometry and graphing calculators appear to find a functional balance.

The emergence of technologies of broader mathematical expressivity can challenge the ways teachers and researchers have historically thought of the mathematics curriculum. Imagine the organization of some future version of this book. Instead of chapters that correspond to content categories (such as numerical, algebraic or statistical thinking), we might see more process-oriented divisions (such as thinking visually, discretely and recursively). While mathematical process standards have yet to achieve the same recognition in most curricula as content standards, they represent, as the latest US curriculum standards (National Council of Teachers of Mathematics, 2000) argue, the fundamental ways in which content knowledge is both acquired and used.

Moving to the right on the grid in Figure 14.3, the program *Autograph* (see http://www.autograph-math.com) has a mathematical depth similar to the graphing calculator or to dynamic geometry, but manages to achieve even greater curriculum specificity. By modularly incorporating functionalities for geometry, functions and statistics, it is more easily mapped to the (equally modular) content strands of the curriculum. A comparison of *Autograph* with dynamic geometry (which occupies a similar place in the grid) might find more subtle distinctions not captured by the graph. For instance, a teacher might find the diverse functionality in *Autograph* to be ordered by a Swiss-army-knife model of presumed equal access and convenience. In dynamic geometry, the same functionality might be ordered by a more hierarchical logic of mathematical structure. This difference, though not obvious, can have a considerable impact upon both the teacher's and the student's experience of the technology as a tool for mathematical exploration and learning.

Fathom, because of its special emphasis on data analysis and on data-based approaches to mathematical ideas, has perhaps a more narrow mathematical expressivity than dynamic geometry, graphing calculators or *Autograph*. But this focused mathematical expressivity helps lend it a greater ease of fit to data analysis or statistics curricula, primarily because of the tight connection between its own emphases and particular curriculum content. One aspect of *Fathom* that the grid does not make evident is its resemblance to statistics software used by research professionals. In contrast, technologies such as graphing calculators and *Autograph*, which have broader mathematical expressivity, bear little resemblance to technologies favoured by research mathematicians. (We return to this important point in the next section.)

Where *Fathom*'s emphasis is recognizable within the strands or topics of most curricula, spreadsheets touch on a mathematically important but – from a curriculum perspective – less familiar set of mathematical ideas. With spreadsheets, students can manipulate numbers and functions, albeit somewhat differently from how they might in other curriculum contexts. More importantly, spreadsheets invite iterative thinking, which occurs everywhere across school mathematics, but is almost never the explicit focus of curricular attention. For now, teachers using spreadsheets in the classroom must identify subtopics and problems which lend themselves well to iterative thinking. They then must help students navigate the differences between the symbols and notation used in spreadsheets with those used in school mathematics. (In this sense, spreadsheets are perhaps closer to the first wave of ICT than other technologies in Figure 14.3.)

In the lower right-hand corner of the grid, we have placed microworlds, a label we are giving to describe specific constructivist environments that instantiate a subdomain of mathematics, such as Hewitt's *Numbers* (see Chapter 3), *MathSticks* (see Noss *et al.*, 1997) or the reworking of old programs like *Monty* and *Counter*. These are thus aimed, by definition, at a particular, very local set of mathematical ideas that usually have very direct connections to the curriculum. For example, *Numbers* focuses on number sense, while *MathSticks* focuses on patterning and pre-algebraic thinking.

Many microworlds have been created using more general-purpose programs such as *Logo*, *Boxer* and even dynamic geometry. The tight focus of microworlds frequently means a short learning curve, since only a limited number of actions are made available to the student. They may therefore be more appealing to a teacher who anticipates a limited use of ICT over the school year. The close attention microworlds can focus on students' thought processes, and on students' behaviour when working in highly specific contexts, has also made such environments extremely useful to researchers (Noss and Hoyles, 1996).

Wave 3: tomorrow's ICT

As we evaluate emerging technologies and project our wave metaphor towards the future, the rising wave of newest ICT seems characterized by yet another expansion of the technology's pedagogic focus. The focus now includes relationships among individual learners, groups of learners, the teacher, the classroom, classroom practices and the world outside the classroom (see Figure 14.4). This wave started to emerge five to ten years ago, when an area of seismic turmoil grew around the problem of trying to democratize the agreed-upon cognitive benefits of ICT.

Important, socially oriented questions began to arise.

- ICT can support the individual learner in the laboratory situation (the first wave, evolving into the second), but how can it support a whole classroom of heterogeneous learners?
- ICT-based cognitive tools can support the development of mathematical concepts, but how can they ameliorate the social issues that challenge less affluent and less well-supported classrooms?
- How is the individual learner's understanding channelled and constrained by classroom norms and interactions?

These types of questions have forced educational technologists to think about broadening or pluralizing learners' access to technology, as well as fostering a more socially sensitive vision of technology. This socially sensitive, third-wave vision insists on explicitly acknowledging the fact that multiple learners are involved in classroom learning. Consequently, technologies must support learners' communication with the teacher, with each other, with the whole classroom – the sources and growth of know-

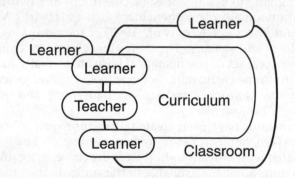

Figure 14.4   Relationships in focus for third-wave technologies.

ledge within it and the interactions among its members – and even beyond the classroom. What kinds of changes to existing technologies or what kinds of new ones could foster such a web of different roles and relationships, where learning is understood as including a social dynamic rather than solely an individual, psychological one?

An early, economically driven instance of transitional second- into third-wave technology is the graphing calculator. These devices effectively democratized student access to ICT by replacing powerful yet expensive computers with less capable but much less expensive units of which a much broader range of schools could afford class sets for their students to use. The newer 'networked calculator' (described in Chapter 8) brings hand-held technology more clearly into the third wave, with its emphasis on collaboration and information-sharing. More recently, the interactive whiteboard (discussed in Chapter 9) has offered 'geographic' as opposed to 'economic' democratization, by providing a common space which can be used and viewed by all students in a classroom – thus supporting the sharing and communicating of mathematical ideas.

As we have identified earlier, there are even more subtle dimensions than economics and geography to the social patterns in a classroom that ICT has only begun to address (Jackiw and Sinclair, 2002). In this chapter's vision of future roles of ICT in classroom learning, we are, of course, interested in continuing the tradition of optimizing ICT features as a cognitive interaction medium for individuals, where learning is construed as being in relation to a machine. But further, we believe that much of the future promise of ICT in the mathematics classroom lies in its ability to develop in ways sensitive to a social knowledge web and that foster the fundamental acts of active teaching and learning in the social space of the whole classroom. We are interested in looking at how technologies can change the way information flows and how it can be shared (as image or as comprehension) and, thus, how ICT can change the way teachers define and control the participation structures of the classroom.

In Figure 14.5 overleaf, we have illustrated the way in which the focus of third-wave ICT on the overlapping, overflowing matrix of learners, the teacher, the curriculum and the classroom inspires a new way of looking at specific technologies. In fact, instead of looking at the particular technology itself, we can start paying attention to the way in which a mathematics-specific, second-wave technology can, with the help of other 'amplifying' technologies such as interactive whiteboards or video-conferencing, become more sensitive to a social knowledge web.

Researchers have identified several strategies which can mediate social interactions, transactions and reflections: for example, small-group discussions and student presentations. How can such strategies be deployed in the prevalent, computer-based environments that promote individual reflection, activity and meaning-making? (We are thinking here of the computer laboratory environment with its individualized work-space

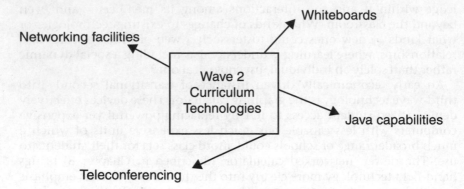

Figure 14.5   Third-wave technologies in mathematics education.

set-up and its 'guided discovery' tasks, where teachers often spend much time putting out technical fires, be they related to the computer itself or the software.) More specifically, how can technologies explicitly encourage socially based behaviour conducive to educative learning experiences?

Social dynamics and ICT

If we revisit from a social perspective some of the technologies that emerged in the second wave, we can identify at least some of the roles individual technologies play in influencing and altering classroom dynamics, modes and conversations. We shall see three roles emerge, two of which relate to classroom dynamics and a third which extends beyond the classroom.

First, technologies can play a role in determining the way in which information is distributed throughout the classroom, illustrated by the graphing calculator. We have already mentioned a first-order, economic effect of the graphing calculator on democratization – namely, reduced cost and size. In Chapter 8, David Wright describes a second-order effect, brought about by the introduction of networking facilities, which allow students to communicate mathematics to each other and to their teacher by sending personal data to a central teacher station.

Wright's example of the networked classroom has its roots in systems such as *ClassTalk* (Abrahamson, 2000), which teachers could use to collect, aggregate and display student responses to questions. This allows the teacher to create new levels of interaction in large classes that contrast sharply with traditional types of interaction where a student would – often painstakingly when diagrams were involved – share a solution on the blackboard. Every student has a personal device, but can use it to achieve a classroom-level goal such as generating solutions to a linear equation. The distribution of information contrasts with that found in a traditional computer laboratory, where the teacher (as well as the students) must physically move to different computers in order to observe or collect student work.

Wright discusses some of the psychological benefits of this kind of distribution of information: properly designed tasks can encourage participation while at the same time removing students' fear of being publicly embarrassed. However, there can also be more mathematical benefits, as illustrated in Hegedus and Kaput's (2003) example of a 'connected classroom'. In that scenario, students are asked to generate equations having a specific y-intercept. Since each student is to choose a different value for the slope, the aggregated result looks like a fan. Thus, student attention can systematically be elevated from individual cases (which he or she might generate) to the family of solutions in such a way as to reveal patterns, structures and higher-order objects not apparent at the individual level. While networking facilities make this kind of student activity feasible, we underline the importance of task design: not all tasks involving graphing calculators and networking facilities will achieve the same psychological and mathematical effects; nor will they foster the same quality of learning occasions.

When a graphing calculator is amplified by networking facilities, the distribution of information can change from a traditional flow from teachers to students to a potentially more democratic and engaging process, predominantly flowing between students and teacher. Might there even be pedagogically more promising ways of distributing information in the classroom, instead of the content and flow of information being completely determined by the teacher, regardless of student goals and progress? Networking facilities could support a more pluralistic classroom dynamic, one where students are free to gain access to and contribute information as they see fit, as they deem appropriate. Yet they will sometimes still need guidance to maintain contact with significant mathematics.

One of the most traditional ways of distributing information in the classroom is through the blackboard, which acts as a large, shared space for teacher–student communication. But when the information is electronic, the chalkboard becomes useless. In his description of networking with the graphing calculator, Wright also discusses the role of the large-scale display, in the form of an interactive whiteboard, which provides classrooms with a shared, blackboard-like space for teacher–student electronic communication. In contrast to other display tools, such as the television monitor or the overhead projector, the interactive whiteboard provides a larger, clearer display, making the mathematics more visible to more students.

Moreover, in Chapter 9, Alison Clark-Jeavons points to a functionality of such whiteboards not exploited by Wright's example, namely the possibility of interacting directly through the whiteboard itself. By dragging or clicking objects directly on the whiteboard, instead of the keyboard, the teacher can make visible, and thus public, actions which were previously private. Students now follow the commands and sequences that someone at the whiteboard (perhaps the teacher or another student) uses to manipulate screen objects. More powerfully, teachers can model some of the processes involved in mathematical reasoning with a given piece of ICT (such as to drag objects to extreme locations, to resample data, to experiment by changing the value of a variable, to graph relations). Thus, in addition to changing the distribution of information, interactive whiteboard hardware also affects the flow of interaction among the teacher, students and various items of software.

While any desk-top software can be used in conjunction with a whiteboard, programs in which dragging is a primary form of interaction, such as dynamic geometry, benefit even more from the whiteboard's interactivity than does keyboard-input software such as spreadsheets or *Logo*. Dragging-based programs provide learners with a shared visual/kinaesthetic learning experience. Interactive whiteboards still require that students and teachers move themselves to the physical location of the whiteboard, in order to interact with the mathematics displayed there. But one could easily imagine a more equitable distribution of information, if students could each have, by means of a networking facility, a mouse at their desk with which they could interact with the whiteboard. Imagine one student working directly at the whiteboard, getting stuck on a problem and another student being able to jump in and, say, drag a few objects so as to create a new, revealing geometric configuration, without the physical disruption or time lag of leaving his or her desk.

One strong appeal of the graphing calculator rests on an assumption, or habit, that every student in a classroom should be doing more or less the same thing at the same time. Within that vision, every student should have the same tool, participate in the same way and work on identical or at least similar problems. But this is not necessarily the only – nor the most natural – organization of classroom activity. How could the flow of interaction among teacher, students and ICT respect and build upon naturally occurring social participation structures? And how can the needs and learning preferences of individual learners still be met in such less rigidly parallel environments?

Consider a problem-solving-oriented classroom with an interactive whiteboard in one corner of the room and a pod of two or three computers in another corner. In contrast with the computer laboratory scenario, or even the classroom set of graphing calculators, this physical setting suggests different students engaging in different ICT interactions at different times. An interactive whiteboard might initially be used by the teacher to present a problem, much as she might have used a blackboard previously. But later, an individual (or even a group of students) might be using it to experiment with a certain model, once they have worked out – perhaps with pencil and paper – the kind of model they plan to use. Their results will be visible and usable by others, who might be inspired by something they see or by a discussion they overhear.

By entering into a more public stage, the whiteboard and the software program being used together could act as a muse for mathematical meaning-making (Jackiw and Sinclair, 2002). Students who prefer to work on their own, or to begin sorting out ideas more privately, may use the pod computers instead. Some students may choose to use these computers merely as reference tools rather than as work-spaces. By saving their work, they can record their ideas, which can then be made available to subsequent users. In this setting, we see ICT taking on multiple modes to suit the learning needs of the classroom, ranging from traditional cognitive modes to more socially oriented ones.

A technology's sensitivity to the social web of knowledge positions can also be assessed based on its relationship with the world outside the mathematics classroom. For example, some of the technologies described in the previous section accommodate additional movement outside the classroom and even outside the curriculum. Both computer algebra systems and dynamic geometry have a vital connection to mathematics and are thus used outside the classroom, by research mathematicians as well as enthusiasts. While these technologies connect beyond the mathematics classroom, tools like the graphing calculator have greater insularity.

This distinction may matter: both teachers and students have objected to the idea of learning or using a distracting piece of technology which will be abandoned before students get to advanced mathematics courses or to real mathematical inquiry, as users of mathematics or as professional mathematicians. It might be argued that tools shared by a number of mathematical communities – learners, academics, hobbyists and professionals – better encapsulate what is integral to good mathematical practice and thus are better positioned to expose students not only to mathematics' concepts, but also to its ways of thinking and inquiring.

Technologies such as the internet, video-conferencing and spreadsheets also reach beyond the classroom; they are productive technologies employed outside the classroom that have been repurposed for mathematics learning. An advantage in using such tools *in* the mathematics classroom is that students will gain technical skill in their use that they will be able to use outside the classroom. In addition, as Chapter 12 suggests, a technology such as the internet can serve to bring together various types of tools – applets, reference guides, communication facilities – that expand the physical and intellectual borders of the classroom.

Closing remarks

The MathsAlive study described in Chapter 10 tells an exciting story about the promise and potential future of ICT in the mathematics classroom. This study complements many others in showing that second-wave ICT has been successful: curriculum and assessment are now less at odds with mathematics learning technologies than during the 1980s. These studies also show that mathematics learning technologies have even succeeded (at least sometimes) in reconnecting the curriculum to important mathematical ways of thinking by increasing the quality and quantity of ways students can acquire and use mathematical ideas.

Additionally, with its extensive use of interactive whiteboards and graphing calculators and with its respecting of the natural participation structures of the classroom, the MathsAlive initiative has begun to move successfully into a third-wave vision of ICT. This vision is based less on attention to the present form or function of today's technologies – their interface, their curriculum and cognitive objectives, their price-to-performance ratio. It instead focuses more on deeper understandings of how the social interpretations of these and future technologies transform the experiences and relationships defining the mathematics classroom. It insists that an ICT can no longer be evaluated in isolation; instead, its potential and meaning will be determined within its wider social context, within the classroom ecology of teachers, learners and – only then – tools and technologies.

How will this vision evolve and change with the coming technologies of the twenty-first century? Will today's dynamic mathematics visualization software merge with high-end 'virtual reality' technologies that exist today only in research labs to define consensual, three-dimensional manipulation environments? Will today's calculator-based laboratory type tools evolve into intelligent, data-sensing and data-collecting robots that could allow students to exercise their mathematics in relation to personally collected and personally meaningful data?

One lesson available from the three-wave model we have adopted here is that not all ICT futures should be imagined in raw terms of technology or hardware functionality alone, but must address evolving pedagogic and social meanings of technology as well. Thus, will the widening reach of the internet across society at large reach a tomorrow in which we not only no longer argue about the 'appropriateness' of internet access in the classroom, but also we no longer can imagine a classroom *without* ubiquitous internet access?

These are provocative scenarios about which to speculate. As with technological soothsaying more generally, certainly the thing they have in common is that they are all most likely wrong. Our purpose in proposing a three-wave model is to provide a framework within which ICT can be thought of less in terms of its specific features or benefits (which – since technology-based – will constantly evolve) than in terms of the roles it may play in the learning situation of a particular student or teacher or classroom. Our hope is that by attending to these roles, you will be better able to evaluate and select future educational technologies – whose shape we cannot yet predict – and to integrate them meaningfully into an overall, developing classroom culture.

References

Abelson, H. and diSessa, A. (1986) *Turtle Geometry*. Cambridge, MA: MIT Press.

Abrahamson, A. (2000) 'A brief history of Classtalk'. Paper presented at the Teachers Teaching with Technology International Conference, Dallas, TX.

Hegedus, S. and Kaput, J. (2003) 'The effect of SimCalc connected classrooms on students' algebraic thinking', in N. Pateman, B. Dougherty and J. Zilliox (eds), *Proceedings of the 27th Conference of the International Group for the Psychology of Mathematics Education held jointly with the 25th Conference of the North American Chapter of the International Group for the Psychology of Mathematics Education*, Honolulu, HI: College of Education, University of Hawaii, Vol. 3, pp. 47–54.

Jackiw, N. and Sinclair, N. (2002) 'Dragon play: microworld design in a whole-class context'. *Journal for Educational Research in Computers*, **27**(1–2), 111–45.

National Council of Teachers of Mathematics (2000) *Principles and Standards for School Mathematics*. Washington, DC: NCTM.

Noss, R. and Hoyles, C. (1996) *Windows on Mathematical Meanings: Learning Cultures and Computers*. Dordrecht: Kluwer Academic.

Noss, R., Healy, L. and Hoyles, C. (1997) 'The construction of mathematical meanings: connecting the visual with the symbolic'. *Educational Studies in Mathematics*, **33**(2), 203–33.

INDEX